TAROT
IN LOVE

ABOUT THE AUTHOR

Elliot Adam is the author of the award-winning *Fearless Tarot*. He began his professional tarot career at the age of sixteen. At age twenty, he opened his own tarot shop, Athena's Oracle, in Milwaukee, Wisconsin. Elliot performs tarot readings for a substantial international clientele that includes Hollywood scriptwriters, high-profile journalists, actors, doctors, and entrepreneurs. A true Gemini Moon, he also holds a doctoral degree in classical oboe. Visit him at ElliotOracle.com.

Consulting the Cards
in Matters of the Heart

TAROT
IN LOVE

ELLIOT ADAM

AUTHOR OF BESTSELLING *FEARLESS TAROT*

Llewellyn Publications
Woodbury, Minnesota

FIRST EDITION
First Printing, 2023

Cover design by Shannon McKuhen
Illustrations on the cover from the Rider-Waite Tarot Deck® reproduced by permission of U.S. Games Systems, Inc., Stamford, CT 06902 USA. Copyright ©1971 by U.S. Games Systems, Inc. Further reproduction prohibited. The Rider-Waite Tarot Deck® is a registered trademark of U.S. Games Systems, Inc.
Illustrations in the interior are from the *Tarot Original 1909 Deck* © 2021 with art created by Pamela Colman Smith and Arthur Edward Waite. Used with permission of Lo Scarabeo.
Interior card spreads by Llewellyn Art Department

Llewellyn Publications is a registered trademark of Llewellyn Worldwide Ltd.

Library of Congress Cataloging-in-Publication Data (Pending)
ISBN: 978-0-7387-6873-1

Llewellyn Worldwide Ltd. does not participate in, endorse, or have any authority or responsibility concerning private business transactions between our authors and the public.
   All mail addressed to the author is forwarded but the publisher cannot, unless specifically instructed by the author, give out an address or phone number.
   Any internet references contained in this work are current at publication time, but the publisher cannot guarantee that a specific location will continue to be maintained. Please refer to the publisher's website for links to authors' websites and other sources.

Llewellyn Publications
A Division of Llewellyn Worldwide Ltd.
2143 Wooddale Drive
Woodbury, MN 55125-2989
www.llewellyn.com

Printed in the United States of America

For Jacob Adam Eernisse
My Knight and Shield,
In my long quest to find you,
I discovered myself.

And to Laughter-Loving Aphrodite and Hera of the Golden Throne
Who were smiling from my desk while I was writing this,
And who mend the hearts of lost lovers even now.

Love thyself.

CONTENTS

Introduction ... 1
  How to Use This Book ... 3
  Avoiding Pitfalls in Relationship Readings ... 5

PART 1: THE MAJOR ARCANA IN LOVE ... 11
  The Fool ... 13
  The Magician ... 17
  The High Priestess ... 21
  The Empress ... 25
  The Emperor ... 29
  The Hierophant ... 33
  The Lovers ... 37
  The Chariot ... 41
  Strength ... 45
  The Hermit ... 49
  The Wheel of Fortune ... 53
  Justice ... 57
  The Hanged Man ... 61
  Death ... 65
  Temperance ... 69
  The Devil ... 73
  The Tower ... 77
  The Star ... 81
  The Moon ... 85
  The Sun ... 89
  Judgment ... 93
  The World ... 97

PART 2: THE MINOR ARCANA IN LOVE ... 101
  Court Cards in Love ... 102
  Pip Cards in Love ... 105

Swords in a Love Reading ... 109

Ace of Swords ... 111

Two of Swords ... 115

Three of Swords ... 119

Four of Swords ... 123

Five of Swords ... 127

Six of Swords ... 131

Seven of Swords ... 135

Eight of Swords ... 139

Nine of Swords ... 143

Ten of Swords ... 147

Page of Swords ... 151

Knight of Swords ... 155

Queen of Swords ... 159

King of Swords ... 163

Cups in a Love Reading ... 167

Ace of Cups ... 169

Two of Cups ... 173

Three of Cups ... 177

Four of Cups ... 181

Five of Cups ... 185

Six of Cups ... 189

Seven of Cups ... 193

Eight of Cups ... 197

Nine of Cups ... 201

Ten of Cups ... 205

Page of Cups ... 209

Knight of Cups ... 213

Queen of Cups ... 217

King of Cups ... 221

Pentacles in a Love Reading ... 225

Ace of Pentacles ... 227

Two of Pentacles ... 231

Three of Pentacles ... 235

Four of Pentacles ... 239

Five of Pentacles ... 243

Six of Pentacles ... 247

Seven of Pentacles ... 251

Eight of Pentacles ... 255

Nine of Pentacles ... 259

Ten of Pentacles ... 263

Page of Pentacles ... 267

Knight of Pentacles ... 271

Queen of Pentacles ... 275

King of Pentacles ... 279

Wands in a Love Reading ... 283

Ace of Wands ... 285

Two of Wands ... 289

Three of Wands ... 293

Four of Wands ... 297

Five of Wands ... 301

Six of Wands ... 305

Seven of Wands ... 309

Eight of Wands ... 313

Nine of Wands ... 317

Ten of Wands ... 321

Page of Wands ... 325

Knight of Wands ... 329

Queen of Wands ... 333

King of Wands ... 337

PART 3: SPREADS FOR RELATIONSHIP READINGS ... 341

Do I Need to Choose a Significator? ... 342

"In a Nutshell" One-Card Spread ... 343

Three-Card Compatibility Spread ... 345

Seeking Love Spread ... 346

Cupid's Arrow Spread ... 348

Should I Stay or Should I Go? Spread ... 350

The Celtic Lover's Knot Spread ... 353

Healing a Broken Heart with the Empress ... 357

Conclusion ... 363

Appendix: "How Does This Person Feel?" Quick Guide ... 367

INTRODUCTION

*Okay, so I just asked my cards how he really feels about me. Why did I pull the Ace of Pentacles Reversed? What does that mean for love? I looked through all my tarot books and even online and they're all talking about business. I'm not asking about money; I'm asking about **him!** Perhaps I wasn't clear with my intentions. Maybe I should concentrate more. I bet I just needed to pick more than one card. Okay, let's concentrate and pull another card…*

*How does he really feel about me? How does he honestly feel about me? How does he **really truly** feel about me?*

The Queen of Swords?! Who is this lady? I've read that the Queen of Swords is a no-good snake in the grass! Is the Queen of Swords an ex? Is she me? Oh no! Maybe he's with someone else! That couldn't be. Maybe that's his mom? He mentioned he suffered abuse from her as a child. I've read that it's normal for people who've suffered trauma to retreat or to build walls around themselves. That's probably why he's not messaging me back…

Aww, he must be super sensitive and sweet. I just need to be more understanding. Poor guy…

This is driving me crazy! What's wrong with me? Why can't I stop thinking about him? This is the third time my heart's been broken this year. Why does this always happen to me? Why are my cards constantly contradicting themselves?

Where did all my power and confidence go?

WHY WON'T THESE CARDS LET ME SEE INTO HIS MIND?

Isn't that how tarot is supposed to work? I remember the day we both met, I pulled the Two of Cups. That was three weeks ago… why are my cards different this time? My favorite YouTube tarot channel says the Two of Cups means you've finally met your soul mate… your twin flame. We must

1

be *"meant to be."* *Who else feels an intense connection like this? He even told me how amazing I am. This can't be a fluke. How can he be the twin flame one day, and then ghost me the next? Why are these cards so confusing? I thought they were supposed to make me feel better.*

I don't want to be alone forever…

What is my problem? Am I just being dumb? What are these stupid cards trying to tell me?

Has this ever sounded like you? Even a long-ago version of yourself?

If you ask any professional tarot reader what questions they get asked most often by clients, "When's he coming back?" is right up there at the top of their list! In fact, it gets asked so often it even begins to annoy some readers. However, if you ask those same readers if they've ever asked their cards a similar question in the past, about someone they felt strongly toward, chances are they will sheepishly say yes. People have been seeking answers about love through divination since we've been painting pictures on cave walls.

Tarot is a language of symbols that speaks directly to the heart. It can be very useful to discover the vibration around a person or situation, highlighting patterns in human behavior and giving you a general idea about what direction events are likely to progress in. However, tarot can be tricky when interpreting hints about the future if your emotions, fears, and expectations are fixed on a desired person. Tarot readings are like mirrors. They reflect *what you carry in your heart* at the time of the reading. The future is always in motion. The future is ever changing based on your decisions and even the unpredictable decisions of others. This means there are no guarantees about a fixed future. This is especially true when using tarot as a predictive tool concerning people you don't know very well yet. Tarot is most effective when it is highlighting warning signs, patterns, or issues that need to be resolved *within yourself* before proceeding with others. When predicting the future with tarot, you must understand that you are seeing a *potential* future, based on the information you carry with you now. Sometimes, tarot is marketed in a way that leads to confusion, especially when it comes to love. Everyone wants certainty. However, tarot will disappoint you if you are looking for guarantees. More than anything, tarot helps you see yourself. This book will dispel some myths about answers to relationship questions when consulting the tarot.

HOW TO USE THIS BOOK

This book will focus on interpreting tarot symbolism for relationships. Although each chapter will provide an interpretation for your love life, you can extrapolate information about many of the archetypes presented in this book to other relationships as well, such as family relationships, professional colleagues, and friendships. This book is not restricted to only interpreting heterosexual partnerships and interactions. It can be applied to any relationship or any gender identity. Although I will use pronouns such as "he" or "she" to describe the archetypes we will encounter in the tarot, any pronoun can be substituted to apply to the person you are inquiring about. Each chapter will provide options for the interpretation of card reversals.

Tarot in Love can be used to answer a quick question you might have about your love life when selecting just one card. I've also included a chapter at the end of the book with multiple tarot spreads that can aid you with an in-depth interpretation of your current situation. Each chapter provides multiple options for how you can apply a card's symbolism to answer questions that pertain to relationships. There is also an appendix in the back of the book that can provide insight into how a particular individual might be feeling about you or their relationship at the time of your question.

Major Arcana chapters (the Fool, the Magician, the Chariot, etc.) and court card chapters (page, knight, queen, king) contain an introductory paragraph describing the *personality traits* of the individual you are inquiring about. This section will describe their character, priorities, strengths, and weaknesses. This section can reveal who the individual is at their core, and what relationship dynamics they value. For numbered Minor Arcana cards (aces, twos, threes, etc.), also called Pip cards, the introductory paragraph will describe a transitory *situation* or *experience* that you, your partner, or the relationship is undergoing. Minor Arcana cards tend to reveal situational events that are impermanent.

A particular tarot card's meaning can change depending on the context of the situation or the question being asked. Therefore, each chapter includes options for how a particular card could be interpreted depending on its context. If the Fool card were selected in response to a question about a potential relationship partner, the card would not be interpreted the same way as it would to describe a well-established relationship. Each chapter will provide a quick reference guide of five categories to help you pinpoint how a card can be usefully applied to your particular situation. The categories are as follows:

New Relationship: This section describes relationships that are just beginning. Here you can discover what sort of vibe surrounds this person or the union. Keep in mind that in the beginning of relationships, people generally show you their best face. It takes time to discover their authentic layers beneath the surface. This section can help confirm your instincts regarding red flags or an individual's best attributes.

Long-Term Partnership: Read this section if you are trying to gain insight into a relationship that has been well established for some time. This segment can also reveal what you, your partner, or the relationship needs to thrive. It can also highlight potential challenges or opportunities for the relationship that you both must confront for your partnership to grow.

Intimacy: This section describes a person's attitude toward sex, emotional intimacy, and vulnerability. It might also highlight deep emotions or desires that a relationship partner might struggle to speak openly about. This segment can also grant insight into how a person needs to feel in a relationship before they open up more.

Seeking Romance: Here you will find advice for people who are single and actively looking for a relationship. This section will describe how a person can use the current energy to their advantage to attract healthy relationships and avoid repeating mistakes of the past.

Desires: This section will describe what a person most desires at the time of the reading. It will grant insight into their priorities, values, and motivations. This section can also describe the attributes a potential partner prizes most in their relationships. Here you can discover if your innermost desires and priorities are in alignment with one another's.

Each chapter also includes interpretations for how to interpret reversed cards. The appearance of reversed cards in a reading should not be considered bad. They reveal an important issue that may need to be examined from a different point of view. If you are dealing with confusing, irrational, or challenging behavior from an individual you are inquiring about, you may want to read the reversed card interpretation to see how that person's shadow might be contributing to their inexplicable behavior. Bringing shadows to light helps you understand them. This allows you to take proactive steps that restore your personal power and keep you from experiencing another person's shadow at your own expense.

At the end of each chapter is a section titled What This Card May Be Teaching You. Here you can discover the deeper lesson that a particular relationship, cycle, or situation could be presenting *you* with. Tarot works best when it is in dialogue with your inner self. This segment provides gentle advice for what your spirit has been trying to communicate to you all along on your quest to discover authentic love. Sometimes you might encounter a particular card over and over in your readings that doesn't seem to describe the person or situation you are asking about. Instead, the card may be trying to get you to understand a particular lesson you yourself are struggling to move beyond. Relationships are mirrors. They can reflect our beauty, charisma, joy, and loving heart. However, relationships also reflect our shadows, fears, issues, and limitations. This section can help you discover the deeper lesson your heart is learning as it heals and transcends past limitations.

AVOIDING PITFALLS IN RELATIONSHIP READINGS

Receiving a reading during a turbulent emotional time can be deeply healing. Not only can you gain insight into the current vibe surrounding another person or a relationship, but you can also gain something far more valuable: *insight into yourself.* This book provides a safe, compassionate space in which to explore some of your deepest vulnerabilities. I have also included a chapter section for finding deeper guidance from your cards during those extra tough times.

All relationships are teachers. They do not exist to complete you. Nor are connections with others meant to endlessly feed something you feel deficient in. Relationships that are built upon neediness, desperation, or cycles of abusive behavior are not healthy. If you are looking to tarot cards to tell you this sort of relationship is okay, you are probably going to be disappointed. Tarot can be very direct. However, its symbolism does not need to be applied cruelly.

I've been working with tarot professionally for nearly three decades, and I can tell you that it can be bluntly honest at times, especially about an issue you may be in denial about. The cards will not bend to your will just because you barrage them with the same question thirty thousand times! If you are asking the same question over and over, hoping to see what your denial *wants* you to see, you will end up more confused and disappointed. If you see a card that appears unpleasant or frightening, it could either be a warning sign about the relationship, or it may be highlighting an underlying issue you need to confront in yourself. In my book *Fearless Tarot: How to Give a Positive Reading in Any Situation*, I reveal how to interpret tarot cards as vehicles for self-empowerment and positive transformation. Challenging cards can be applied to achieve a constructive result in yourself *if* you are open to examining them at a deeper level.

Within each person is an awareness I call the Higher Self. Some people call this awareness the unconscious, the spirit, your better angels, your best self, or your soul. Tarot is language that speaks in pictures. This is the same language the Higher Self speaks in. This language is not literal, it is *symbolic*. Tarot can speak directly to the deepest part of you, beyond your fears, wants, and needs. Although, I've found that when tarot reveals truths, it's usually for your own good. When listening to your Higher Self, you can view the truth of your present situation with love and compassion. Your Higher Self will always lead you to opportunities to grow and transcend challenges. Tarot works best when it is partnered with your Higher Self. You will receive substantive clarity rather than hollow hope.

Every person also has an ego. This is the part of you that desires immediate gratification and comfort. **The ego resists change!** It grasps for words like *mine, now, unfair,* [insert chosen curse word], *always, forever,* and ***I need!*** The ego has also been called the Lower Self by some. It is concerned with survival. The ego is often best friends with your fear. The ego worries constantly. "Am I too fat?" "What does he think of me?" "How come she is happy and I'm not?" "Will I be enough?" "Does she think she can replace me with *that*?" "Does he want ME?" "When will I finally get what **I** deserve?" **"I hope she burns in hell!"**

Tarot is adept at communicating to the Higher Self, but it does not effectively appease the ego. If you sit down for a tarot reading hoping to hear a rationalization for neediness or desperation, you will likely walk away from your reading hurt, angry, or confused. Divination will not always provide you the information you *want*, but if you are open to your Higher Self and its direction, tarot can provide the information you *need*.

Performing a reading for yourself works best when you are open to hearing the deeper wisdom being whispered beyond the shallow layer of ego and fear. Tarot is a transformative tool. The Higher Self encourages evolution, change, personal empowerment, accountability, and courage.

If the ego is running a reading, it is unlikely you will get the closure you seek. The ego will pick card after card, asking the same annoying question over and over until it sees something that affirms the image it *wants* to see. For example, "Is he coming back?" The Tower. "No … but is he possibly coming back in a few weeks?" Death. "No—but will he text me?" Ace of Swords. "Hmm … what does that mean? Looks better. Does he love me still?" Two of Cups! "See! I knew we were meant to be! Am I doing this wrong? I still feel anxious! These cards don't work … why would I get the Tower, Death, and the Two of Cups? I'm so confused …"

Examples of better questions to ask are, "What is this relationship helping me grow beyond?" "What am I not understanding about this person at this time in their life?" "What do I need to understand *about myself* to receive closure about this situation?" "What personal standards do I need to raise to attract a partner who will treat me with the respect I deserve?" "What do I need to love in myself right now?" "Am I accepting a relationship that is not worthy of my best self?" "How can I restore my self-esteem?" "What do I need to surrender?" "What do I need to accept about my current partner?"

The answers you get to questions like these will often be clear and give you the exact medicine you need. Your ego may dismiss the initial answers you receive because it hates altering its preconceived assumption it stubbornly wants to hold on to. The ego will resist change even if your transformation promises your goal of being happy and eventually getting into a relationship that is worthy of you. The ego wants to stay fixed, blameless, unaccountable, and stuck. The ego yells, fears, and wails until it gets pacified like a cranky baby. People confuse this obsessive single-mindedness with loyalty and true love … it's not. It's a desperate attempt to hold on to something that is destroying you. Showing up as a victim in your relationships will never lead to happiness. Loving yourself enough to courageously change what you know deep down must be changed will result in your breakthrough.

Each person you connect with on this planet can teach you something profound. Relationships hold up a mirror that helps us see ourselves more clearly.

That's why it feels so good when we are first approved of or admired by a love interest. The person admiring us is reflecting to us the beauty we possess but may not be able to see clearly. If we don't authentically love ourselves, we might feel the admiration from another as the first hit of an addictive drug. This often leads to the person we desire becoming an addiction, not a healthy relationship partner. On the road to finding true love, you will discover that the journey is really about learning to love yourself. This is why you hear icons like Ru Paul say, "If you can't love yourself, how the hell are you going to love someone else?"[1] This statement is so true! But this is often easier said than done. It takes self-work.

Often an abusive or needy relationship is teaching your spirit how to love yourself more than your addiction to the acceptance, desire, or approval of another. This lesson in *true love* is a tough one. It might just be one of the most difficult lessons you are on this planet to learn. Everyone will get their heart broken at least once in their lifetime. Some people will find their heart getting broken over and over until the lesson of *loving themselves* and raising their standards finally sinks in. It's not the duplicitous relationship partner keeping you in a state of suffering, **it's you!** Tarot works best when you are accountable. It can also help you find what needs to be replenished in your own heart before you place expectations on others to fill it for you.

All romantic relationships you experience are "meant to be," though not necessarily in the context of being your "soul mate" or "twin flame." Some relationships teach us hard lessons, such as when it's time to raise your standards, how to maintain your dignity in the face of heartache, or how to be accountable. At the end of each chapter, I encourage you to read the What This Card May Be Teaching You section. This will help you check inward and resolve your own challenges before navigating what to do with others.

No relationship is perfect. All relationships take work. The healthy relationship you do eventually settle down with will constantly challenge you to be a better version of yourself. As a little girl, Liza Minelli once asked her mother, Judy Garland, "Mama, what happens after Happily Ever After?" Judy Garland

---

1. Denes Fernando, "If you can't love yourself, how in the hell you gonna love somebody else?" https://youtu.be/l8AyBlNpePQ. Ru Paul closes every episode of *Ru Paul's Drag Race* with this self-affirming message to her viewers. This particular YouTube link is a compilation of the iconic quote.

paused before wryly responding, "You'll find out!"[2] Love doesn't stay a fairy tale forever. If your relationship is based on true love, maturity, and respect, it will be more substantive than fiction. It will be a safe space to grow and improve together; this is where the work really begins. Make no mistake, true love and relationships require effort, personal evolution, and compassion. However, the work is well worth it.

People are constantly changing. Every day we grow (and hopefully evolve) into new and better versions of ourselves. If you are asking the tarot to affirm permanence to the feelings and life stage of a specific person, you may see that same person transform into something completely different. That is why a reading can sometimes appear contradictory to an *earlier* reading about the same person or subject. People are changeable and contradictory! We like to think nothing changes about ourselves and others, but this is just not true. Tarot can best help you understand what is happening *right now*. Your power is in the present. If you are asking for permanent future assurances from the tarot, you won't get them. Nothing is fixed in stone.

You are not in control of what another will do, or the choices they will make. You cannot dominate their thoughts or will them into acting the way you want them to. All you have control over is your chosen response to what the relationship is teaching you at this time. You are in the driver's seat. You choose whether you walk through life as a victim or a victor.

Bettering *yourself* is the swiftest route toward true love. If you want to attract a partner with confidence, success, and self-esteem, work on those attributes *in yourself first!* Like attracts like. If you are resistant to a particular card's message, that's a big red flag that your ego is running the reading. Try to dig deeper than superficial fears when consulting the cards. Your romantic interest is likely reflecting something you need to understand about yourself. To give yourself an effective and positive relationship reading, tune inward, and let the best version of yourself take the lead.

---

2. "Larry King Live Interview with Liza Minelli," CNN Transcripts, October 5, 2010, trascripts .cnn.com/show/lkl/date/2010-10-05/segment/01.

Part I
The Major Arcana in Love

The archetypal personalities of the tarot are a powerful group. They reflect the characteristics that are found within each of us. The Major Arcana consists of twenty-two cards that express the diverse archetypes that reside within each person to varying degrees. When Major Arcana cards appear in a general reading, they can express the unconscious forces that affect one's life from within. The Major Arcana can also be used effectively for spiritual development. However, tarot is contextual. The meanings of the cards change depending on what you are asking about, your current state of mind, or what position of the spread a card appears in. That is why no one tarot book can give you fixed definitions that apply to every concern. Tarot is a nuanced tool. It can go far deeper than simple yes or no answers to your questions, but you must have the courage to see what is truly there. When performing a relationship reading, the Major Arcana cards can reveal deep insight into the unconscious attitudes at play within yourself and others.

Just as everyone has varying degrees of masculine and feminine attributes expressed within them, so, too, does each person embody varying degrees of the twenty-two archetypal qualities of the Major Arcana. However, at any given time, one archetype may seem dominant within a person depending on their situation or life phase. For example, someone who exhibited freedom-loving qualities of the Fool card for years may now be entering a life period where they are making sacrifices for the future, more in line with the Hanged Man archetype.

The following interpretations of the Major Arcana will reveal to you the priorities and archetypal traits being expressed in yourself and in the other people who accentuate your world. The following section will illuminate how each archetype is expressed when an individual is empowered, and how each archetype is expressed when someone is grappling with their shadow, which is exemplified in the reversed version of each card. The shadow is the hidden, repressed, or "out of power" part of us. Everybody encounters their shadow from time to time. The shadow resides in the unconscious. It dwells deep within us and is linked to the most primitive part of our brains. The shadow is not necessarily evil, but it can be expressed in some destructive behaviors. If you are encountering baffling or hurtful behavior coming from a person you care about, look at the reversed section of the Major Arcana card to gain further insight into how their shadow may be affecting the situation.

Each chapter will give you greater insight into the many personalities that color your life. If you are struggling to understand what a card is teaching you about yourself in a relationship, there is also a section that reveals what *you* may be learning through this experience. Remember, each relationship in your life exists to teach your soul a valuable lesson. As much as you may want to use the cards to know another person more intimately, ultimately you are interacting with a mirror, provided by the eyes of the other, to truly know yourself.

THE FOOL

The Fool is the archetype of freedom. He represents an individual who resists restriction, pressure, or conventionalism. The Fool will always go his own way and possesses a great sense of humor. He operates best in relationships that retain a sense of freedom, adventure, and fun. If you are trying to capture his interest, use humor and mischief. There is a lighthearted quality to relationships with the Fool. An individual who embodies the Fool's best qualities will never be boring. The Fool will love to travel and try new things. You cannot possess or own the Fool. The moment he feels stifled, shamed, or restricted is the moment he will pack his bag and seek adventure elsewhere. The Fool can also represent an individual who is youthful or young at heart. At his best, the Fool is hilarious, unique, unconventional, exciting, open-minded, and unafraid of taking risks. At his worst, he is immature, foolish, infantile, thoughtless, chaotic, inconsistent, and struggling with responsibility.

In a Love Reading
New Relationship
The Fool prefers to bond as a friend first. He can settle into a long-term relationship; however, he needs to feel unrestricted, or he will naturally rebel. There is a "wait and see" quality to this card. Although off to a good beginning, this card will caution that events need to play out a bit more. In the meantime, have fun!

Long-Term Partnership
The Fool can appear when it's time for a fresh start in a settled partnership. This card will encourage you to create new conditions for intimacy to reawaken. A new goal that both partners can get excited about, such as an eagerly anticipated trip, a new home, or a shared interest, can bring you closer together.

Intimacy
The Fool is thrilled by uninhibited spontaneity. Lovemaking should include playfulness and unpredictability. Keep the Fool guessing, and he'll stay interested. Overly serious, stifling, or controlling energy will immediately turn him off.

Seeking Romance
This card encourages less predictability. The Fool craves newness, lack of restriction, and adventure. If you've fallen into a slump, it's time to change up the energy. The appearance of the Fool encourages travel, new friendships, and exciting new places. The Fool never seems to grow up, and so he could encourage you to be more playful.

Desires
The Fool desires freedom, laughter, and fun. Friendships are important to the Fool. He will never make one sole individual the focus of *all* his attention. You

may need to make room for the Fool's friends if you want to have a relationship with him. He seeks an uninhibited partner who isn't controlling in relationships.

Reversed
New Relationship
The Fool Reversed can signify an individual who hasn't acquired all the emotional tools necessary to contribute to a practical relationship. He may not give much thought to the long-term success of relationships. Upright or reversed, the Fool is charming company, although he acts with a thoughtlessness that is never malicious.

Long-Term Partnership
The Fool Reversed can signify a partner whose persistent immaturity or inability to face responsibilities has become challenging. Discussions about bills, finances, or the future are often avoided. This card can also highlight neglected practical concerns. The Fool Reversed will often let his partner take on all the responsibility when it comes to sticky situations.

Intimacy
The Fool Reversed can indicate a pervading sense of *distance* within this relationship. There will always be some aspect of this person that is just out of reach. This relationship will thrive on independence and may even experience periods when the partnership is long-distance.

Seeking Romance
The Fool Reversed may encourage you to release your fear of failing before you even try. If you've been secluded or are expecting love to come to you, you may need to take the initiative and courageously get out into the world again. Start with reaching out to friends and having fun. Stop overthinking yourself and let go. You might actually have a good time!

Desires
Upright or reversed, the Fool desires freedom. Plans, schedules, and obligations give him the heebie-jeebies! The Fool Reversed just wants to have a good time and does not like to project too far into the future. Although the Fool Reversed is merry company, he can often act with thoughtless insensitivity.

What the Fool May Be Teaching You

The Fool is teaching you to let go of planning, controlling, or forcing life to follow your expectations. Numbered zero, the Fool governs new beginnings and the first shaky steps leading toward a happier future. Your growing process may seem chaotic at this time, but it will teach you how to let go of all you no longer need. When the Fool appears, you are likely learning to free yourself from outdated, rigid views and adapting to a new reality. The Fool is unpredictable, and when he appears, he turns all your expectations on their head … for your own good. Stop worrying about what others will think. Act on your intentions or speak up. The Fool could also be teaching you to be less inhibited and go for it! Keep things light for now and give your relationship life room to grow organically. Release the need to be in control or to know everything. Set yourself free from overthinking. This is your time. Own it!

THE MAGICIAN

The Magician represents an intelligent person with a brilliant mind. He thrives within the realm of ideas, imagination, communication, education, writing, or technology. As a natural leader, the Magician is goal-oriented and will resist any attempt to restrict his personal interests or autonomy. Even in relationships, he will insist on being in control of his own destiny. The Magician will resist anyone who pressures him into a "normal" life. Instead, he aims to be exceptional. The Magician's attention span is fleeting if he is not stimulated mentally. Unimaginative or intellectually incurious people bore him to death. Shared interests and a compatible communication style are essential to maintain a long-term relationship with him. At his best, the Magician's personality is mentally curious, charismatic, brilliant, witty, captivating, and funny, and he's a great conversationalist. At his worst, the Magician is flighty, changeable, unpredictable, and easily bored, and he can detach with little warning.

In a Love Reading
New Relationship
The Magician's interest can be piqued by displaying your knowledge, passions, and authentic interests. He loves all sorts of subjects and appreciates a sharp wit. Even if he does not share the same pursuits, he will be intrigued by learning something new. The Magician seeks an intellectually curious partner who is interested in his mind.

Long-Term Partnership
Communication is all important when the Magician appears. Make time to talk to one another—not just about problems or needed improvements, but, more importantly, about the common interests you share and enjoy. Good communication requires you to also be a good listener. Both partners succeed when they feel their ideas are truly heard and respected.

Intimacy
The Magician is turned on by what he hears, imagines, or visualizes. Something as simple as your tone of voice could excite him far more than planning out the perfect evening. He loves clever language and double entendres. Insecure or needy people are an immediate turnoff. Never use tactics like guilt or pressure to leverage him, or he will abruptly detach.

Seeking Romance
Place yourself in surroundings where you can engage in intellectual discourse or share in common interests with others. Love will likely manifest where your mind and heart meet. Gravitate toward physical or online spaces where people of like mind gather.

Desires
The Magician desires a true meeting of the minds. Magician personalities thrive in environments where their creativity, interests, and independent brilliance are not stifled. The Magician can also be a bit of a nerd, feeling a special kinship with a partner who shares this lovable quality.

Reversed
New Relationship
The Magician Reversed is a charmer. This card can warn of flattery, trickery, or words that just don't add up. If what he is saying sounds too good to be true, it probably is. The Magician Reversed can also represent an uncontrollable flirt. If you are possessive, you may get frustrated by his shameless glances at the attractive server or bistro.

Long-Term Partnership
The Magician Reversed can highlight communication problems in a relationship. This card can also represent a partner who is using passive-aggressive behavior to get their point across. When the Magician appears reversed, be direct, clear, and honest without abandoning kindness or the ability to listen.

Intimacy
The Magician Reversed can be detached or self-centered. Communication (or the lack of it) about difficult subjects is usually at the root of intimacy problems. One partner may be feeling unfulfilled. However, they may struggle with putting their feelings into words.

Seeking Romance
The Magician Reversed can represent an individual who enjoys being single for now. This could lead to hard feelings if this person glibly expressed an interest in forming a deeper connection. This card can also represent self-improvements you are making that are hard to stay committed to. Keep your word with yourself.

Desires
The Magician Reversed is often indecisive and may struggle to articulate what he truly wants. He desires the freedom to change his mind at any time, which makes him struggle with commitment. Upright or reversed, the Magician desires to maintain control over his own destiny.

What the Magician May Be Teaching You

The Magician could be teaching you that your predominant thoughts are the magic spells creating the current reality you are experiencing. The beauty of the Magician's message is that if you don't like what you are experiencing, seeing, or feeling, you can change it! However, you must redirect your thoughts toward fully supporting yourself, rather than continuing to diminish yourself on whoever (or whatever) makes you feel small. The Magician encourages you to take command of your mind to restore your personal dignity and self-esteem. Before you can profoundly connect with the best in another, you must embody what is best in yourself. The Magician encourages you to grasp the wand of your personal authority instead of fruitlessly waiting for another person to grant your power to you. When you wield the limitless wonder of who you truly are, the magic will begin to happen in your life.

THE HIGH PRIESTESS

The High Priestess is a mystery. She is interested in understanding her partner at their deepest level; however, it is much trickier to get to know her. Everyone displaying the traits of the High Priestess has integrated and embraced the feminine receptive principle within themselves. Even when young, the High Priestess personality will demonstrate a wisdom beyond her years. The High Priestess guards her privacy and will resent any unwelcome intrusion into her innermost landscape. Try not to prod, probe, or pressure when the High Priestess personality needs to retreat. When the High Priestess appears, you may also experience a strong feeling of *déjà vu* as if you've already connected with an individual in times long past. At her best, the High Priestess personality is extremely intuitive, otherworldly, insightful, experienced, and wise. At her worst, she is overly secretive and emotionally aloof and can regularly withdraw when feelings get too intense.

In a Love Reading
New Relationship
The High Priestess personality radiates a seductive and enigmatic aura. This person appreciates someone who also exudes an air of mystery. Try not to reveal everything about yourself right away. The High Priestess personality values depth, complexity, and substance over image. Never wear a superficial mask; it won't work anyway.

Long-Term Partnership
You can know your partner for years only to discover new mysteries still being unveiled. This relationship is fundamentally bonded at the soul level. There could be such a strong sense of connection that you can finish each other's thoughts or sentences. Both partners intuitively know far more about the other than what is outwardly shared. This is truly a soul connection.

Intimacy
The High Priestess archetype loves mystery. Passion is ignited by not revealing everything right away. The High Priestess likes the subtle nuances, flirtations, and slow progression leading up to intimacy. Be real. The High Priestess is repelled by artifice or superficiality.

Seeking Romance
The High Priestess reassures you that your current experience is just another lesson in your initiation toward wisdom, authentic love, and wholeness. The High Priestess reminds you that the Great Mystery will lead you toward the right person and place when the time is right … and not before. Listen within and trust the part of you that is ageless and wise for your next step.

Desires

The High Priestess personality desires a partner who embraces their authenticity. She will know if you are trying too hard to craft an image or if you are truly being yourself. The High Priestess also likes to keep her mystery and secrets. She requires someone who will allow her periodically to withdraw and who respects her privacy.

Reversed
New Relationship

The High Priestess Reversed can represent an enigmatic person who abruptly alters their behavior without warning. One moment it feels as if a deep connection is being forged only to find this person abruptly retreating when feelings become too intense. The High Priestess Reversed protectively guards her emotional vulnerabilities.

Long-Term Partnership

This card will highlight one partner in the relationship who struggles with understanding and expressing their innermost feelings. They would rather retreat than confront and will need to periodically withdraw into their own private world to restore their equilibrium. This partner conceals a deep love and intense emotions but may struggle to put them into words.

Intimacy

The High Priestess Reversed can represent someone who may have a hard time trusting and may constantly test others to ascertain if they are being authentic. Getting close to this person is extremely difficult. They have likely erected a series of emotional barriers. The High Priestess Reversed can be emotionally unavailable or distant.

Seeking Romance

The High Priestess Reversed can reveal recurring patterns of irrational behavior that is leading to misunderstandings or confusion. If you are experiencing baffling behavior from another, you may have to accept that there isn't a rational reason as to why.

Desires

The High Priestess Reversed carefully guards her private thoughts. If you continue to prod and pry into her innermost feelings, she will likely retreat from you. This personality desires the avoidance of uncomfortable conflict and will try to leave unspoken hints as to how they truly feel.

What the High Priestess May Be Teaching You

The High Priestess will always teach you to reconnect with, and trust, the intuitive voice within. She reassures you that you possess everything you need to pass the present emotional initiation stretching before you. Your inner priestess deserves to be honored and respected. She is both wise and ancient. If an external worry is pulling you to a lower vibration, it is time to transcend it by remembering the old soul residing in your core. Relationship partners who can truly see and marvel at the person you truly are at your center are extremely rare … however, that doesn't mean they don't exist. Trust where the Mystery leads, and your soul's mate will find their way to you. The High Priestess gently invites you to the quiet place within. Away from all the drama and noise. Her whisper will tell you exactly which next step must be taken. Trust her gentle guidance.

THE EMPRESS

When it comes to matters of the heart, the Empress is in her element. She is instinctively nurturing and affectionate. Empress people also embrace the feminine side of their nature, no matter their gender. The Empress possesses an unmatched ability to create soothing, reassuring environments where love can flourish. She understands the magic of an enchanted evening and will expose her partner to the finest things in life. Empress personalities love to pamper their mates with thoughtful little presents and sumptuous meals. They also make skilled chefs. In a love reading, the Empress will represent someone who is extremely devoted to whomever she considers to be her family. A sure way to turn off an Empress personality is to criticize her family, friends, or community. At her best, the Empress is kind, nurturing, loving, giving, and compassionate. At her worst, the Empress can be smothering, needy, or a doormat.

In a Love Reading
New Relationship
The Empress archetype is a true romantic and cherishes the courtship phase of a relationship for as long as possible. Her archetype thrives on romance. Handwritten notes of affection and decadent meals lovingly prepared will capture her heart. The more chivalrous you are in the early part of the relationship, the better.

Long-Term Partnership
The Empress oversees nurturing, growth, and deepening commitment in relationships. It may be time to give birth to new conditions, such as buying a new home, creating a new business, or even expanding your family through children or pets. When the Empress appears, your relationship is likely entering a new cycle of love, success, and plenty.

Intimacy
The Empress adores indulging in the pleasures of the senses. As the Great Mother of the tarot, the Empress is also an extremely fertile card. The appearance of the Empress is a fortuitous sign if you are thinking of starting a family. If you are able to have children and don't want a family now, take your necessary precautions!

Seeking Romance
The Empress is a sensuous archetype and will encourage you to flirt and freely express your romantic nature. It may also be time to connect with the goddess of love and beauty within. Indulge in life's delights. The Empress is a welcome guide toward your heart's bliss.

Desires

The Empress archetype desires beauty, peace, romance, and harmony. She represents a person who maintains extremely high standards. Never be crude, rude, or trashy with an Empress personality. She is a class act who is repelled by vulgarity. The Empress can also symbolize a desire to begin a family or to have children.

Reversed

New Relationship

The Empress Reversed can signify a budding relationship where one partner is overbearing, smothering, or needy. This might have the unintended effect of turning off the very person they are trying to impress. If you are coming on too strong, back off a little. The advice of the Empress, upright or reversed, is always to let them come to you.

Long-Term Partnership

The Empress Reversed can represent a partner who needs to be needed. Although this person likes to think that she is selflessly acting for those she cares for, this may be masking her insatiable desire to feel wanted or loved. This card will alert you to a partner who gives much while silently expecting a lot in return.

Intimacy

The Empress Reversed is high maintenance. Atmosphere and appearance are very important to her. Romantically, she will insist on finery. Messy environments or sloppiness will make her nose turn up. This queen requires a romantic environment that is not only sensuous, but luxurious as well.

Seeking Romance

The Empress Reversed can highlight issues around past mothering or nurturing that are unconsciously affecting one's adult relationship life. A lack of adequate nurturing from early family life may be at the root of extreme aloofness or excessive clinginess in adult relationships. A counselor or another professional may help with healing past issues.

Desires

The Empress Reversed can represent the desire to raise your standards. She alerts you if you've been allowing yourself to be walked over like a doormat in relationships. This card encourages you to stop placing yourself in situations where you feel disrespected or dishonored. Upright or reversed, the Empress archetype encourages you to command respect.

What the Empress May Be Teaching You

The Empress lovingly teaches you that caring for yourself is what is needed now. Loving yourself is your best shield. It is better to walk away from all disrespecting your majesty than to continuously cast your pearls before swine. The Empress reminds you that it isn't enough to just pour all your love on a partner. You must also maintain a standard to receive an equal measure of love and respect in return. The Empress does not understand the concept of scarcity. If you feel you can't have healthy relationships or that negative experiences are all you can get in this life, the Empress smiles reassuringly at you. She asks you to trust in the concept of divine timing. She knows that with self-love and patience, in the right season, at the right time, the love that is meant to be will blossom.

THE EMPEROR

The self-confident Emperor is a leader who never follows. Whether young or old, an Emperor personality is most comfortable when he feels in control. Emperor personalities are tough and will persevere in the face of life's challenges, asserting the empowered masculine attributes of their nature, no matter their gender. In life and love, the Emperor seizes the initiative. If the Emperor feels his personal

authority is being usurped, he will inevitably reassert control over his own destiny. In love, it can often be difficult to gage what the Emperor is truly thinking or feeling. Communication does not always flow easily with him. For the
Emperor, actions speak louder than words. To understand his inner motivations,
look at what he is *doing*, and not at what he is saying. At his best, the Emperor is
strong, stable, assertive, and fiercely protective of those he loves. At his worst, he
is irritable, tactless, belligerent, unexpressive, and autocratic.

In a Love Reading
New Relationship
The Emperor is all in at the start of a relationship when everything is still fresh
and new. He will struggle if the relationship becomes routine and ceases to offer
new excitement and challenges. Like the astrological sign of Aries, the Emperor
thrives on new beginnings. For this relationship to work, there must always be
something fresh and exciting to look forward to.

Long-Term Partnership
If the Emperor has made a commitment, he is one of the most stable figures in
the tarot for the longevity of relationships. He is protective and a responsible
role model for children. However, the Emperor tends to be stubborn. You may
have to be the one who compromises more in the relationship.

Intimacy
The Emperor is extremely passionate. Lovemaking for him is very physical, and
he will require an active sex life to maintain his interest. If an Emperor personality has been consistently cranky, he may be feeling sexually frustrated. Physical activity, getting out of his head, and getting outdoors can help revitalize his
passions.

Seeking Romance
It's time to make the responsible choice for your love life to improve. Allow
your inner adult to call the shots right now. Stand up for your dignity, boundaries, and self-respect. Don't waste your time with anyone who's proven they are
beneath you.

Desires

Although the Emperor appears outwardly confident, he may harbor a hidden insecurity about holding the supreme place within his partner's passions. He can be warm but tends to require trust before revealing his sensitivity. The Emperor desires a partner who vocally validates his importance and value. The Emperor needs to feel appreciated to open up.

Reversed
New Relationship

The Emperor Reversed is no poet! If you are looking for this individual to gush on you with romantic accolades describing your beauty and best qualities, you probably won't receive these flowering words. Competition, sports, business, and the drive for external success are the arenas he thrives in.

Long-Term Partnership

The Emperor Reversed can represent a domineering and autocratic partner. He will insist on being in full control and will resent any attempt to coerce or pressure him. If he feels insecure in his authority, he may display his temper or attempt to bring others down a notch to soothe his wounded pride.

Intimacy

Mountains will often appear on the Emperor card. When the Emperor is reversed, the mountains can symbolize remoteness when it comes to intimacy. This person can often appear detached to protect their vulnerabilities.

Seeking Romance

Sometimes the Emperor Reversed can represent either an absent father or a relationship partner who has many issues surrounding a complicated history with his own father. The lack of a father's approval and validation can create deep insecurities for people in their adult relationships. It may be time for you or your partner to tackle old issues from the past.

Desires

Upright or reversed, the Emperor will not beat around the bush. When an Emperor personality sees what he wants, he will be very clear about what his intentions are. He will desire a partner who doesn't play games or create drama.

This person will always let you know where you stand by his *actions* rather than his words.

What the Emperor May Be Teaching You

The appearance of the Emperor will teach you the importance of maintaining your dignity and power. Instead of looking to others to take the lead, the Emperor reminds you that the only person who can properly address your current challenges is you. The Emperor could also appear to strengthen your resolve as you take a stand for yourself. Establishing strong boundaries clarifies to others how you expect to be treated. You must let others know what is acceptable or unacceptable with your *actions*, much more than with your words. The Emperor encourages you to bask in the feeling of personal empowerment that comes from taking the lead in your own life, rather than passively waiting for someone else to rescue you from it. The Emperor is a warrior. You may need to fight for your dignity and respect at this time. The Emperor also wears armor. You may need to protect yourself while still getting to know a person or situation. If someone is violating your personal honor code, you must be willing to say the word *no*! The Emperor will always encourage you to be more assertive and to stand up for yourself and your values.

THE HIEROPHANT

The Hierophant is ever devoted to those he feels responsible for. He has a strong sense of right and wrong. Family and tradition are important to him. The Hierophant has ardent beliefs about everybody and everything. He might also hold strong spiritual views that inform how he shows up in the world. He does not necessarily proselytize his beliefs or opinions, but if you ask him for honest feedback, you will receive the unvarnished truth. For balance, the Hierophant will periodically retreat to his sacred inner sanctum to reconnect with his sense of purpose. If the Hierophant is set on a course, he will see it through to completion. In relationships, his stubbornness can be both a blessing and a bane. After knowing a Hierophant personality for a short time, you will recognize that he follows a predictable routine. At his best, the Hierophant is faithful, devoted, traditional, and steadfast. At his worst, he is stubborn, resistant, and close-minded, and he believes *his way* is the only *right way*.

In a Love Reading
New Relationship
The Hierophant can be a little shy at first. He might attempt to avoid conversations that are too direct, especially when it comes to his feelings. Try not to rush or pressure him into moving forward faster than he is ready. The Hierophant is often interested in a partner who unselfishly honors a commitment to a purpose greater than themselves.

Long-Term Partnership
Many Hierophant people are either married or expect to be. The Hierophant will always honor his commitment to his family and their traditions. Although he is often uncompromising, his intentions most often originate from a good place. Like the Emperor, the Hierophant is extremely stubborn and seeks a partner who can bend where he cannot.

Intimacy
Intimately, the Hierophant may be self-conscious or even prudish. Be patient. When the Hierophant opens his heart completely to you, lovemaking will feel transcendental. The Hierophant will not play games; however, he does occasionally need to be encouraged to loosen up a bit.

Seeking Romance
The Hierophant encourages you to seek a partner who shares your *values*. You may be establishing higher standards; as such, you should require honor, trust, and consistency from others before you make a commitment. Superficial and disingenuous people will no longer cut it.

Desires

Being dedicated to consistency and ritual, the Hierophant secretly desires a partner who can introduce some excitement and spontaneity into his life. However, he must also feel like a deeper connection can be established. For a Hierophant relationship to work, you must both share the same values and a shared commitment to something larger than your individual desires.

Reversed
New Relationship

The Hierophant Reversed may represent someone who is already married or committed to another person, family, or obligation. Image is everything to the Hierophant Reversed. He may not want to upset the maintenance of the status quo. Projecting an image can sometimes come at the expense of his truth.

Long-Term Partnership

The Hierophant Reversed can represent a partner who is fixed, uncompromising, and set in his ways. If you remain in this partnership believing you can eventually change his ways, you are mistaken. Once he has made up his mind, it will be difficult to persuade him to see things otherwise.

Intimacy

At his core, the Hierophant Reversed is emotionally conservative. It may be difficult to gage what he is truly feeling about others. The Hierophant Reversed is extremely adept at locking away his emotions and throwing away the key. The Hierophant Reversed is always hesitant to share his vulnerabilities and doubts.

Seeking Romance

Upright or reversed, the Hierophant encourages you to have faith that all will work out under the benevolent guidance of the universe. You may have to release your need to control and allow what is yours to come to you. Trust that the romance meant to find you will be. Let go of negative beliefs surrounding what you think is truly possible for you.

Desires

The Hierophant Reversed may represent a person who desires absolute control over their own destiny. He may have experienced constant pressure from an overly dominating parent or an equally controlling ex. As a result, he will steer clear of anyone he perceives as trying to control or pressure him.

What the Hierophant May Be Teaching You

The Hierophant may be teaching you about faith. Faith is the part of us that perseveres even when the path ahead is shrouded in shadow. Faith is love's twin sister. Faith is tested when life events aren't going perfectly. Faith will help you discover the higher meaning within your greatest challenges. Everything happens for a reason. The Hierophant teaches that the highest expression of love can always be reclaimed by realigning with the divine light that emanates from your center. *You* are forever; the fleeting challenge you are currently confronting is not. The Hierophant will help you find meaning in even the most harrowing experiences of the heart. Although this challenge will pass, the wisdom it is imparting will remain if you can recognize its gift. Have faith that a future overflowing with love, joy, and bliss still waits for you. Angelic hands are gently guiding you toward the correct next step.

THE LOVERS

In a love reading, the Lovers are a welcome sight! They amplify the effects of positive cards and moderate the challenges found in others. The Lovers can signify an intense, mutual attraction or the deepening of an existing bond. Whenever the Lovers appear, it's time to share, open your heart, and connect. They suggest that you allow *love* to choose your next move. If you've been single ... that may be about to change. If the Lovers signify a personality type, they can represent someone who is on a quest to find their perfect match. This individual may be ready for romance; however, the Lovers also represent *choices*. The person you are asking about is undoubtedly attracted to you; however, they may still be weighing all their options. Trust that when love is true, relationships will evolve organically. At their best, the Lovers represent someone who is attractive, affectionate, and ready for love. At their worst, they are indecisive and impractical and may not face harsh realities regarding the person they are intensely attracted to.

In a Love Reading
New Relationship
Love is in the air! This is an exciting card that promises intense mutual attraction. Time (and other cards) will reveal if this passion develops into something deeper. For the moment, know that your personal rapport with this individual is off to a very good start.

Long-Term Partnership
For a long-term partnership, the Lovers can indicate marriage or the strengthening of a lasting commitment. No matter where you go or what happens in your lives, the bond between you both is eternal. Compromise, communication, and compassion will be the tools to help this partnership overcome its obstacles.

Intimacy
The Lovers represent intense sexual chemistry. Your lover will have no trouble discovering what pleases you. The nakedness of the Lovers can represent un-self-consciousness. Do not fear baring your true feelings when the Lovers appear. The Lovers herald romance and increased affection. When it comes to sexual matters, the Lovers is one of the best cards to appear.

Seeking Romance
If you are single, romance is in the air! Your self-esteem is on the rise, and it's time to flirt, play, and express yourself. Make the extra effort. Adorn yourself with flattering clothes, complementary colors, or any other accoutrements that highlight your attractiveness. Allow subtle smiles and smoldering eyes to set your personal magnetism ablaze.

Desires

Whenever the Lovers appear, smiling Aphrodite is looking down upon you with favor. This card can represent a person who feels great desire for you. The Lovers may inspire you to act on your own desire to connect. Take a risk and bare your feelings.

Reversed
New Relationship

The person you are drawn to is likely your complete opposite. Although opposites attract, they may not share your priorities, values, or goals. Time is needed to gather more data and to reveal if love is true. Lovers Reversed challenges you to honor your authentic values, even when your perception may be distorted by intense attraction.

Long-Term Partnership

The Lovers Reversed can highlight a relationship challenge that can be resolved with healthy communication. Try to consider that there are two sides to every story, and that your manner of communication may not be identical to your partner's. If the relationship is normally healthy, harmony will likely be restored by understanding the other person's perspective.

Intimacy

Even reversed, the Lovers will signify attraction and sexual chemistry. Your partner will likely be turned on by something you find very different from what stimulated you in the past. However, this card can signify passionate excitement if you can stretch beyond familiar perimeters and open yourself to new ways of expressing intimacy.

Seeking Romance

You are either healing from a breakup or can't seem to get over a past relationship. This card can represent a relationship that you continually try to resurrect, even when nothing changes. The harmony you seek will not come by reviving a dysfunctional past.

Desires

You may hold two conflicting desires in your heart and may feel unclear about which pathway to take. Resolve internal conflict by steering your heart toward truth, even if you feel resistant to accepting it. Make the choice that empowers you, and you will find what you truly want.

What the Lovers May Be Teaching You

If disharmony is at your center, the Lovers may be teaching you how to look upon yourself with perfect love, trust, and self-acceptance. The Lovers also represent choices. This card can represent the transformative decision to love yourself more than your desire for validation or approval from someone who is emotionally unavailable to you. The angel smiles down on the naked, unashamed Lovers without judgment, accepting them just as they are. This symbolizes the importance of allowing your Higher Self to take the lead when it comes to assessing yourself. All begins to mend when acceptant love for yourself resides within your center. Cherish the gifts you bring. Make the choice to love and accept yourself unconditionally, no matter where you currently find yourself on your path. The angel whispers this eternal truth you can trust in: "Be Love, and you will find love."

THE CHARIOT

The Chariot personality is confident, proud, and bold. He tenaciously drives toward success. The Charioteer's passion ignites most fervently when there is a goal to attain. In love, the Charioteer is especially ardent when trying to win the affection of the person he desires. However, if the conquest proves too easy, he quickly loses interest. The Charioteer prefers a challenge. Though the Charioteer exudes implacable confidence, he is also surprisingly sensitive. Like all armored figures in the tarot, it may take time before he reveals his vulnerabilities. The Charioteer is protective of those he cares for. When his heart is invested, he will loyally fight for his love to the end. Many Chariot people are called to *serve* in some manner, for a cause greater than themselves. At his best, the Charioteer is confident, assertive, passionate, driven, strong, and sensitive. At his worst, he can be overly controlling and will often bottle up his feelings. He can also be a ruthless competitor and prone to obsessiveness.

In a Love Reading
New Relationship
When dating the Charioteer, be confident. He is attracted to strength of character and presence. Don't be too eager to please. Chariot people retreat when they catch the slightest whiff of desperation. The Charioteer respects individuals who hold firm convictions and know their own mind. This card can also signify progress or movement in a relationship.

Long-Term Partnership
The Chariot can describe a partnership where both people are leaving their comfort zones and are about to embark into uncharted territory. Although there are challenges or conflicts that are sure to be confronted, the Chariot promises victory. Overcoming adversity brings out the best in this relationship.

Intimacy
The Charioteer is simple to understand when it comes to sex. He is a conqueror. Once he achieves his objectives, he will quickly grow bored. The Charioteer must always feel as if there is something more to attain. A person who maintains an aura of mystique will fascinate him.

Seeking Romance
If you are single, the Chariot encourages you to be bold and go for it! Don't let the fear of looking a certain way keep you from your happiness. Leave your comfort zone and have courage. You won't win your heart's desire if you retreat from every opportunity to achieve it.

Desires

Though a Chariot personality will often appear like they want to move fast, slow down a bit and prolong the excitement. The Charioteer is passionate, but he's really looking for someone who maintains their standards and boundaries. People pleasers never satisfy him.

Reversed
New Relationship

The Chariot Reversed can represent a love interest who is obsessed with appearing impenetrably confident. This may be a mask for an unacknowledged insecurity within.

This card can also represent someone who retreats into their shell when they don't understand their emotions. You can't make the Charioteer reemerge. He must come to you.

Long-Term Partnership

The Chariot Reversed may describe a partner who feels they've lost control over their life's direction. Although this person appears emotionally impenetrable, they are likely feeling extremely vulnerable. Discussing underlying issues compassionately may help them get back in the driver's seat.

Intimacy

This reversal can represent a person who is insecure and craves validation. Affirming what makes him attractive, sexy, and desirable will ignite his passion. Upright or reversed, the Charioteer must feel his partner only has eyes for him, especially when it comes to sex.

Seeking Romance

A past heartbreak may be tempting you to retreat behind fortified impenetrable walls. Focus on pursuits that bolster your confidence. Physical activity can be one tool to help restore vitality and passion. Resist rushing into a rebound relationship to avoid feeling the discomfort of a past loss.

Desires

The Chariot Reversed can represent a desire to seek a meaningful relationship while also feeling pulled in two opposite directions. Two paths spread before you, and only one can be chosen. Choose the path that takes you away from feeling powerless and small.

What the Chariot May Be Teaching You

The Chariot may be teaching you to bravely leave an emotional rut behind. Many decks show the Charioteer leaving a walled castle. This represents a psychological need to leave behind comfortable yet stifling patterns. Two mysterious sphinxes often pull the chariot, one black and one white. The answers to love's questions are rarely black and white and, like the sphinxes, may pull your heart in opposite directions. In the old myths, the sphinxes pose riddles to a hero. Even though the Charioteer may feel confusion and inner conflict, he bravely steers his vehicle toward empowerment. It takes courage to leave disempowerment behind. The Charioteer courageously drives forward, reminding you to not get stuck in the past. You are in the driver's seat of your life. Passively believing that it is someone else's responsibility to drive you toward wholeness can waste precious years. Take the reins and steer your life's chariot toward the path that restores your power and dignity. Your best life waits before you, not behind.

STRENGTH

The person embodying the Strength archetype has a noble bearing and loves being in the spotlight. Heads turn when this dynamic presence walks into the room. A Strength personality, regardless of gender, is passionate and proud. In love, they are warmhearted and demonstrably affectionate. Strength people spend a great amount of time trying to harness their irrepressible inner fire.

Activities that help them tame their energy, like working out or perfecting a talent, can be extremely beneficial to them psychologically. However, Strength people insist on *self-correcting*. Critical feedback from others may provoke the lion's roar. In love, Strength people look for a warmhearted person who is loyal and can match their charismatic energy. They prefer to venture out into the world and do things rather than endlessly sit with their partner at home. At their best, Strength people are robust, warm, charismatic, and strong. At their worst, they can be vain, combative, and needy for validation.

In a Love Reading
New Relationship
A Strength personality will seek a mate who is as vibrant as they are. They don't seek a perfect partner but do desire someone who is improving their life in some way. A Strength person will be repelled by anyone who appears unmotivated. In the beginning of a relationship, this person seeks energy, attention, passion, action, and fun.

Long-Term Partnership
Strength can signify a relationship that has weathered many challenges. This card can also appear when one partner must exert self-control over their own desire to maintain the balance of the union. Strength often implies a continuing challenge that must be habitually confronted. However, the foundation of this partnership is strong.

Intimacy
Intimately, Strength can symbolize a passionate, instinctive attraction. The chemistry can feel overwhelmingly intense, especially in the beginning. Savor the building passion of the courtship phase, but take your time. This will ensure the smoldering passion doesn't burn out too quickly.

Seeking Romance
If you are single, Strength appears to advise you to engage in some form of self-improvement. Work out at the gym. Seek a more fulfilling job. Return to school. Engage in spirit work. Cultivate a talent. Participate in activities that strengthen your confidence and self-esteem. This will stoke the fires of your presence and confidence.

Desires
Strength can represent a desire to reclaim power; however, this requires that some difficult emotions be tamed. The lion on the card can represent overwhelming feelings to rein in, such as jealousy, anger, pride, or passion. Self-improvement is required and will be reinforced by making better decisions and making the choice to be strong.

Reversed
New Relationship
Strength Reversed can represent a relationship partner who requires validation. They may not feel confident or strong and will struggle with taking the lead. This person requires encouragement, not criticism, before they feel they can be more vulnerable.

Long-Term Partnership
Strength Reversed can represent a connection to a person who struggles with self-restraint. This can manifest as an addictive tendency or the inability to restrain their impulses. Sometimes this card will appear as a warning not to enable a destructive behavior, just to placate the raging lion. Stand up for your values and hold high standards for what you know is right.

Intimacy
Intimately, Strength Reversed can represent a person in the relationship who is withdrawing to nurse their wounded pride. They may think of sex as the ultimate validator of their desirability. This person is very sensitive to rejection. If they feel undesired or shamed, they may fight about an unrelated issue, which is used as a smoke screen.

Seeking Romance
Strength Reversed can signify a person who is seeking love but still harbors uncomfortable, bottled-up emotions surrounding rejection, anger, or humiliation from the past. Before a new partnership can be initiated, self-confidence must be restored. Exercise, engaging activities, or creative expression are wonderful ways to nurse the wounded lion back to health.

Desires

Strength Reversed can represent a person who struggles with a desire that feels out of control. This card usually tests one's willpower. Upright or reversed, Strength requires us to tame the lion within while also infusing our self-correction processes with compassion and love.

What Strength May Be Teaching You

Strength may be teaching you to courageously rein in a fear, passion, or inner weakness. In the tarot, Strength symbolizes self-control. Many decks feature a woman taming a lion. The lion can represent an internal issue that is self-sabotaging. If allowed to run loose, the lion can consume your every thought and emotion. The lion is different for everyone. For some, the lion represents unresolved rage or sorrow from a past betrayal, which unconsciously telegraphs a disempowered vibe to others. For others, it's the yearning for a past abusive relationship that has proven to be destructive. The lion can also come in the form of the fearful voice within, which continually sabotages one's confidence. A lion on the loose can wreak havoc in your relationships. The woman on the card is at peace with the lion and teaches you to be gentle with yourself as you make self-corrections. The best way to tame the lion is to redirect its energy toward actions that restore wholeness. Working out, engaging with your community, seeking therapy, or following your bliss through creative expression are just some ways you can subdue the lion. Perhaps the thing that seems to endlessly thwart your best life can be overcome by taming the beast within.

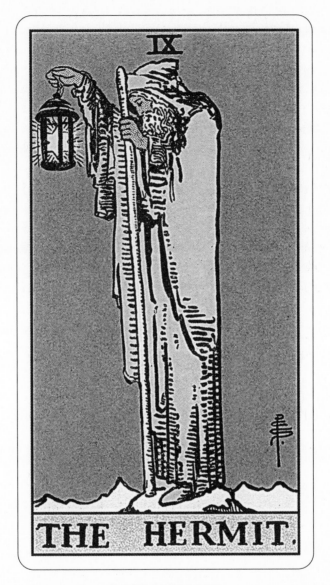

THE HERMIT

The person embodying the Hermit archetype is an introvert. Although he can survive in social settings, he thrives best when allowed to retreat to his inner world. For his sanity, the Hermit will often withdraw from external pressures to study, create, or process his emotions. Any person who enters a relationship with the Hermit must be comfortable with his desire to retreat. In love, the

Hermit is attracted to maturity. He is not impressed by people who strive to maintain a superficial image. The Hermit peers directly into the spirit of the person he is connecting with. The independent Hermit never looks for a relationship to complete him. This can lead to misunderstandings with a partner who desires ceaseless attention. A Hermit personality thrives best with a partner who is equally independent and self-reliant. At his best, the Hermit is wise, intelligent, thoughtful, sensitive, trustworthy, and authentic. At his worst, he can be reclusive, remote, and overly serious or a depressive curmudgeon.

In a Love Reading
New Relationship
Even in the beginning of a relationship, a Hermit partner will habitually withdraw to recenter and process. Although this person cares, he will frequently be absent due to physical proximity or other obligations. If both partners are independent and self-reliant, this connection holds potential. However, mutual affection must be communicated and understood.

Long-Term Partnership
Hermit partnerships thrive on independence. There is likely a deep bond between both people, but also a desire to periodically retreat, replenish, or work on independent goals. Both partners might even prefer to sleep in separate places. The Hermit is a natural scholar, artist, or deep thinker who lives more in his inner landscape than he does with others.

Intimacy
Intimately, the Hermit archetype will want to move slowly. He is often uncomfortable with public displays of affection. It may take time to gain his trust. This card can also signify a person who can be shy when it comes to physical intimacy.

Seeking Romance
The appearance of the Hermit does not mean you are doomed to be alone! Seeking an authentic love takes time. This card often mirrors a feeling that you are walking through the dark. Much like the Hermit, you can't see your way fully through the passing shadow. Your inner light is illuminating the next step to take. Choose the wise path. Love will follow.

Desires

The Hermit can represent a person who desires to retreat or withdraw to feel happy and secure. This individual will resent feeling pressured out of their seclusion. The Hermit can also signify a person who feels they need to detox from a painful experience that is still being processed.

Reversed
New Relationship

The Hermit Reversed might find it awkward to connect with others, having "gone it alone" for so long. This person truly desires to connect in a meaningful partnership but may lack some basic relationship skills. This person will also retreat when his feelings are hurt or he feels misunderstood. Communication does not always come easy for the Hermit Reversed.

Long-Term Partnership

The Hermit Reversed can represent an overly critical partner in a relationship. He is a scorekeeper and will analyze his partner's every word, looking for inconsistencies. Instead of self-reflection, he may focus on what he thinks everyone else needs to improve. This is often a smoke screen for feeling neglected or not knowing how to ask for what he needs.

Intimacy

The Hermit Reversed can represent a person who *avoids* intimacy even while expressing a desire to connect. Anxiety can lead to this individual bottling up their true feelings. The Hermit Reversed will often send mixed signals while attempting to maintain a comfort zone of impenetrable privacy.

Seeking Romance

The Hermit Reversed can signify that it's time to rejoin the world of the living. Becoming too isolated can feel safe and comfortable because you are never challenged to grow. It may be time to take slow and steady steps into society again. Don't be afraid of calling more attention to yourself and sharing your light.

Desires

The Hermit Reversed can represent a deep desire to connect with others again, while also feeling unresolved about an issue that needs time to heal. This card will usually appear after a period of seclusion to heal and process old wounds.

The best advice for the Hermit Reversed is to move forward slowly. The numbing ice around the heart will thaw in its right time.

What the Hermit May Be Teaching You

The Hermit may be teaching you to listen inward. It is time to withdraw from the energy of others to truly know *your own* mind and heart. The Hermit shines a light on those internal landscapes we mistakenly believe are empty. Sometimes we are fooled into thinking the only thing that could fill this illusion of emptiness is another person's love, desire, or validation. The Hermit leads you into your shadows and shines a light on what needs to be loved in yourself. You don't have to wait for someone else to love what lies hidden within you. The Hermit thaws the frigid ice around your heart with his warm, illuminating lantern. You are safe enough to allow uncomfortable emotions to be felt, *loved,* and released. Your current journey isn't about another person's path to you. It's about your pathway toward yourself.

THE WHEEL OF FORTUNE

Wheel of Fortune personalities are the unpredictable rogues of the Major Arcana. They radiate an aura of destiny, surprise, and excitement. Falling for them can be a thrilling roller-coaster ride, which can easily disorient you. In love, Wheel people throw all caution to the wind. The tumultuous drama they gamble in can be both stimulating and addictive. Wheel of Fortune personalities will expose you to the highest highs *and* the lowest lows. As a result, relationships with them are notoriously erratic. Try not to get too attached to how a Wheel personality may be behaving at any given moment; their minds change as swiftly as their moods. One day they burn hot, the next day they blow cold. A relationship with a Wheel of Fortune personality often exhibits an on-again, off-again dynamic. At their best, Wheel personalities are fun, exciting, hilarious, entertaining, resilient, passionate, and charming. At their worst, they are changeable, detached, manic, inconsistent, and erratic, and they struggle with breaking negative behavioral cycles.

In a Love Reading
New Relationship
This connection is both unpredictable and exciting. This person may express fervent passion one day, only to ghost you the next. Although they may behave inconsistently, in time you will begin to see patterns. For a new relationship, this card advises you to stay grounded. Gather more information before allowing your hopes to rise too high.

Long-Term Partnership
The Wheel of Fortune can symbolize a relationship that feels consistently changeable. Although the variability of the partnership may have shocked you in the past, it is now clear that it follows a consistent pattern. There is no need to guess what is likely to happen in the future with this relationship. All the answers you seek can be found in the cycles of the past.

Intimacy
Wheel of Fortune relationships will display intense bouts of passion, followed by equal periods of detachment. This card can also highlight an intense attraction to a "hot and cold" personality. Although their passion will periodically cool, it is also likely that their passion will cycle back with force.

Seeking Romance
If you are single, you may be feeling exhausted with the yo-yo that is your love life. However, the Wheel of Fortune can appear when a change in luck is at hand. Take chances. Be less predictable. Break the old cycle that's been keeping you stuck. The Wheel of Fortune rewards change. It's time to find your center and flip the script.

Desires
The Wheel of Fortune can represent a desire to break a predictable cycle. Remember that you are in control of your life. You don't need to maintain unfulfilling cycles just because it's what you've always done. You also don't need to leave your future to chance. Take a risk and create your own luck. The Wheel grants good fortune to those who can change.

Reversed
New Relationship
The Reversed Wheel can represent a partner who tends to move through life in reverse. This individual might be so stuck in a behavioral cycle that it seems involuntary. This card can also represent a partner who struggles with relapsing into old destructive patterns. Although they often act thoughtlessly, their behavior isn't malicious.

Long-Term Partnership
You and your partner have overcome countless dramatic plot twists. Although this relationship requires lots of emotional energy, it has also granted you both a full panoply of emotional experiences. For all the ups and downs, this partnership's cycles are now as predictable as clockwork.

Intimacy
The person you are asking about is much like a magpie—constantly attracted to the shiniest new thing. This card can represent someone with fleeting affection. The Wheel Reversed can also represent a person who is both thoughtless and impulsive when it comes to sex.

Seeking Romance
A Wheel that moves backward will take you in reverse. This card can highlight a present situation that seems to echo the past. What will you do differently this time around? Revisiting old cycles also grants the opportunity to break them. It's time to begin anew.

Desires
Upright or reversed, the Wheel of Fortune represents a strong desire to break a cycle. Although it feels like you haven't been making progress, this is an illusion. You may have repeated old lessons, but with each return, you've gained

new wisdom. You finally possess the sense to get off the hamster wheel. Trust your desire to establish a healthier pattern.

What the Wheel of Fortune May Be Teaching You

The Wheel of Fortune is composed of two parts: the rim, and the hub. The rim of the wheel represents all external forces that are outside of your control. The rim can include other people's approval, disapproval, actions, or behaviors, none of which you have any control over. If you consistently attach yourself to the rim of the Wheel, you are doomed to rise and fall with each validation or rejection you receive. However, the Wheel also has another component: the hub. The center of the wheel is a symbol for *your* center. Your center is where your best self can be found. Your center whispers these reassuring words: *Let go of trying to control… destiny will unfailingly bring what is yours to you.* Your center is the eye of the storm. It is where self-love is found. You cannot control the unpredictable actions of others. You can only choose which part of the Wheel you attach yourself to. Remember who you are and return to your wise center. It is only from this place of power that you can finally change your luck.

JUSTICE

Justice personalities value truth, honesty, and integrity above all else. They are charming, tactful, and diplomatic. They also strive to embody grace, good manners, and beauty. Justice people seek a well-rounded partner who leads a balanced, orderly life. They loathe chaotic, sloppy energy. Often, men who embody the Justice archetype will possess a pronounced feminine nature, while women will exhibit qualities traditionally identified as masculine. In love, Justice people secretly desire to allow their passions to run wild; however, their self-restraint usually inhibits their ardor. Justice people possess great kindness and strive to avoid conflict. However, don't mistake their genteel manners for weakness. Justice people have extremely high standards. They won't give a second thought to cutting out anyone who does not meet their exacting expectations. Once they've detached, they don't look back. At their best, Justice people are intelligent, charming, honest, and elegant. At their worst, they can be haughty, cold, detached, or indifferent.

In a Love Reading
New Relationship
Justice can signify a new partner who is attracted to intelligence, beauty, and elegance. They are repelled by crudeness and have refined taste. Proper etiquette is required when courting this person. They are most attracted to intellectually curious people. Justice people also love to debate issues … so long as the discussion doesn't become too heated.

Long-Term Partnership
Justice can symbolize a well-balanced, complementary partnership. Each person strives to uphold the relationship's integrity through honesty. Often this card will appear when an important truth needs to be confronted with neutrality. Justice can also indicate legally binding contractual matters that may make your lives together more official.

Intimacy
Justice people live more in their head and benefit from being aware of the sensations in their bodies. They often feel they need permission to let loose. Pique their passionate interest by stimulating their imagination. A Justice person will unselfishly strive to give as much pleasure to their partner as they receive.

Seeking Romance
If you are single, Justice encourages you to seek a relationship partner in an intellectual environment, such as a university, class, or community organization. Broaden your horizons and open your mind to people who aren't your physical type. You may discover a connection of common interest that leads to something far more substantive.

Desires

Justice often accompanies a desire for truth. You are beginning to take an honest look at your love life and make the decisions you've been avoiding. Although being honest with yourself isn't always easy in matters of the heart, the truth shall set you free. Rely on *facts* rather than on *hopes* to ensure your breakthrough.

Reversed

New Relationship

Justice Reversed can signify a person who may lack honest self-awareness. They may strive to keep up appearances. Avoiding reality can stunt their own opportunities for growth. Upright or reversed, Justice demands truth. Honesty, authenticity, and accountability must be added to your list of relationship non-negotiables.

Long-Term Partnership

Justice Reversed can represent a partner who habitually has difficulty being honest with themselves or others. This is not because they have nefarious motives, but rather they feel terrified of facing a difficult truth they've avoided. Justice Reversed can also signify a messy legal issue or an elephant in the room that must be confronted.

Intimacy

A Justice Reversed personality can often appear detached and may be hard to get close to. They may have trouble getting in touch with their authentic feelings. This person also has difficulty tuning in to their physical body. Intimacy can be a particular challenge unless their mind is stimulated.

Seeking Romance

You may be trying to process an unjust situation that hit you in the heart. Life isn't always fair and can send you circumstances you don't deserve. If you attempt a new partnership while still feeling emotionally unbalanced, love may continue to elude you. Take the time to restore your equilibrium and reclaim your power. You won't regret it.

Desires

It is time to gather all the facts before following what your heart desires. Upright or reversed, Justice insists that you be honest with yourself. You may be feeling trapped between two opposing wishes. Your heart must be reconciled with your head. Let logic and common sense take the lead in this situation.

What Justice May Be Teaching You

Lady Justice may be gently guiding you to be honest with yourself. You may have to open your eyes to an uncomfortable truth within yourself or another to restore equilibrium to your emotions. Lady Justice's lesson may appear cold at times, but that isn't because she is cruel or unfeeling. She is the rational part of you that acts in your own best interest even while your emotions rail against change, clinging to the source of their turmoil. Lady Justice is the little voice in your ear that whispers an inconvenient fact. However, when you accept her wisdom and good judgment, tensions dissipate, and you can breathe a deep sigh of relief. It is time to honestly call out any false imitations in your life you've fooled yourself into accepting. For exceptional love to be experienced, the highest standards must be maintained. Denial, self-deception, and delusions may offer temporary relief, but they will always fall short of the real deal. Lady Justice whispers from the seat of your soul, "Only the truth can set you free."

THE HANGED MAN

The Hanged Man places the needs of others first. He will sacrifice every ounce of his energy to external demands. Although this may sound noble, this often comes at the expense of himself. In love, the Hanged Man often seeks a partner who is just as selfless as he is. He may become resentful if he feels his partner isn't making the same level of sacrifice to family, work, or the relationship. The

Hanged Man focuses on working toward future security, even if it means suffering through an unfulfilling job in the present. His level of selflessness can quickly deplete his spontaneity, passion, and joy. Habitually caving into pressures applied by others can take a toll on his physical body, leading to stress ailments such as headaches or chronic muscle pain. He benefits from a partner who allows him to periodically unplug and tend to his own needs. At his best, the Hanged Man is selfless, unselfish, and hardworking, and he will sacrifice everything for those he loves. At his worst, he is depressive, stagnant, and a resentful martyr.

In a Love Reading
New Relationship
The Hanged Man often represents a love interest who is tied to many external obligations. He will likely sacrifice his time and energy to a larger cause. The Hanged Man rarely has the freedom to make his lover the center of his world. However, he possesses integrity and will try to do the right thing. Few people are as loyal to those they care for as the Hanged Man.

Long-Term Partnership
The Hanged Man can represent a relationship where many sacrifices are being asked of a partner. There is likely a long stressful ordeal that both individuals are working through. A Hanged Man personality benefits most when his partner shares in the responsibilities. Conflicts may arise if only one partner is invested in the maintenance of the relationship.

Intimacy
The Hanged Man routinely avoids giving himself over to pleasure or relaxation. He will often use the excuse of some pressing external demand he believes needs more of his attention. This card can highlight repressed desires that are never explored because of external stress.

Seeking Romance
If you are single, the Hanged Man can represent a feeling that your love life is in a state of suspension. Although this may not be the most romantic time, sacrifices made for yourself, studies, or work will result in your future happiness. Your present efforts may indirectly lead you toward the love you seek.

Desires
The Hanged Man can represent a desire to move past a frustrating state of suspension. It may feel like life has been turned on its head. However, current challenges and sacrifices are leading you toward greater wisdom and self-awareness. Be patient with the process. Before you can proceed, a sacrifice is required. Let go of any attachment that perpetuates suffering.

Reversed
New Relationship
The Hanged Man Reversed can represent a love interest who is currently placing their own needs first. They may need a partner who can step back and allow them to tend to the deeper issues within their life and heart. This person requires time for self-reflection and care before they can commit their energy to the needs of another.

Long-Term Partnership
The once upside-down figure of the Hanged Man is now back on his feet. This card can often symbolize a relationship that has just completed a difficult rite of passage. That which was stuck or suspended in the partnership is now progressing again. There are new options available and opportunities to succeed. Overall, this card embodies a period of relief.

Intimacy
The Hanged Man Reversed is attracted to people who can stand on their own two feet. He likes his partner to take the lead. He is reticent to take on a lover who appears as another helpless individual who cannot care for themselves.

Seeking Romance
The Hanged Man Reversed can also represent a personal breakthrough. Having done the hard work on yourself, there is now the possibility of more fun and romance moving forward. No matter what trials and tribulations have been faced, this card reassures you that you can always pick yourself up, dust yourself off, and move on to happier days.

Desires
The Hanged Man Reversed desires a connection with someone who knows what it feels like to endure difficulties and overcome them. He gravitates toward

sober-minded individuals who don't sugarcoat reality. This card can also signify a desire to get back in the saddle after a challenging period.

What the Hanged Man May Be Teaching You

The Hanged Man teaches you the necessity of stretching beyond an immediate desire for gratification. He asks you to do the right thing, even if the right thing is hard. Often he appears when your life feels like it has been turned upside down. The message many of us unconsciously receive from the world is that *all* discomfort is bad. It needs to be medicated, numbed, or forgotten about as soon as possible. Society also tells us we should always be with someone and happy all the time. However, sometimes life requires us to endure uncomfortable work on ourselves and our relationships. It's time to free yourself from a current hang-up. Although you may be going through some temporary discomfort for now, it is all in the service of improving your relationships and your life. The Hanged Man knows that the thing making you uncomfortable is also where your growth is happening.

DEATH

Death personalities are dark, intense, and tantalizingly seductive. Their mysterious aura can be intoxicating. This person might place you in touch with your deepest fears and forbidden desires. No matter who they become involved with, Death people transform their partner's lives in momentous ways. The changes they bring are always *significant*. In love, Death can describe a relationship partner who is currently embroiled in a major life transformation, such as a breakup, death, crisis, move, or other ending. Death personalities are no strangers to loss and may still be grieving. They will often come across as subtlety detached and not completely transparent. A Death card partner will likely have a tumultuous past. It can be hard for this person to begin anew if old endings aren't resolved. A new day can dawn, but first the past must be put to rest. At their best, Death personalities are sensual, intense, and passionate and can bring positive change. At their worst, they are abrupt, unfeeling, harsh, and uncompromising.

In a Love Reading
New Relationship
The appearance of Death can indicate that the person you are interested in is still undergoing a major change. You may have to be patient and not make anything official until after their transformation is complete. Once they cross this major threshold, they won't likely be the same person you initially fell for. Inevitably, you will have to accept who they are becoming.

Long-Term Partnership
Death can indicate a major ending in the life of one or both partners. There is much transformative energy that can feel difficult to process. Some of the changes occurring may also trigger feelings of loss or grief. This partnership must face its current challenges and transformations with honesty and compassion. Everything is in flux.

Intimacy
The Death personality is seductive and will not shy away from sexual taboos. Their calm exterior hides an intense, hidden passion. However, it takes time and patience to gain the trust of this individual. This individual radiates passion and even danger when you're caught by their hypnotic gaze.

Seeking Romance
If you are single, Death can highlight a difficult ending that you are still processing. Let the past be the past. Although Death can highlight a difficult change, it is truly leading toward a better future. Accept what needs to end so you can move on to happier times.

Desires

Death can represent a deep desire to escape from the grief of a major ending. This card often appears when someone is still processing a death, breakup, divorce, or other difficult transition. The sooner this individual can accept that they can't re-create the old ways, the sooner they can welcome new happiness. Acceptance is the last stage to overcome grief.

Reversed

New Relationship

Death Reversed can represent an individual who may display possessive, jealous, or obsessive behavior. Although their intensity can feel flattering at first, their behavior over time may raise red flags. This card advises one to trust their instincts and enforce their boundaries.

Long-Term Partnership

Death Reversed can represent a resistant partner who is extremely averse to change. They may cling to unhealthy habits or people, even if these attachments create suffering. It's important to encourage them to let go of the old to make room for new, authentic happiness.

Intimacy

Death Reversed can represent a person who resists getting close to others because they fear the change that will occur. Although there is intense physical attraction, the ability to emotionally connect seems to hit a ceiling. This person may also fear major commitments because of the way they will irrevocably transform the structure of their lives.

Seeking Romance

Death can appear reversed when you've already undergone a long process of loss, grief, and transformation within your love life. It's time to move on from fruitless shadows and revitalize your vibrant spirit. Like the phoenix, you are rising out of the ashes, and hope is rekindled.

Desires

Death Reversed represents a desire to hang on to the past. The person in question may be having a hard time letting go of a person or a fixed expectation of what they wanted their life to look like. When Death appears upright or reversed, it demands that change be accepted. This process can move as fast or as slow as this person allows, but change will inevitably happen.

What the Death Card May Be Teaching You

Death appears when it is time to let go of something that no longer serves you. It may feel very difficult to surrender an attachment to a long-nurtured expectation even when it is no longer proving useful to your progress. The thing you are most resistant to releasing within yourself is often the last major barrier preceding your breakthrough. Death can also teach you to let sleeping dogs lie. If an unhealthy relationship is over, don't resurrect it. If you are experiencing a difficult change that evokes sadness or grief, be gentle with yourself. The light will return when you accept the wisdom found within the dark. You are moving on to a completely new way of life. This will attract new people and opportunities. Although that past held its share of grief for you, the sun is rising again on a new landscape. Summon your courage as you boldly step over this important threshold. Death is *always* accompanied by rebirth. In truth, endings are new beginnings in disguise.

TEMPERANCE

Temperance personalities have a knack for making people feel completely at ease. They are social chameleons and can adjust their energy to meet the needs of whomever they are interacting with. They desire a relationship partner who is both sensitive *and* strong, playful *and* practical, idealistic *and* realistic. Temperance people strive to be moderate in all things. They can love intensely but will not allow their relationship to consume their whole lives. They are repelled by extreme behavior of any kind. Temperance people are attracted to intellectually well-rounded companions who are open to learning. They often take the role of the teacher in their relationship, exposing their partner to worlds previously undiscovered. Temperance people adhere to a strong ethical compass and consistently strive to do the right thing. At their best, Temperance people are moderate, compassionate, calming, and wise. At their worst, they can be passive, dull, or invisible, or they avoid taking a strong stand when required.

In a Love Reading
New Relationship
For a budding partnership, Temperance advises taking things slow. Put your toe in the water before taking the plunge. This relationship will thrive when it progresses gradually and organically. Temperance relationships thrive with easygoing, harmonious exchanges of energy.

Long-Term Partnership
This complementary relationship has created much healing for both partners. Although there is a preference for calm, this relationship may need to be exposed to more excitement from time to time. Plan adventures to exotic places or focus on a shared goal. This card can also signify a need to restore relationship bonds through emotional intimacy.

Intimacy
A Temperance lover melds into the energy of their partner. This person will prefer lovemaking to be slow and sensuous and to achieve a higher vibration. Temperance harmonizes opposites. The differences in temperament of both partners will likely complement one another beautifully.

Seeking Romance
If you are single, Temperance can indicate that you are still healing. Be patient and gentle with yourself. Delve into self-care to gain insight into your deepest needs. By caring for yourself, you will increase your ability to open your heart authentically with another.

Desires

Temperance can represent a person who desires a partner who possesses a calming, reassuring presence. This individual is repelled by too much intensity, loudness, or pressure. Temperance advises moderation and advises that love be approached gently rather than aggressively.

Reversed
New Relationship

Temperance Reversed can signify a partner who is likely prone to excess. They may exhibit a tendency to do something too much. They might also obsessively fixate on one aspect of their lives at the expense of all else. This card can also signify a person who appears excessively needy or insecure.

Long-Term Partnership

Temperance Reversed can signify a partner who feels neglected or depleted. This may cause them to act out excessively or extremely. Temperance Reversed will encourage both partners to respond proportionally to the relationship issues before them. Beware of being swept up in impulse or reactivity.

Intimacy

Intimately, Temperance Reversed can represent a partner who is still healing past trauma surrounding sex or sexuality. This card advises proceeding gently and taking all the time that is needed. This individual will open their heart when they feel safe, validated, and reassured. Trust is slowly being reconstituted.

Seeking Romance

Temperance Reversed can also signify an obsessive rut that is fueling a current state of emotional disharmony. This card advises to mentally switch gears. Upright or reversed, Temperance always holds the potential for healing if you can reclaim a state of balance within yourself first. Inner harmony must be restored before meaningful connections can be established.

Desires

Temperance Reversed can highlight an unsatiated desire. There is likely an excessive all-or-nothing attitude. You may have to make peace with two contradictory thoughts residing in your head at the same time. Upright or reversed,

Temperance encourages you to replenish your sense of balance. Stop fixating on what isn't working, and step back to restore your perspective.

What Temperance May Be Teaching You

Temperance teaches you the importance of restoring balance, moderation, and inner calm. It's time to check in with your own feelings before seeking to fulfill needs or desires. Stop pushing so hard to *make* life do what you want. Instead, go with the flow. Temperance encourages you to be self-aware of how you are showing up in the world. Sometimes the fervent desire for something has the unwanted effect of driving it away. Temperance calls you inward to soothe any signals you are sending that come across as too frantic, desperate, or intense. Let go of your attachment to control. Inhale a slow, deep, nourishing breath. Hold it for a moment. Exhale all your worries, obsessions, or anxieties about the future. When you surrender tension, you transform your aura. Suddenly the vibrant beauty of your authentic self is reignited. Watch how easily your desires begin to manifest when you release your feeble attempt to control. The moderating waters of Temperance promise healing when you allow your heart to flow in harmony with this natural course.

THE DEVIL

Devil personalities are seductive, mesmerizing, and achingly beautiful. He can hook you with angelic eyes tinted with trouble. From the start, your intuition will siren *DANGER* in flashing red lights. However, the Devil's smooth-talking ardor can be hard to resist. Soon, you are tricking yourself into believing him. At first, he appears madly passionate for you, promising you the moon. Then he flips the script, abandoning you to desperately beg for his intoxicating attention. The exhilarating drama the Devil offers is an addictive drug. Once you begin to detox, he predictably reappears, swearing his love for you, and promising he's changed. Every apology you've longed to hear is whispered in your ear. However, his behavior never changes. Rinse and repeat. The Devil never becomes what he promises…but deep down, you already knew that. At his best, the Devil is sexy, attractive, and alluring, unleashing his lover's repressed passions and darkest desires. At his worst, he is destructive, manipulative, addictive, and a liar.

In a Love Reading
New Relationship
The Devil can signify a smooth talker whose slippery words are too good to be true. Your instincts are likely warning you, though you may try to rationalize them away. Follow your common sense rather than your hopes or desires. Unfortunately, people with low self-esteem who are desperate for love get suckered by the Devil all the time.

Long-Term Partnership
The Devil can highlight a destructive relationship pattern that must be faced honestly. It's time to bring this issue to light, honestly. Destructive cycles are broken when something is *done* about them, not when they're avoided. Seek out appropriate caring professionals for added support. The Devil can also represent a partner who struggles with addiction.

Intimacy
Hands down, the Devil archetype could give you the best sex you've ever had. If you've been without passion or attention for a while, the Devil will hit your system like an intoxicating drug. However, beware of becoming addicted to a person who dangles you along. *Great sex does not equate to true love.*

Seeking Romance
If you are single, the Devil represents repeated destructive patterns it's time to break free of. You must remain vigilant against the manipulative intentions of people who could prey on your vulnerability. Don't repeat the destructive cycles of the past. Know your triggers and what deceptions you are susceptible to.

Desires

The Devil will often appear when you are playing with fire and know it. This card often appears when you must be completely honest with yourself about a relationship you don't want to see honestly. Be on guard for inventing an alternate reality to match your desire. You will know you are in a destructive cycle if you are continually rationalizing it away.

Reversed
New Relationship

The person you are asking about has a difficult past they are still overcoming. They are no longer ensnared by a former limitation. The past they are walking away from will attempt to pull them back. Time will tell if they keep progressing. Gather more information before allowing yourself to fall head over heels.

Long-Term Partnership

The appearance of the Devil Reversed does not doom your relationship life to ruin. However, uncomfortable truths and repressions must be addressed honestly. The Devil Reversed encourages breaking destructive habits. Beware of excusing behaviors you once considered inexcusable. It's time for the relationship to be raised to a higher standard.

Intimacy

For a healthy relationship, the Devil Reversed can represent hidden desires that one or both partners are hiding. Instead of avoiding their passion, it might prove fun to explore their forbidden desires. This also may have the added effect of bringing them closer together.

Seeking Romance

The Devil Reversed can signify that you've overcome a destructive relationship pattern that was depleting your power. Hope for a brighter future emerges, and the chains of the past are slipping off. You may feel your first steps are wobbly, but trust that a better future awaits. Keep making good choices.

Desires

The Devil Reversed can symbolize freeing yourself from a self-destructive desire. It's time to exert some self-control. Leave any person, relationship, or destructive cycle that has been keeping you stuck in hell. Breaking a bad habit feels the most difficult in the beginning. Be gentle, and take it one day at a time.

What the Devil May Be Teaching You

Everybody has a devil within. The Devil represents repressed fears of unworthiness, obsessions, addictions, and negative patterns that continually sabotage our aspirations for happiness. The Devil is the voice within that tells us we aren't worthy of love, and that we'll never find happiness. He tricks us into believing that we are just stuck with the way things are because they've always been that way. Our repressed shadows often appear mirrored in relationships that continually let us down. The Devil highlights any untruths you may be telling yourself that are keeping you chained in a self-destructive pattern. You must honestly assess if obsession, addiction to approval, neediness, desperation, or expectations are distorting your ability to see the uncomfortable truth staring you in the face. When the Devil appears, it's time to seek a higher vibration and leave the underworld. Send love to the part of you that's been hurting. Seek emotional support from those who want the best for you. Stop accepting a reality that isn't worthy of your best self. By embodying your better angels, the Devil will lose all power.

THE TOWER

Tower people avoid reality by walling themselves away from unpleasant truths. They are experts in avoidance. They resist changing any behavior that has kept them in comfort, even if it's harmful to their self or others. On the surface, Tower people try to exude the illusion of security and impenetrability. They are very concerned with maintaining their image. In relationships, Tower people are attracted to partners who enable their fantasies. If their relationship is built on shaky foundations, they pretend everything's okay. They quickly sweep unpleasant facts under the rug. Cracks rapidly form in their well-manicured facade. Inevitably, their beautiful delusions crumble. However, relationships with Tower people can initiate the breakdown that results in a breakthrough— *for Tower people merely serve as a mirror for the denial you yourself refuse to face.* At their best, Tower people are intelligent and imaginative and can initiate great change for themselves and others. At their worst, they are superficial, deluded, and volatile.

In a Love Reading
New Relationship
The Tower advises that you gather more information before entrusting your heart. People always show you their best attributes in the beginning. Try not to buy into the initial image that is presented. You have nothing to lose by taking your time. The Tower can also warn you of tricking yourself into believing what you *hope* to see rather than what is truly there.

Long-Term Partnership
For a healthy relationship, the Tower can signify a breakdown that results in a breakthrough. In any relationship, conflicts inevitably arise. This card can symbolize tremendous healing by releasing toxic emotions that are negatively affecting the relationship. When confronting instability honestly, the Tower can be immensely cathartic.

Intimacy
Tower people are explosive in the bedroom. This card can signify passionate excitement but also warns of playing with fire. It can be tempting to confuse a passionate sex dynamic with true love when the Tower appears. Try not to overly attach yourself to the fantasy over reality.

Seeking Romance
The Tower encourages you to stop rationalizing and face the truth your instincts are alerting you to. Hopes and expectations may be drowning out your common sense and inner wisdom. Your heart will heal, open, and connect only after it accepts reality. Step out of the rubble and begin anew. You will not find fulfillment by reliving past disasters.

Desires

The falling tower can symbolize the desperate desire to be loved, which can result in accepting substandard relationship conditions. The Tower places you in direct contact with the current source of your instability. This shaky fault line has been ignored until now but can no longer be avoided. Let go of all that no longer serves you. Time to reinvent yourself.

Reversed

New Relationship

Upright or reversed, the Tower warns against rushing into rebound relationships. Make sure enough time has passed after a previous breakup. If you are just beginning to form a connection, start with friendship. The Tower Reversed advises that both partners bring closure to past unresolved issues before initiating something new.

Long-Term Partnership

The Tower Reversed can represent a recovery process after crisis. One or both partners require healing, understanding, and patience. An attachment to an outdated structure has crumbled. This individual must clean up the debris in their own heart first before focusing on the needs of the relationship.

Intimacy

The Tower Reversed can represent someone who is not stable in their feelings. They may still be overcoming an upheaval or crisis that is interfering with their ability to be intimate. More time may need to be devoted to self-care. The Tower Reversed can represent a period of withdrawal to repair past damage.

Seeking Romance

You may be healing from a breakup or the ending of another intense attachment. Although it may not feel like it now, the dust is settling, and the hope of a brighter future will soon make itself known to you. The storm has passed; however, the pieces must now be picked up.

Desires

The Tower Reversed represents a desire to reconnect after an immense personal transformation. Difficult truths have been accepted that have reshaped your reality. Trauma has been overcome. Slow and gentle progress is needed now.

Even if past changes felt harsh, momentous healing is happening. Leave the imprisonments of the past behind.

What the Tower May Be Teaching You

The Tower serves as a wake-up call. It forces you to honestly confront illusions or attachments that are keeping you stuck. Despite its destructive imagery, the Tower is one of the most healing cards in the tarot. A symbolic lightning bolt is blasting away past destructive cycles. Although this can feel like a painful shock, you stand at the precipice of immense personal transformation. The past storms you've endured may feel unfair, but they carry within them cleansing magic. The Tower does not allow you to stay attached to the fantasy that, somehow, second-, third-, or fourth-best is good enough for you. The Tower compels you to stop returning to whatever keeps you trapped in a state of suffering. A happier time is still possible for you, but first you must accept the truth of how much you matter. It's time to escape the prison of illusions. Raise your standards. You deserve the best. Release anything less.

THE STAR

Star personalities have that little something extra, often described as the It Factor. They stand apart from everyone else, possessing a magical charisma. Star people are used to being desired for their presence, talent, or abilities. Everyone seems to want to bask in their glory. Star people are friendly to most everyone but are emotionally available to only a select few. When first meeting them, you may even feel intimidated and may be unsure as to where you stand within their affections. Star people are attracted to farsighted individuals who know their own mind. They tire quickly of people who are overly dazzled by them. They seek a partner who shines in their own right. *Stars also need space to thrive.* If you are with a Star personality, you must not impede their ability to share their sparkling light with others. Stars don't orbit around other people; others orbit around them. At their best, Star personalities are fascinating, talented, unique, magical, and charismatic. At their worst, they are remote, guarded, and self-absorbed.

In a Love Reading
New Relationship
When first getting to know a Star person, they can come across as rather distant. This is a defense mechanism they learned to protect themselves from the pressure they often feel from others. The Star card can signify that your new interest holds a lot of potential. However, you will have to let this connection intensify slowly. Try to establish a firm friendship first.

Long-Term Partnership
A relationship with a Star personality can radiate an aura of destiny. No matter what life changes may unexpectedly alter your path together, the bond you share is eternal. At the core of this partnership are two souls, joined in friendship, journeying through the ages. Star relationships are rare and can often stand the test of time if the friendship remains intact.

Intimacy
Equity of passion is often an issue in Star relationships. One partner often burns hotter than their lover can reciprocate. A Star relationship will burn out quickly if the relationship is ignited by passion alone. Intimately, Stars want sex to be so much more than a mere physical act. Stars seek enchantment. They want a partner who expends the extra effort.

Seeking Romance
If you are single, the Star advises you to spend time with your friends. Release your expectations. Express yourself freely and socialize again. Enjoying time out in the world with friends can increase your chances of finding a potential romance. Don't be afraid to let yourself shine!

Desires

Sometimes the Star can signify a person who desires space. This individual can alternate between intense passion and aloof coolness. They will want their partner to pick up on nonverbal clues as to when they want to be left alone. You cannot possess a Star personality. They must come to you when they feel ready.

Reversed
New Relationship

A Star Reversed personality will have the same It Factor as their upright counterpart but may lack the wisdom to know how to wield it. They can sometimes come off as self-absorbed or emotionally cool. They may also be a bit one-dimensional, making their charisma the center of their personal universe while leaving little room for anything (or anyone) else.

Long-Term Partnership

Upright or reversed, a relationship with the Star person is special. When reversed, the Star warns of imbalance for one partner. External demands may be adding a lot of pressures to this person's plate. They may be too available to the outside world. Boundaries may need to be established around the expenditure of energy so that this little star does not burn out.

Intimacy

The Star Reversed can signify struggling with self-doubt or feeling insecure about what others think. This card can warn of trying to please all the wrong people while passing over those who truly care. Although the Star is dazzling, they may not know their own worth.

Seeking Romance

When the Star appears reversed, your energy is better spent on developing your talents and friendships for now. If you keep working on yourself, you will shine brightly. What better magic is needed for attracting love? Invest your energy into whatever makes you emanate excellence. Don't waste precious feelings on barren pursuits.

Desires

The Star Reversed can also illuminate a desire for someone who may serve better as a friend than as an intimate partner. Distance or circumstance may be getting in the way of a connection at this time. If a relationship with a Star person is ultimately meant to be, destiny will make it so, without your need to control it.

What the Star May Be Teaching You

The Star may be teaching you to see the big picture, placing your current situation in a universal context. Destiny is destiny. What will be, will be. There is likely a great desire to feel settled and secure in a partnership, but you are being reminded to honor your own sacred light first. Sometimes romance is not the center of our universe, as much as we'd like it to be. Sometimes we are attracted to someone else's distant light because we need to recognize it's mirroring our own brilliance. The Star can appear when you need to make best friends *with yourself*. Go as far as you can with your talents, connections, and abilities. Don't be dazzled by the light of others, thinking that is what will make *you* special. You may be learning to take your brilliance to the absolute limit. Perhaps you need to radiate your full splendor and let others orbit around you for a change. By shining in your own right, you will attract what is yours. It's time to reconnect and cherish the divine spark within. When you truly believe in your light and its value, magical and synchronistic things begin to happen!

THE MOON

Moon personalities are magnetic, romantic, and alluring. For a relationship with a Moon person to work, the magical glow of an enchanted evening must survive the glaring light of day. For Moon people, mysterious, unconscious feelings constantly pull at them. Although Moon people feel deeply, they often struggle to articulate their emotions. In love, Moon people desire a fairy tale and struggle with facing realities that are too harsh. Relationships with Moon people can be of unsurpassed romance but will also cycle through a roller coaster of emotional highs and lows. Moon personalities feel every emotion to their limit. Many Moon people find it extremely difficult to dissolve attachments, even when they've proven destructive. They can become obsessed with their exes and may need extra support when trying to let go. At their best, Moon people are sensitive, compassionate, beautiful, magnetic, alluring, and magical. At their worst, they are delusional and moody and fall into cycles of victimization.

In a Love Reading
New Relationship
A partner embodying the Moon archetype can touch a part of your heart that every lover before seemed to miss. Although the relationship can initially feel spellbinding, its true test will be if the attraction can withstand the real-world challenges that will inevitably arise. Attractions are intensified when the Moon appears.

Long-Term Partnership
A healthy Moon relationship will feel as if nature herself brought this union together. The attraction is chemical, and the bond is lasting. However, for an unhealthy relationship, the Moon can ensnare both partners in a repetitive cycle of irrational, destructive behavior. One or both partners must be wary of acting on their emotional impulses without understanding them.

Intimacy
Moon personalities are seductive and imaginative and will have no trouble pleasing their lover. They mirror their partner's energy, orbiting around their deepest desires. A Moon union results in magical lovemaking. Try not to allow desire and fantasy to sweep you too far away into a beautiful dream. Keep one foot firmly in reality.

Seeking Romance
If you are single, the Moon tells you to follow where your intuition is leading you, whether it is to an activity, job, or place. This may put you at the right place during the right time. Notice the subtle signs and signals the universe

seems to be sending you. Also, trust your first impressions and instincts. They are correct.

Desires

The Moon can signify an intense, magnetic desire for someone. You may be mesmerized by all that remains to be discovered. As difficult as it can be to resist, never be too aggressive when the Moon appears, or you'll break the spell. In Latin, the moon is called *luna*, which the English word *lunatic* derives from. Moon relationships can drive you crazy, in the best and worst ways.

Reversed

New Relationship

Moon Reversed can describe a deep connection that erratically changes with no explanation. Although behaviors constantly shift and change, a cycle may be revealed in time. The Moon Reversed can represent a relationship that is founded upon illusions. Although spellbinding, you must be honest about its less attractive realities.

Long-Term Partnership

A Moon Reversed personality may behave irrationally or display excessive moodiness. The shadow of the Moon is often expressed by one partner being in a state of denial about a glaring issue. They may have difficulty facing facts or taking responsibility for their behavior.

Intimacy

The Moon Reversed can also appear when there is a hidden feeling that should be openly expressed in your relationship. If not expressed, this unresolved feeling will continue to interfere with intimacy. If both partners are willing, healthy communication can do wonders for creating a safe space and repairing bonds.

Seeking Romance

The Moon Reversed can signify you've been powerfully imprinted on by a past emotional attachment. This connection is replayed in your mind, over and over. Although you may say you are looking for someone new, others may unconsciously perceive that your heart is already occupied. Past attachments may need time to dissolve before new bonds can be established.

Desires

A Moon Reversed person can become obsessive when their love is unrequited. If they feel strongly, they can't conceive of how this other person isn't equally as obsessed with them. A powerful bond with a Moon Reversed personality can be established in one evening but may take far longer to break.

What the Moon May Be Teaching You

The Moon teaches you to face your habits and cycles honestly. Are you feeling empowered in your relationships, or swept up in obsessive feelings that are making you lose your sensibility? If a relationship issue is driving you crazy, it may be time to understand what is unconsciously motivating *you*. It's time to reflect upon your needs and desires at their deepest level. The Moon can draw you into understanding the past. Your personal history will reveal the reasons behind why you feel so strongly about the issue you are struggling with. It may be time to seek therapy and address the love that may not have adequately been met. Each month, the Moon begins anew. This reminds you that you can always start again, whether healing from a current relationship issue or facing a personal shadow you've struggled with. Although you may feel the magnetic pull of deep desire, you do not want to be ruled by it. The Moon always calls you home to your luminous center where you can regain personal power.

THE SUN

Sun personalities light up any room they walk into. They are laughter-loving and vivacious, becoming the center of attention without effort. Their energetic charisma can brighten almost anyone's mood. Sun personalities gather many admirers but can also be targeted by the insecurities of others. In love, Sun people are attracted to partners who are upbeat and optimistic. They adore compliments and admiration. Sun people are also drawn to color, creativity, vibrancy, and music. They loathe spending time around depressives who endlessly moan or complain. A Sun person will avoid needy or insecure partners like the plague! Being a natural performer, a Sun person appreciates a good audience. For a relationship with a Sun personality to work, their partner must also be their biggest fan. At their best, Sun people are fun, energetic, entertaining, warmhearted, charismatic, optimistic, and never boring. At their worst, they can be fair-weather friends, self-centered, egotistical, and fools for flattery.

In a Love Reading
New Relationship
The appearance of the Sun indicates a positive new beginning! As with any new relationship, you will want to be practical and gather more information, but this partnership is off to an amazing start. Sun relationships thrive with enjoyable activities. Try not to heap too many heavy expectations on the relationship until after commitments have been established.

Long-Term Partnership
A Sun person thrives most with a partner who doesn't mind playing the "supporting cast" role. Sun people are used to being the center of attention and need to shine. The Sun can also signify a relationship rooted in healthy self-esteem for both individuals. One partner may need more attention than their relationship can provide. External activities are encouraged.

Intimacy
Intimately, Sun personalities like it hot! This relationship will thrive on physical vitality and uninhibited passion. Sun people are attracted to confident partners who possess powerful self-esteem. They are repelled by apathy, preferring partners who get out of the house and get active.

Seeking Romance
If you are single, don't be coy. Be bold, uninhibited, and passionate. Flirt, play, and don't allow the quest for romance to become too serious or dark. This time of your life should be enjoyable. No matter what has happened in the past, a new day is dawning. Radiate the joy you are seeking to attract. You can always begin by smiling more!

Desires

The Sun can signify a desire for more fun or enjoyment when it comes to love. If life has become too serious, it may have the unwanted effect of driving people with good vibes away. Engage in activities that elevate the mood. Travel, outings, dates, exercise, sex, or other adventures can restore vitality.

Reversed

New Relationship

When times are good, there is no better company than the Sun, upright or reversed. In the beginning of a relationship, this is never a problem. The challenge of the Sun Reversed person is that over time they may avoid heavy subjects like commitment, planning for the future, or challenging relationship issues. The Sun Reversed needs positive incentive to stay engaged.

Long-Term Partnership

Even reversed, a long-term partner represented by the Sun is a pleasure to be around. The only negative tendency they tend to express is their desire to sugar-coat problems. The Sun Reversed can represent someone who blatantly ignores a difficult issue their partner is experiencing if it makes them uncomfortable. Honest conversations about challenges aren't easy for them.

Intimacy

Upright or reversed, Sun people cannot thrive in gloom for long. Passion is very important to them. If enthusiasm is missing in their relationships, they will naturally gravitate toward where they will be better admired. Sun people need to know their partner is physically attracted to them to make the relationship work.

Seeking Romance

The Sun Reversed encourages you to check in with your energy. If it feels dark, needy, or depressed, know that others can pick up on that, too! Even when reversed, this card is an encouraging and optimistic omen for the future. The Sun rules joy and happiness. If you get happy, your love life may experience a burst of renewed excitement.

Desires

The Sun Reversed can represent a desire to place a positive spin on personal challenges and vulnerabilities. Honesty is the best policy, especially with yourself.

Avoid any toxic positivity that is becoming a barrier to authentically connect. Quality partnerships thrive when both partners can be honest, especially about the hard stuff.

What the Sun May Be Teaching You

The Sun could be teaching you to be aware of the energy you are sending out into the world through your *presence*. Your presence is the aura of energy that surrounds you. It cannot be seen but is unconsciously felt by others. If you've been moping, needy, negative, or jaded, you must be self-aware enough to know that other people can perceive that energy, too! Don't look to someone else to validate your light. It may be time to increase your self-esteem. One way to improve the way you feel about yourself is to get moving. Get active and exercise. Engage in self-care and self-improvement. Go outside. Connect with the people and activities that make you feel good. The Sun is confident in its central place in the solar system and looks to no other body. Don't underestimate your value and what you bring to the table. Time to raise your personal vibration. The Sun reminds you of your light and worthiness. Let your *presence* communicate this truth to others.

JUDGMENT

Judgment people are survivors. Like the Sun archetype, they are eternally optimistic; however, they are also *realistic* about life's challenges. They've experienced their share of loss, grief, and endings. In love, Judgment personalities are attracted to strength of character. They want to know that their partner is also a self-sufficient survivor who doesn't give up when life gets tough. Those who whine about their lives make Judgment people's skin crawl. Having survived their own challenges, they hate to feed into someone else's delusion of helplessness. Judgment people will always seek to assist those they care for. They are just the sort of person you want by your side in a crisis. Judgment people are often of service to their family, friends, or greater society. You may have to share a Judgment person with those they support. At their best, Judgment people are realistic, optimistic, refreshing, resourceful, and resilient. At their worst, they are reactive, judgmental, and uncompromising, and they pressure others to change before they are ready.

In a Love Reading
New Relationship
Judgment can symbolize that one or both partners have undergone a major life change and are now ready to start the next chapter. This might make both people rather cautious. Although past difficulties have been experienced, a fresh breeze is blowing through. As of this moment, the future is wide open. Enjoy this time of revitalization and renewal.

Long-Term Partnership
The appearance of Judgment symbolizes new beginnings after many trials and tribulations. It's time to release dead energy within your partnership to experience a positive renewal. You may also recognize where you have been taking your partnership for granted, and you are beginning to see the relationship again as if for the first time.

Intimacy
Judgment can represent reigniting the fading embers of passion. It's time to reawaken romance. Elevate the amorous atmosphere with music, candlelight, gifts, compliments, and suggestion. Revive the magic in your relationship by putting in the extra effort.

Seeking Romance
If you are single, Judgment can signify that the opportunity for love will be more likely if you open yourself to new experiences. The old ways don't work anymore. The past is the past. It's time to move on and start anew. Like the phoenix, you are rising from the ashes.

Desires

Judgment represents rebirth, renewal, and awakening. The old ways have been swept away. This card often appears when there is a strong desire to pick up the pieces and start over. Say yes to invitations. Seek new environments and different company. Engage in any activities that make you feel beautiful, self-confident, and alive again.

Reversed

New Relationship

Judgment Reversed can appear as a warning to not begin a new relationship if an old partnership has not completely ended physically, psychically, or emotionally. Judgment Reversed can also appear if you are rushing into a rebound relationship to avoid the discomfort of being alone with unresolved issues.

Long-Term Partnership

Sometimes Judgment Reversed appears when there is a negative past relationship cycle rearing its ugly head again. If an outdated relationship pattern has repeatedly proven destructive, it's time to end it. Resuscitating unhealthy patterns only delays the inevitable process of finally moving on with your life.

Intimacy

Judgment Reversed can represent a glaring, unresolved issue that needs to be confronted maturely by both partners. Upright or reversed, Judgment encourages you to wake up and pay attention to what is really happening. Truths must be heard and expressed if intimacy is to be restored.

Seeking Romance

Judgment Reversed can often signify a major loss, troubled childhood, or personal struggle that is interfering with current relationships. This card can also represent a person who is not using their best judgment or common sense. This card encourages seeking support to resolve the past so that a better future can be created.

Desires

Judgment Reversed symbolizes a strong desire for a new beginning. You are no longer sleepwalking through life. Abandon the old ways that weren't working. Upright or reversed, Judgment will appear just before a pivotal breakthrough.

What Judgment May Be Teaching You

Judgment often appears when it is time for personal restoration after a major loss or challenge. This card reassures us that the end of one part of our lives isn't the literal end of our entire lives. Judgment also encourages you to step out of any mental graves you find yourself in. This grave often manifests as fear, low self-image, or the avoidance of your best life. You deserve all the great things life has in store for you, but you must seize the good things in life today. Let the past be past. Surrender the ineffective approach you know needs to die. Like the blazing phoenix, the death of an old partnership, habit, mindset, or experience isn't the end of you. It's just the beginning. Out with the old and in with the new! It's time to say yes to the best life has to offer. No matter what's happened before, you deserve better now. Your heart is about to experience a revitalizing renaissance. The long-abandoned hopes and dreams of your heart are stirring again with new life. Allow yourself to rise again.

THE WORLD

World personalities are the total package. They are high-achieving visionaries who see the big picture. They tend to be complete in themselves and are natural leaders. They are self-motivated and possess an irrepressible drive to win at life. World people are self-actualized, which makes them mature enough for substantive relationships. In love, they are attracted to people who also value success, perseverance, and achievement. They've worked hard to get where they are in life and expect the same tenacity from their partners. They are attracted to people who are aspirational, well-rounded, and practical. Immaturity, passivity, and apathy are major turnoffs for them. World people need enough room in their lives to achieve goals and rise toward excellence. They tend to prioritize their personal ambitions and career over pleasing others. At their best, World people are self-actualized, mature, successful, farsighted, and complete in their self. At their worst, they can be ruthlessly competitive, insular, and patronizing.

In a Love Reading
New Relationship
The World signifies a partnership brimming with potential. However, one or both partners are striving toward an achievement and must be given the freedom to follow their ambition. Striving for success in their career or creative goals is often the first priority. You may have to share this individual with their desire to achieve.

Long-Term Partnership
This partnership likely consists of two individuals who are at their best when they are working toward a goal. If the relationship has been feeling stagnant, it needs a goal to aim for. World relationships work best when they are working toward something. This card can also signify the graduation from one phase in a relationship to the next.

Intimacy
The World symbolizes synergy in intimate relationships. Each partner exemplifies the opposite energy of the other, while still being able to blend that energy harmoniously. Both partners instinctively strive to give and receive equally.

Seeking Romance
If you are single, the World can signify feeling self-confident and complete in yourself. When the World appears, it can sometimes take longer to find a person of quality. However, it is well worth the wait. Don't settle for less than the best. Keep reaching toward your loftiest goals and true love will gravitate toward you.

Desires

The World can represent a desire to complete a relationship phase in order to grow. This can manifest as transitioning from flirting to dating, dating to seeing each other exclusively, or becoming engaged to marrying. In the rare case that the World indicates the conclusion of a relationship, the partnership ends with a feeling of completion for both partners.

Reversed

New Relationship

When asking about another person, the World Reversed can symbolize an individual who procrastinates or avoids maturing. Although they have great potential, they also harbor a lot of fear about their own success. The World Reversed can also represent a frustrating situation that you are trying to get someone else to change with little success.

Long-Term Partnership

When the World is reversed, it may feel as if your relationship life is constantly spinning on repeat. There is likely an ingrained pattern that needs to be broken. Although the World Reversed represents repeated lessons, it can still herald eventual success if counterproductive habits are changed. Challenge yourself to apply a new approach to break old cycles.

Intimacy

The World Reversed can signify a partner who lives in the past when it comes to intimacy. They may mentally replay experiences that were both thrilling and traumatic. They may also feel a strong attachment to a past person they are no longer with. The World Reversed encourages breaking past attachments that have proven to be disempowering.

Seeking Romance

The World Reversed might appear when you are hesitant to abandon a counterproductive cycle because of the comfort you get from its familiarity. For a new door to open, the previous one must be closed. The World Reversed can also represent hanging on to someone who isn't meeting your best standards. It's time to graduate from second best and go for number one.

Desires

Sometimes the World Reversed can highlight a fear of commitment. The person in question desires freedom and fears losing their autonomy. If you are waiting on another person to make a commitment, establish healthy perimeters around how *long* you are willing to wait. Upright or reversed, the World encourages you to complete cycles that are keeping you stuck in limbo.

What the World May Be Teaching You

The World may be teaching you to complete a cycle in your life that feels unfinished. It is time to move on from old, repeated lessons you've outgrown. The World is the tarot's culmination card. It indicates that your journey has taught you much, and now it is time to apply that wisdom to restore wholeness. In love, it's time to expect the world in your relationships and not settle for anything less than the best. The World reassures you that you're ready to cross this important threshold. Make the all-important choice to reclaim your power once again. With the completion of this past important journey, a new pathway is opening to you. It is time to be courageous as you step out into the wider world and exemplify the completeness found in yourself. Limitless possibility awaits you when you allow yourself to come full circle. Completing an outworn cycle can feel frightening and unfamiliar. However, the appearance of the World reassures you that you are ready.

PART 2
THE MINOR ARCANA IN LOVE

The Minor Arcana consists of four suits: swords, cups, pentacles, and wands. In a love reading, each suit is associated with whatever issues are currently taking precedence in the relationship. Swords are concerned with communication and mindsets, including what you or your partner are mentally wrestling with. Cups are associated with love, feelings, and the full range of emotional experiences affecting the partnership. Pentacles have to do with issues of emotional security, values, priorities, family obligations, and money. Wands correlate with passion, individual ambitions, and whatever is currently growing in the relationship.

Whereas the Major Arcana reveals the major archetypal forces influencing us from within, the Minor Arcana reveals transitory situations that affect a relationship's development. Tarot cards are contextual. Their meanings can subtly change based on the question asked, how a situation is evolving, or where a card appears in a spread. The Minor Arcana will reveal passing situations or events that can be enjoyed, worked through, or learned from.

Never despair if you see a challenging card in your reading. Life is full of ups and downs, and the appearance of the positive and challenging cards of the tarot reflects this. Remember, no matter how resistant you may feel when encountering an image, each card carries an important lesson for you. Pay attention to the appearance of many cards from the same suit in your relationship tarot spread. This will illuminate what major issues and priorities currently dominate the relationship.

COURT CARDS IN LOVE

Each of the four tarot suits (swords, cups, pentacles, and wands) contains a royal family of four noble characters: a page, knight, queen, and king. These regal figures are called court cards. Court cards can be extremely helpful when interpreting the personalities that accentuate your life. They can signify the other people around you, including relationship partners, and their current priorities or states of mind. Court cards can also reveal the hidden attitudes and outlook of the person you are inquiring about. Much like the archetypes of the Major Arcana, court cards can portray the qualities you or your partner are currently exhibiting. They can also describe situations you or your partner may be currently facing. Again, context (and common sense) must be considered when interpreting court cards. If a court card seems to perfectly reflect the person you are asking about, then it should obviously be interpreted as referring to that person. However, if a court card's archetype does not seem to reflect the current people affecting the relationship, then they can be interpreted as a situation or as important messengers delivering a solution. The archetypes found in the tarot court can sometimes serve as models of behavior that can aid you in making better decisions for yourself.

In years past, court cards often adhered to strict gender roles in tarot instruction books. For example, kings were always men, and queens were always women. Over the last century, society has been reexamining the rigid attitudes toward gender roles and our conformity to them. We are fortunate to live in an age where there is greater understanding of the nuances of gender identities. We now recognize that men, women, and gender nonconformists exhibit a diversity of gender traits within themselves. Women can be strong, competitive, ambitious, and assertive. Men can be sensitive, loving, tender, and beautiful. When looking at court cards, keep in mind that although someone may identify themselves as a particular gender, the card that represents them may depict a figure of the opposite gender. It is more important to perceive the *qualities* of the court card being described rather than its gender depiction. I've known many strong women who've appeared as kings in a reading. I myself have also been known to appear as a queen from time to time!

Court cards have also been traditionally interpreted to describe someone's age. Pages were considered children or young girls. Knights were thought of as strapping young men in their twenties. Queens and kings were considered older than thirty. Although this simplification can make it easier to identify who a court card is referring to, I have found that the card offers less description of someone's age, but rather their *maturity level*. A man in his forties can appear as the Page of Cups if he is creative and poetic and possesses an eternally youthful spirit. A sagelike young lady who is wise beyond her years can also appear as a king or queen. Tarot cards reveal who people are beyond their outward facades. Try not to get too hung up on social identifiers and how they match up with the gender or age of the figure on the card. Court cards adeptly describe the personality traits, maturity, interests, and priorities of the people you are inquiring about. Here are some interpretations of what each member of the royal court may reflect about a person's maturity level, priorities, or state of mind when it comes to love.

Pages

Pages possess an eternally youthful spirit. They are still growing and often haven't reached full maturity in their relationships, profession, or life. Pages like to play and experiment and are still finding their voice. They are likely engaged in discovering their place in the world. In relationships, pages are somewhat childlike and extremely sensitive. They might act out unresolved childhood issues in their partnerships. Pages are creatives who aren't restricted by the heavy responsibilities or ambitions the other court cards contend with. They are rarely boring and are usually a lot of fun to be around. Like Peter Pan, most pages never want to grow up. At their best, pages exhibit unfettered freedom, creativity, talent, beauty, innocence, and youth. At their worst, pages can be immature, childish, thoughtless, unaccountable, and irresponsible.

Knights

Many tarot decks will depict knights riding a horse. Knights are always in motion, ever coming and going. In a love reading, knights are passionate, vigorous, and electrifying individuals. They lack the stable nature of kings ... and yet, that's what makes them so attractive and exciting. However, the youthful vigor that makes knights so captivating is also what makes them resistant to being tied down. Their behavior is notoriously erratic and inconsistent. Knights usually appear very confident in themselves, even when they don't have life completely figured out yet. They are still on a quest of personal development and rarely make their relationship partner the main focus of their life. At their best, knights are sexy, passionate, exciting, confident, vigorous, and chivalrous. At their worst, they can be unfaithful, inconsistent, and noncommittal.

Queens

Queens are receptive, feminine, and often ready for a relationship. They are mature and make stable partners who are often protective and nurturing to their partner, family, or relationship needs. Queens are often successful in the area of their life that their suit governs. In relationships, queens are rarely selfish. They often place the needs of their partner ahead of their own. With the exception of the Queen of Swords, most queens have to be reminded to care for their own needs. Queens are faithful in relationships and will be true to their partner and relationship as long as they continue to be honored and respected. At their best, queens are mature, receptive, faithful, loving, and patient. At their worst, they can be codependent, clingy, reactive, and passive-aggressive, and they will tolerate intolerable relationship conditions even at the expense of themselves.

Kings

Kings are mature, successful, self-actualized, and stable. In relationships, kings are not interested in playing games and seek a partner who also has their life together. Kings can either represent an older person or an individual who is truly wise beyond their years. For the most part, kings strive to be honest and direct. However, their stoicism can sometimes make them difficult to read in relationships. With the exception of the King of Cups, most kings struggle with expressing their vulnerabilities. Kings appear on stable thrones in the tarot. They are settled and resist changing. Often their personality traits are baked in, making it difficult to teach an old dog new tricks. The very qualities that make kings stable relationship partners can also make them somewhat boring. Kings often need encouragement to leave their comfort zone or spice things up for their relationships to experience more passion. At their best, kings are respectable, stable, successful, self-actualized, and fiercely protective of those they love. At their worst, kings can be dull, sedentary, tyrannical, immovable, stubborn, and controlling.

PIP CARDS IN LOVE

The numbered cards (ace through ten) in each suit are also called Pip cards. The Pip cards often depict different action scenes that tell a story. In love readings, they describe *situations and circumstances* the relationship is currently experiencing. Some Pip cards look happy and vibrant, while other cards look dark and depressing. Life is a mixture of positive and challenging experiences. The tarot's Minor Arcana appropriately reflects this.

When interpreting the Pip cards in a love reading, look for patterns. One of the most noticeable patterns are multiple cards appearing from the same suit. Another pattern you might notice is the appearance of two or more numbered cards that cluster together. The more of the same numbers that appear, the more powerful the message. Major Arcana cards can also be included with Minor Arcana cards of the same number. Double-digit cards can be reduced. For example, Justice, numbered eleven, can be reduced to the number two by adding both digits together (1+1=2). Tens are unique. They can stand on their own or can be reduced to the number 1 (1+0=1). Here are some numerological correspondences to aid you in interpreting clusters of the same number appearing in your relationship reading.

Multiple aces in a love reading represent *renewal and new beginnings*. Perhaps a new relationship is just starting, or an existing partnership is entering an exciting new phase. Aces introduce positive change and the opportunity to begin anew. Aces in a reading are like reset buttons. It doesn't matter what may have happened in the past; the appearance of multiple aces promises a fortuitous time to begin anew. Multiple aces can also signify time frames, such as one day, week, month, or year.

Multiple twos in a love reading will often point to *choices or compromises* that affect the partnership. When multiple twos appear, you may have to compromise your needs and expectations with the priorities of another. Twos are best brought into harmony through communication and compromise. The appearance of multiple twos may herald a time to consider another person's point of view. Multiple twos can also signify time frames, such as two days, weeks, months, or years.

Multiple threes in a love reading will inspire you to *express yourself*. Threes encourage you to be more confident and let others know what is in your mind and heart. Threes are also concerned with restoring joy and passion. Threes can also let you know when your heart needs healing. When threes appear, it is time to pay attention to the physical needs of relationships. Multiple threes can also signify time frames, such as three days, weeks, months, or even years.

Multiple fours in a love reading represent *reestablishing stability* to regain a sense of firm footing in your relationship life. Fours can encourage you to work on self-improvement in the real world. This could include establishing new routines to improve your appearance, physical health, vitality, or career. Fours can also indicate that self-discipline is required. You know what is truly best for you and how to be strong... so be it! Multiple fours can also signify time frames, such as four days, weeks, months, or perhaps even years.

Multiple fives in a love reading can highlight *conflicts or challenges* that need to be overcome in a partnership or within yourself. Fives are traditionally considered challenging cards to receive in a tarot reading. Fives are also the halfway point between one and ten. This could be a pivotal turning point in your own life. It can be difficult to witness the destabilization of past hopes and plans, but the current changes will lead to a better version of yourself. Multiple fives can also signify time frames, such as five days, weeks, months, or (rarely) years.

Multiple sixes in a love reading represent the *restoration of harmony*. Sixes can also portend the resolution of conflicts and the ability to progress. The tarot's sixes are cards of offering and giving. Sixes also bring in good karma to balance out past struggles and selflessness. Past troubles are far behind, and new possibilities await. Sixes encourage you to be loving and nurturing to yourself or your partner. Multiple sixes can also signify time frames, such as six days, weeks, months, or (rarely) years.

Multiple sevens in a love reading represent *transcendence and illumination*. Sevens appear when you begin to receive answers as to why something didn't go exactly as you planned. Often the reason is because something even better awaits. Sevens are magical numbers that reveal the synchronistic twists and turns of fate. Sevens will often appear when divine timing is at work in your life. When sevens appear, what is *meant to be* will be. Multiple sevens can also signify time frames, such as seven days, weeks, months, or (rarely) years.

Multiple eights in a love reading can highlight *perpetual cycles* in your relationship life. Eights are shaped like the infinity symbol. The infinity symbol can illustrate the continuation of a predictable behavior. Multiple eights reveal that the best predictor of future behavior can be found by examining past patterns. Eights can alert you to a harmful cycle that should be broken or to continue a healthy process that is working for you. Multiple eights can also signify time frames, such as eight days, weeks, months, or (rarely) years.

Multiple nines in a love reading highlight a cycle of learning that is *nearing completion*. Each nine in the Rider-Waite-Smith tarot depicts a solitary figure. The ninth Major Arcana card is the Hermit himself. Nines indicate that there is independent work that needs to be done. Nines can lead you away from what you *think* you want and toward what you *need*. Nines may lead to a period of retreat or introspection. Multiple nines can also signify time frames, such as nine days, weeks, months, or (rarely) years.

Multiple tens in a love reading symbolize *completions and new beginnings*. Ten is a cyclical number. When adding both digits (1+0), you arrive back at the ace, a harbinger of new beginnings. When multiple tens appear, life events are culminating, and exciting changes are about to occur. When tens describe a relationship partner, they may highlight an individual who has completed a major life chapter, the next remaining unwritten. Multiple tens can also signify time frames, such as ten days, weeks, months, or (rarely) years.

SWORDS IN A LOVE READING

The swords suit is associated with the element of air and rules our current thoughts, mindset, and fears we may need to communicate. Many dark and frightening images appear in the swords suit. This is because many of us carry negative expectations, shadows, and fears that show up in situations that happen over and over until we finally learn the lesson. Sword cards can highlight current or past traumas that are still affecting your mind. They can also reveal underlying issues that need to be communicated with your partner or a trusted counselor. Swords can reveal how to transform yourself from being mentally victimized (by yourself or others) to being clear, empowered, and ready to act. Although swords are not considered romantic, they are extremely important. Swords represent the unvarnished, dispassionate truth. Sometimes we need to confront and clear the shadows within ourselves so we'll be ready for an honest and loving relationship with another person.

In a relationship reading, swords illuminate the predominate thoughts you harbor about your love life and relationship experiences. Darker cards do not doom you to experience terrible things. They reveal a challenge you may need to confront honestly before you can progress. The challenge can be with another person or within your own mind. Darker cards can also represent harmful situations and expectations that need to be cut out of your life. Not all sword cards are challenging. Even the harshest sword cards are extremely empowering. Swords show how someone currently thinks about their role in the world around them. They can also reveal what an individual may think they deserve. Many times, our own limiting beliefs about what we can attain are the very thing thwarting our best efforts to make our dreams come true. We might think it is the cheating spouse or the guy who won't call back who is causing our misery. The swords suit will turn the tables on your assumptions and bluntly ask you, "If this situation is unworthy of you, why are you tolerating it? Why not cut this person out of your life if they continue to harm you? What ingrained beliefs are contributing to your acceptance of the unacceptable? Why do you think you aren't being respected when you haven't been respecting yourself?" The swords suit will demand that you courageously confront your fears, challenges, and victimhood. Although it can be harsh at times, it can lead to a huge personal breakthrough if you have the courage to take your authentic power back.

When many sword cards appear in a love reading, it indicates that there is a lot brewing mentally for either you or your partner. Swords also rule *mindsets*. A person's mindset will often determine how successful they are in their relationships and in life. Swords will challenge you to take responsibility for your thoughts and cut away anything that depletes your personal power. Swords can also rule old issues that need to be confronted and released. Communication and understanding the *why* behind an issue will often prove the greatest healer when many swords appear. Most importantly, swords represent power. They will reveal whether you are wielding your personal power or surrendering to someone else's validation or approval.

ACE OF SWORDS

All aces in the tarot signify that a positive new beginning is at hand. In the case of the Ace of Swords, wonderful things begin to happen when you reclaim your personal power and take control of your life's direction. Instead of passively waiting for another person to take the lead, the Ace of Swords urges you to take charge. The Ace of Swords encourages you to be assertive in relationships. Stop avoiding the issue that makes you most uncomfortable. Resolve inner conflict by having an honest conversation or allowing your common sense to show the way. The Ace of Swords inspires you to restore clarity by being honest and direct. If there is something you really want to say, *say it*! Although you can't control what choices others will make, or what surprises happen in your own life, you can always choose your response. If you have been unhappy, this card reminds you that your choices can shift your energy from victim to victor. The message of the Ace of Swords is clear and direct. *Take your power back!*

In a Love Reading
New Relationship
The Ace of Swords can signify an electric attraction. The spark between the two of you is definitely there. Your new love interest will excite your imagination with unlimited possibility for the future. Try to appeal to this person's intellect and love of conversation. This card signifies a true meeting of the minds. Be assertive and don't hide your intelligence.

Long-Term Partnership
The Ace of Swords represents a relationship between two powerful personalities. Your partner must feel they can speak openly about their personal ambitions. Restore clarity through honest communication. This partnership thrives when both people feel in control of their own destiny. Mutual interests can reignite the spark between you.

Intimacy
The Ace of Swords represents renewed passion. Instead of waiting for your partner to act, you may want to take the initiative. This card can also signify a need for space and independence so that each partner has room to grow. The Ace of Swords can also warn you not to cling too tightly to this person, or you will smother the spark.

Seeking Romance
If you are single, the Ace of Swords urges you to take charge of your love life. Clothe yourself in self-confidence and power. Remember that your choices give you control. Gravitate toward people and activities that affirm your power instead of sapping it. Visualize yourself wearing a crown to your first date and watch how your energy shifts.

Desires
The Ace of Swords signifies a strong desire to take charge and start over. No matter what has happened in the past, the promise of new possibilities awaits. However, action must follow whatever decision you make. Make the choice that restores your personal power and stick with it. This card can also symbolize the establishment of new boundaries.

Reversed
New Relationship
The person you are asking about may have trouble trusting and is a bit guarded. The Ace of Swords Reversed can represent someone who is still a bit unsteady and needs a lot of support. It is better to wait and see before rushing toward the next step.

Long-Term Partnership
When the Ace of Swords appears reversed, you must protect healthy new habits or boundaries you've just established in your relationship. The positive changes haven't fully taken root yet and need time to be reinforced. Stay committed to your mutual goals and defend what you both hold dear.

Intimacy
The Ace of Swords Reversed can represent a guarded partner. They may be so stuck in their head that they feel disconnected from their body. Instead of waiting for the other person to make the first move, you may need to take the initiative. Upright or reversed, the Ace of Swords urges you to confront issues directly instead of avoiding them.

Seeking Romance
The Ace of Swords can appear reversed if you've made an important decision for your own good but still feel shaky about it. You are getting your life back on the right track, but time is needed for positive new patterns to be established. Stay strong and keep yourself from anything or anyone who will tempt you to cave to past weaknesses.

Desires
Ace of Swords Reversed can represent a desire to avoid change or conflict; however, this no longer serves you. You can create the life you want to live, but you

must take ownership of it. Maintain your values and guard the truth. A choice must be made. Choose the path that supports your independence and power.

What the Ace of Swords May Be Teaching You

The Ace of Swords may be teaching you to reclaim your power. For this to happen, you may need to allow your head to rule your heart at this time. Follow your common sense, especially if it urges you to grow beyond old patterns that have kept you in a state of suffering. It is time to be honest with yourself about what's been disempowering you. The appearance of the Ace of Swords signals that a new beginning is at hand. Your crown and sword of power are finally being returned to you. Use this blade to cut away the illusions that have been keeping you scared and stuck. Remember the person you were when you felt most powerful, beautiful, confident, and alive. *You are still that person*; however, now you have the gift of added wisdom. No matter what storms you've endured in times past, it's time to get up, dust yourself off, and reclaim your power. Take charge!

TWO OF SWORDS

The Two of Swords represents the state of being in-between. In a love reading, the Two of Swords often represents a person who is in the midst of personal transformation. They may be transitioning out of an old pattern, life cycle, or relationship. Although you may want definitive answers at this time, they simply aren't available. The Two of Swords often accompanies the process of waiting.

Waiting for an answer. Waiting for more information to come to light. Waiting for a commitment. Waiting to see if a partner will follow through. The Two of Swords encourages you to make peace with the in-between phase you are wading through. Release anxiety and reestablish calm. Breathe deeply into your wise center. It may feel like you are walking blindfolded; however, your inner sight will guide you through this transition. The place in your life that feels unresolved is precisely where life's greatest magic is happening. Trust yourself. You are exactly where you need to be, and everything is transitioning as it should.

In a Love Reading
New Relationship
The Two of Swords often represents a love interest who is still in a state of in-between. They may be transitioning out of a past relationship or they could be in the process of a personal transformation. Be patient, manage expectations, and move slowly. You may have to accept where this person is at in their life now, instead of falling in love with their future possibilities.

Long-Term Partnership
The Two of Swords can signify a long-standing issue that remains unresolved. Perhaps an honest conversation can result in a compromise. It's time to bring clarity to amorphous issues. The Two of Swords can also symbolize a truce. You may be in the process of making peace with your partner or their position.

Intimacy
This card can signify the importance of *listening* to your partner. Before working on the more intimate aspects of your partnership, your partner requires patience, compromise, or understanding. He or she is likely undergoing a confusing life change or is balancing other demands. Sex may be inconsistent or on hold at this time.

Seeking Romance
If you are single, you are likely undergoing a process of personal transformation that is still incomplete. Although you feel in limbo now, you will soon find the closure you seek. Slow and steady steps are needed now. Sometimes the Two of Swords is also associated with friendship. Socializing with friends may indirectly place you in the path of a potential admirer.

Desires

The Two of Swords can signify a desire to get clear in your own mind before placing your focus on relationship issues. A transformation needs to happen internally before it can be reflected in your world. An empowering new life phase is opening to you, but first you must change how you've been thinking or feeling. Seek the wisdom found within to restore your equilibrium.

Reversed

New Relationship

The Two of Swords can signify a person you've been waiting on for a long time. They may avoid commitment or making decisions. The clarity you desire can only be possible if you address this issue head-on. You may feel uneasy about letting go and moving on, but this may be the time to do it. Waiting hasn't been working. It's time to change course or change tactics.

Long-Term Partnership

The Two of Swords Reversed urges you to set an honest deadline with yourself for when you expect to experience resolution around an important relationship issue. If the same unfinished cycle keeps recurring, it is a sign that the situation will not change unless you change. If your current reality is no longer support-ing your best life, you may need to consider moving on.

Intimacy

The Two of Swords Reversed can signify dormancy in a sexual relationship. You may be coming out of a time when one or both partners have felt the need to withdraw. This card encourages you to step out of limbo by seeking answers. You may need to initiate the conversation. This card can also signify a need for more compromise in the partnership regarding sex.

Seeking Romance

You've worked on yourself enough. It's time to take decisive action and step out of limbo. You've sought to bring closure to the past and now it's time to move on. Put your toe in the water before taking the plunge. The world is calling and it's time to connect again. You can now put your self-work into practice.

Desires

The Two of Swords Reversed can signify a desire to bring closure to a situation that has been suspended for quite some time. For the next door to open, that last one must be shut. Stop waiting for another person to make you *feel* ready to get your life moving. Be decisive and make the choice to step out of limbo.

What the Two of Swords May Be Teaching You

The Two of Swords is teaching you to make peace with being in-between. Although it can feel unresolved and unsettling, you are exactly where you need to be at this time in your life. There will be plenty of time in the future to focus on the needs of others, but right now your most beautiful transformation will happen when you focus inward. The Rider-Waite-Smith tarot depicts a blindfolded woman sitting serenely before a seascape. The blindfold represents not being able to see the future clearly at this time. However, her serene posture assures you to trust in the magical transformation occurring in your life. That which remains unresolved will not remain that way forever. The Two of Swords represents the restoration of inner peace if you can accept your current place on your path without judgment. Change is in the air. Be gentle with yourself. Like the phases of the moon, the current appearance of your situation will shift into something different in time. The Two of Swords offers an opportunity to shift your perspective and to eventually transition out of this twilight time. You don't need to pick at yourself or control. Just *be*.

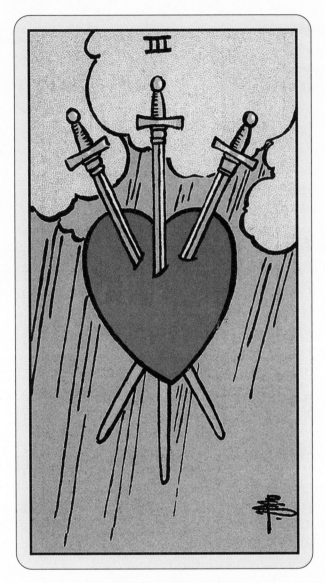

THREE OF SWORDS

You don't need to be a tarot expert to take one look at the Three of Swords and know it symbolizes a broken heart. In a love reading, the Three of Swords often symbolizes a wound, *either past or present*, that needs healing before positively progressing again. Many available definitions for this card include betrayal, sadness, love triangles, and heartbreak, and, indeed, this card can reflect those feelings and situations. However, the Three of Swords does not automatically mean that your partner is going to cheat on you or stab you in the back *every* time it appears. Instead, it highlights where you *already know* you've been hurting. Often, the Three of Swords compels you to face residual trauma, hurt, or heartbreak that has continued to negatively impact your perspective for far too long. Painful truths can be difficult to acknowledge. However, if you can honestly name the swords that perpetually stab at your heart, you can draw them out and release them. This allows the wounded heart to finally mend.

In a Love Reading
New Relationship
This card can signify that another person, interest, or thing is pulling your love interest's attention away from fully investing in a partnership with you. This card can also warn of beginning a rebound relationship, where one partner's heart has not completely recovered from a past breakup or emotional betrayal before rushing into their next relationship.

Long-Term Partnership
The Three of Swords can represent a partner who consistently leaves you for another love. However, sometimes the other love isn't a paramour, but rather a family obligation, a friendship, a career, a creative pursuit, or an ambition. You will have to decide if you are willing to share your partner with this other obligation.

Intimacy
The Three of Swords can represent deception, lies, or even cheating from your partner. If you ask your cards the direct question "Is he cheating on me?" and this card appears, the answer is most likely yes. If you even need to ask that question about your partner, this should serve as a huge red flag that the relationship is not rooted in transparency or trust.

Seeking Romance
If you are single, it's time to release old wounds and make some room in your life for a new love. However, you may have to let go of an old emotional attachment that is still hurting you. It's time to allow for new beginnings and healing. Before beginning the next chapter, the baggage of the past must be released.

Desires

The Three of Swords can represent a desire to surrender painful emotions that have been obscuring your perspective for far too long. The rain depicted in most decks can symbolize tears and sorrows, which can be released through crying. It's time to honestly confront the cause of your suffering and finally let it go.

Reversed
New Relationship

It may be time to do some self-work before attempting to form a deep connection with the other. Using another person to avoid what is uncomfortable within will not result in true love or happiness. Only you have the power to draw your own swords from the wounds in your heart. Confront the uncomfortable things that need to be released gently and courageously.

Long-Term Partnership

You (or your partner) are rationalizing away a relationship issue that has been causing inexcusable pain. It's time to stop deflecting and communicate honestly about what is being experienced. This card can also signify that time has begun to heal a wound from a difficult past episode of your relationship.

Intimacy

There is an uncomfortable elephant in the room of your partnership that must be acknowledged openly and honestly. The partnership cannot progress without transparent communication about damage to the relationship's issues surrounding intimacy, past or present. It's time to face facts.

Seeking Romance

The gray clouds that appear on this card in many decks can symbolize the use of old mental narratives that convince you there is no hope. This is an illusion, as you can absolutely be happy again. In the Rider-Waite-Smith deck, one cloud is drawn unfinished. Your future is still unformed and provides unlimited opportunities to create a happy life.

Desires

The Three of Swords Reversed can signify a desire to put the pieces back together. An important inner threshold has been crossed, and now it's time to walk away from the source of great harm. An old obsession or wound ceases to sting as it once did. Time will aid in the healing of this wound.

What the Three of Swords May Be Teaching You

The Three of Swords can highlight emotional blockages rooted in negative past experiences. For the wound to heal, the swords must be released from the heart. The wounds the swords represent could have been inflicted last night, or as far back as childhood. We've all clung to a harmful person or behavior longer than we should have at some point in our lives. Soon the heart is tricked into thinking the possession of the thing causing your pain provides comfort, but this just isn't true. For the heart to heal, the toxic shrapnel must be *named, honestly confronted,* and finally *removed.* If you choose to hold on to a past person or issue that continues to destroy your happiness, then you are habitually betraying yourself. It's like wearing a sign on your head that says, "Hey, betray me! I do it myself all the time!" The people you try to connect with will unconsciously perceive it. Predators will exploit it. A potential partner might feel pressured or uncomfortable that they must fix your issues. Only you can truly address your wounds and compassionately heal them by making the choice to do so.

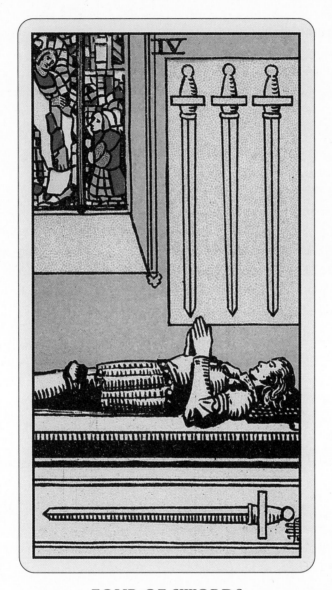

FOUR OF SWORDS

The Four of Swords can represent rest or retreat from an intense person or situation. In a love reading, this card encourages self-reflection. Looking inward allows you to extract yourself from the muddling energies of others. This will empower you to get clear in your own thoughts without needing someone else to provide that clarity for you. It may be time to detach from an emotionally tumultuous situation and give yourself some time to breathe. The Four of Swords can also appear when it's time to walk away from a confusing situation to regain your peace of mind. The lesson of this card is to make peace within *yourself* before tending to relationships with others. The Four of Swords can also appear when it's simply time to take a break or schedule a vacation. This card reminds you that when you're at peace, you are truly empowered. Throwing more stress at an already stressful situation will only serve to exhaust and deplete you. The heart and mind will make better choices when they are calm.

In a Love Reading
New Relationship
The Four of Swords could indicate that your budding relationship may not progress quickly at this time. Be patient. The person you are asking about may periodically need to retreat to regain clarity or may simply need more time to make up their mind. This card can also represent a love interest who is involved in some sort of recovery process. Take it slow.

Long-Term Partnership
For a long-term partnership, the Four of Swords could indicate that one or both partners will benefit immensely from periodic alone time. You may also find that your relationship works best when you can both focus on your independent interests. It may also be time for a vacation to rest, replenish, and rejuvenate your bond.

Intimacy
It may feel like your sex life has been in a long slumber. It may be time to reawaken the passion by speaking candidly about your needs. This card can also indicate that external stress is interfering with the intimacy you and your partner share. A relaxing, romantic retreat is in order. Engage in activities that release tension.

Seeking Romance
If you are single, you may be feeling rather isolated. Counterintuitively, you may have also become very comfortable being on your own. This can result in unconsciously sending out signals to others that you're not actually looking for a relationship.

Desires

The Four of Swords can represent an introverted personality who periodically desires solitude or privacy. Try not to force this person into participating in social activities they'd rather avoid. Everyone is different, and not everyone loves to interact with boisterous groups. This card encourages respect for someone's space or boundaries.

Reversed
New Relationship

The Four of Swords Reversed can signify someone who has social anxiety that interferes with their ability to connect with others. Take baby steps with this person. They mustn't feel pressured or rushed. This card can also signify a person who hasn't dated in a long time and is awkwardly getting off on the wrong foot. Time and patience are needed.

Long-Term Partnership

The Four of Swords Reversed could indicate that both you and your partner have been so inundated with the needs of others that you would benefit from some rest and relaxation. Embarking on a romantic retreat can do much to restore the bonds you share.

Intimacy

Romantic opportunities await if you can stretch beyond your comfort zone. You may have become isolated for too long and now it is time to allow yourself to open up and be more vulnerable with others. This card can also signify physical or emotional space between you and your partner. Compromise may help build a bridge over this widening chasm.

Seeking Romance

You may have been feeling restless or anxious about your love life. Something about the past remains unsettled and you are hesitant to move on. Take all the time you need to heal and make peace with the past. Your heart has needed detachment and rest so that it can heal; however, it's preparing to wake up. A reawakening is just around the corner.

Desires

Upright or reversed, the Four of Swords encourages you to reject frantic thinking. This card can signify a desire to restore inner peace. Take a time-out and remember to breathe. If you have accumulated anxious or restless energy, channel it into something constructive. Let your restlessness become fuel for self-improvement.

What the Four of Swords May Be Teaching You

The Four of Swords is teaching you to calm your mind and decrease the intensity surrounding relationship expectations. It may not feel like being alone is useful to you now. However, taking time to retreat and recenter will do wonders for reclaiming your sanity and composure. Sometimes when we anxiously want or need something, we witness the undesired effect of driving it away. If the cause of your stress is another person, the Four of Swords dispels the illusion that you can't heal. It's time to retreat to get clear on what *you* need right now. The Four of Swords encourages you to restore clarity before tending to others. Be kind to yourself during this process of emotional recuperation. Your love life may need to undergo a period of slumber to detox and heal. Now is the time for self-care. The Four of Swords reassures you that life will open its wonders to you when both head and heart are at peace.

FIVE OF SWORDS

The Five of Swords can symbolize feeling overwhelmed by a messy situation that impairs your judgment. Mixed signals, unclear communication, or internal conflict is resulting in confusion. Your head may be saying one thing, while your heart says another, and yet both experiences *feel* equally true. The Five of Swords reminds you that *feels like* doesn't always translate to *is like*. You may be dealing with someone who acts in a contradictory manner. Their words may tell you one thing, while their actions explicitly show the opposite. The Five of Swords encourages you to restore clarity to messy situations by *being clearer*, first with yourself, then with others. Reason must take precedence over feelings. The Five of Swords also challenges you to restore order by establishing clear boundaries. Only you can dictate what is acceptable or unacceptable in your relationships. *Common sense* will always be your greatest ally when navigating through the confusing landscape of the Five of Swords.

In a Love Reading
New Relationship
The Five of Swords can represent a new love interest who is a fixer-upper. They might meet many of your standards, but certainly not all of them. Your strong feelings may rationalize away their flaws. Be wary of tolerating more of this person's issues than you can handle. This card can also signify someone who isn't quite ready for a commitment yet. Be honest, clear, and direct.

Long-Term Partnership
The Five of Swords can signify a partnership of conflicting opposites. One partner may be cool and cerebral, while the other partner is sensitive and volatile. It may seem as if you speak two different languages altogether. Counseling or other resources may help you both clarify what you are attempting to communicate to the other.

Intimacy
The Five of Swords can symbolize feeling inundated with external issues that are negatively impacting your sex life. This card usually indicates the feeling of being overwhelmed. Tune in to your partner's needs and see if there is some way to help alleviate stress. Sometimes this card can signify a person who is not being transparent about their sex life.

Seeking Romance
If you are single, you may be feeling overwhelmed by the messiness of dating. Past nightmare scenarios may have left you feeling defeated or disheartened. Take your time before diving into the next emotionally intense situation. Walk into new partnerships with clear and sensible boundaries. Make sure your standards are being respected.

Desires

The Five of Swords can represent the desire to extract yourself from a messy emotional situation. Although you didn't have control over all that's happened, you do have control over your response. This card can signify a relationship that's hit an impasse due to someone's issues. Let your head govern your heart if you are confused by what you should do.

Reversed
New Relationship

It may be time to walk away from a relationship that is giving you more sorrow and stress than joy. Although it may be difficult, you will fare better if you turn away from disempowering partnerships. This card can also signify that you need to be clearer about your relationship expectations from the beginning.

Long-Term Partnership

You have been engaged in an argument, conflict, or struggle, and your energy feels scattered and messy. You may need to walk away from the conflict to get clear about what it is you want. Difficult conversations are necessary in any relationship but cease to be productive if they repeatedly devolve. Know your non-negotiables and adhere to them.

Intimacy

This card can warn you about a person who plays games. Use your common sense when addressing any blatant untruths that are staring you in the face. Don't rush forward blindly. Time and repeated patterns reveal this person's true character. Sometimes, this card can indicate that something is being done behind your back.

Seeking Romance

There is an overwhelming conflict between your head and heart that needs to be resolved. Keep your word with yourself. If you say you are going to uphold a better standard, *stick with it*. If you are experiencing a moment of weakness, seek the support of people you trust who want the best for you.

Desires

The Five of Swords Reversed will often appear when you've been pushing too hard toward your desire and feel like you are repeatedly hitting a wall. Remember, the definition of insanity is doing the same thing over and over while expecting a different result. It is time to change tactics. Take a step back to notice any counterproductive pattern you feel ensnared in.

What the Five of Swords May Be Teaching You

The Five of Swords teaches you to trust your common sense. This inherent gift will always steer your heart away from confusion and harm. Although the Five of Swords can refer to a period in your life when you are overcoming a series of setbacks, it is not a hopeless card. A turning point is occurring. It's time to pick up the scattered pieces of past sorrows and reestablish clarity. Before blindly picking up *all* the pieces from the past, consider which pieces actually contribute to your best life. Any outdated baggage that has been fueling your fears, shadows, or self-limiting beliefs are no longer helpful. Reason must govern feelings at this time, even if it creates temporary discomfort. In the Rider-Waite-Smith deck, the cold winds of reality are breaking up the gray clouds of illusion. The fresh breeze of truth is empowering, even if its winds can sting when first hitting you—but be comforted. The winds will not blow cold forever. Even your common sense will concede that next summer's breeze is on its way.

SIX OF SWORDS

The Six of Swords signals movement. The movement could be literal, such as moving in with a partner, changing residence, or traveling. Or the movement could be symbolic, such as moving beyond an old attachment that no longer serves you. In a love reading, the Six of Swords usually signifies *benevolent change*. Although you may be leaving behind the familiar, your progress will likely feel gradual and natural. It may seem as if there is a steady current, smoothly propelling you toward your next appropriate course. The Six of Swords can also appear when your instincts are telling you it's time to leave behind an emotionally turbulent situation. However, when this card appears, you will likely feel *ready* to progress. Sometimes, the Six of Swords can signal long-distance relationships or meeting someone new from a far-off place. Whatever its context, the Six of Swords encourages you to go with the flow. Surrender to the natural current sweeping through your life, and you will arrive at a safe harbor.

In a Love Reading
New Relationship
The Six of Swords signifies progress. The advice of this card is to not rock the boat. If it feels like your relationship is progressing on the right track, *let it be*. For now, just enjoy the ride. Sometimes this card can also signify a long-distance relationship or a new love interest who travels often.

Long-Term Partnership
The Six of Swords can indicate that your relationship is moving out of a turbulent period. Both partners are about to enjoy a calmer time. This card can also signify a change of residence or researching potential homes to move in to. Finally, the Six of Swords can indicate that it's time for a vacation. Any place by the water will do.

Intimacy
The Six of Swords can indicate a desire for change, movement, or newness. It could also indicate increasing activities, such as physical exercise, to make you feel better in your own skin. Travel to exotic places may also reawaken the passion in your sex life.

Seeking Romance
If you are single, it's time to change *where* you've been looking for love. New places and opportunities are opening to you now. This card will alert you when it's time to seek out a new scene. Once you embark toward your new destination, you'll wonder how you could have stayed stuck for so long. Let go and move on.

Desires
The Six of Swords assures you that you will attain your heart's desire when you let go of your need to control. If you are not sure what to do, surrender to the current that is flowing toward empowerment. Change is happening. Stop fighting the waves. This card can also signify a desire for a person who lives far away or frequently travels.

Reversed
New Relationship
The Six of Swords Reversed warns you not to settle for any port in the storm. You may have to move past a person who clearly isn't meeting your standards. This card can also indicate a new love interest who seems a bit stuck. Making a choice, *any* choice, is preferable to sitting, hoping, and waiting for this person to take the initiative.

Long-Term Partnership
This card can signify feeling stagnant in your relationship. An important issue needs to be resolved before you can move forward. Upright or reversed, the Six of Swords is a benevolent change card. Sometimes this card appears when one partner is making improvements while the other feels stuck. Try to motivate them through shared interests and activities.

Intimacy
One or both partners may need more physical activity to work out their anxiety. This will help them feel better about their health and physical appearance. If you've both been stuck in a rut, increased exercise may improve intimacy. This card can also signify an unfulfilling routine that must be changed.

Seeking Romance
If you are single, the Six of Swords Reversed can symbolize that you've been feeling stagnant. It's time to shake things up and transform the energy. Romance will not be found by repeating the same cycles or revisiting the same places. Open yourself to new experiences, locations, and activities. Plan a trip, or simply get out and about. It's time to get the energy moving again.

Desires

This card signifies a desire to progress. It's time to ask yourself what choices are perpetuating the same unfulfilling result. Get your life moving again. You may need to face your fear of leaving past drama far behind. Upright or reversed, the Six of Swords rewards positive change.

What the Six of Swords May Be Teaching You

The Six of Swords teaches you to accept the spontaneous tides of change and *surrender*. It's so easy for us to become transfixed by our desires that we work against the natural current. When you fight the waves, you will likely experience exhaustion, panic, or defeat. The Six of Swords advises you to sail beyond the rough waters you've been floundering in. Take a deep breath, relax, and let your shoulders drop. Instead of resisting where these unknown tides are leading, whisper to yourself, "I accept." Shift your energy from combatively fighting this natural current to working with it. The universe is benevolently leading you toward a safer harbor; however, the turbulent waters of the past must be left far behind. *Trust* that you haven't been led all this way to sink. The most joyous experiences in life often happen in unexpected places and at unplanned times. Relax and let go of your need to control. Serendipitous experiences will come together if you can surrender to destiny's current.

SEVEN OF SWORDS

The Seven of Swords has long been associated with tricksters, manipulation, and deception. If this card represents a new love interest, they are cunningly intelligent and thrilling company. However, they are also a bit dangerous. In many tarot decks, the Seven of Swords depicts a thief. In a love reading, this can warn you of getting your heart stolen by someone who won't take care of it. The Seven of Swords can also signify a partner who possesses a rebellious nature. They flout the rules and are resistant to feeling controlled or obligated. The Seven of Swords will always ask you to take an honest look at what is currently *happening*, without getting carried away with what you *hope to see*. Many times, the deception emphasized by the Seven of Swords is *self-deception*. This can happen if you are still clinging to an unhealthy attachment, even when the inconvenient truth is staring you in the face. At its most innocent, the Seven of Swords is associated with fibbing and false flattery.

In a Love Reading
New Relationship
The Seven of Swords can represent a thrilling new love interest; however, resist throwing all caution to the wind. Trust your instincts if something feels off. Watch this person's actions instead of believing their words alone. They may defy the rules or even the law. This card can also represent a heartbreaker who flirts with everybody.

Long-Term Partnership
For a long-term partnership, your partner may be rebelling against something in the relationship that feels overly restrictive. They might protest established norms in the relationship. This card can also indicate dishonesty by omission. You may have to read between the lines to get at the heart of what they truly need.

Intimacy
The Seven of Swords will warn you to stay vigilant with sexy flatterers who are up to no good! If you are hearing words from someone that aren't matching up with their actions, trust what you are seeing. This card can also signify a person who *shows* you who they really are through their actions, even if their words are telling you the complete opposite.

Seeking Romance
If you are single, a past betrayal from a dishonest partner may be interfering with your ability to trust. Don't allow the past to make you paranoid about the future. The past experiences have sharpened your wits. Trust your inner wisdom. You can no longer be fooled unless you choose to ignore warning signs.

Desires

The Seven of Swords can represent a desire to cut through deception and reestablish the truth. Instead of being anxious or paranoid about a glaring issue, be honest and direct. Define your values and boundaries and make them clear. This card encourages you to face the truth in yourself and in others, even if you feel conflicted.

Reversed

New Relationship

The Seven of Swords Reversed can signify learning how to trust again. You may have been tricked in the past, and you are having a hard time opening up. Don't close the door on new relationships without obtaining more information. Sometimes you have to take a chance, even when there are no guarantees. Gather more data.

Long-Term Partnership

This card encourages you to be cautious where love and money intersect. This card can signify a partner who is unwise with money. Be clearheaded with your finances. If there is a risk of losing big, consider a prenuptial agreement or other protective financial agreements. If you have a shared credit card or bank account, know your balance at all times!

Intimacy

The Seven of Swords Reversed can indicate a change of luck. If a little black rain cloud has been hovering above your romantic prospects, this card could indicate that it is finally dissipating. Expect chance encounters or unexpected excitement.

Seeking Romance

It may be time to change your own luck in love. There is an anonymous quote that states, "Luck is what happens when preparation meets opportunity." Review where you are in your life right now and how you feel. *What personal improvements do you feel ready to make? How could you get your life ready for the right person?* Invest in your best life.

Desires

The Seven of Swords Reversed can represent a desire to stop playing with fire in relationships. You may have lost your patience with a love interest who says all the right things but doesn't deliver. This card encourages you to change your luck by removing yourself from a situation that you just can't win.

What the Seven of Swords May Be Teaching You

The Seven of Swords could be teaching you to establish healthy relationships rooted in truth. In a healthy relationship, you will not have to wonder if your partner is telling the truth because they will have established trust through their words *and their deeds*. In healthy relationships, you won't have to rationalize bad behavior away, or rush to defend the indefensible. In a healthy relationship, you won't need to excuse a partner's emotional unavailability because of their past trauma or because they had an emotionally abusive parent. In a healthy relationship, you won't have to run to the nearest tarot reader to reassure you that a partner isn't cheating or that they will finally leave their marriage. Sometimes, the Seven of Swords forces us to face inconvenient truths that we would rather rationalize away. This card alerts you to any denial that *is perpetuated from within*. The Seven of Swords teaches us that *true love* cannot subsist on *love* alone. It also requires the *truth* part.

EIGHT OF SWORDS

The Eight of Swords represents destructive passivity in relationships. In a love reading, it can appear if you are waiting for *someone else* to rescue you or validate your worth. The Eight of Swords can also reflect residual sorrow from past rejection or abandonment. These past hurts can fuel self-limiting fears of being worthless, alone, hopeless, or stuck. When the Eight of Swords appears, you may have convinced yourself that your hands are tied, and that you have no choice—that somehow your sadness is just the cost of love. You may endlessly wait for your savior to return or obsessively check your phone for a sweet message from the very person who devastated you. When the Eight of Swords appears, you must resist coddling the person (or belief) that is keeping you stuck in passivity. You must believe in your own worth, rather than waiting for someone else to prove it to you. Only *you* have the power to save yourself. The Eight of Swords will often appear as a final test to reveal what you really think of yourself.

In a Love Reading
New Relationship
The Eight of Swords will alert you if you are setting yourself up for failure in new relationships by energetically showing up as a victim. Maintain your dignity, power, and self-respect. Watch out for being too eager to please or passively waiting for the other person to recognize what a wonderful person you are. Know your worth walking in.

Long-Term Partnership
The Eight of Swords can warn of unhealthy dependency in relationships. One partner might rely on the other to make them feel good, solve all their issues, or take care of their responsibilities. Relationships work best when both people show up in their power. This card can also signify a partner who is being passive-aggressive or needy.

Intimacy
The Eight of Swords can symbolize feelings of rejection, embarrassment, or abandonment. One partner may suffer from low self-esteem, depression, or unhappiness with their body image. This card can also signify a sexual issue that one partner feels too embarrassed or ashamed to talk about.

Seeking Romance
If you are single, the Eight of Swords could represent feeling hopeless as you endlessly wait for your ideal relationship to arrive. *A watched pot never boils.* Switch mental gears. Engage in activities that empower you. This will have the added benefit of making your aura much more attractive to be around and will get the energy moving again.

Desires

The Eight of Swords can signify a desire for an unhealthy person who has dishonored you. If your question is, "Are they coming back?" this card asks you *why* you are surrendering your self-respect to someone who has proven they don't deserve you. Victimhood is beneath your dignity. This card always encourages you to free yourself from a disempowering situation.

Reversed
New Relationship

The person you are asking about is likely coming out of a difficult situation and may need more time. Try not to rush them into commitments they are not ready to make. Be patient and compassionate. If the love is meant to be, it will be. The less you try to control the situation, the better it will turn out.

Long-Term Partnership

Your role in your relationship is just one part of you, not the whole you. You are far more than the other half of another person. You are a whole within yourself. Remind yourself of the other roles you play in this life. It's time to restore balance. There is work to do on yourself independent from your partner.

Intimacy

You are wriggling out of the trap of feeling you are less than you truly are. It's time to invest in yourself and free yourself from any person, attitude, or situation that makes you feel powerless. Take off the blindfold and see yourself clearly. This card can also signify addressing past issues of sexual rejection or trauma and working through them.

Seeking Romance

You are distant enough from a bad relationship that you can finally see it clearly. You may be wondering, "How did I put up with that garbage for so long?" Thank your heart, mind, and spirit for not breaking during that trying time. You are set up for success now. Smile at the future that is coming into being. Your heart is bouncing back.

Desires

You've embraced your desire to become a more courageous version of yourself. Your self-work is paying off. You are no longer allowing fear to dominate your approach to love. The blindfold is off, and you see yourself clearly now.

What the Eight of Swords May Be Teaching You

Although your heart may sink when you see the Eight of Swords in a relationship reading, don't despair. The dark cards of the swords suit often play out *in your mind*. Disempowered thoughts and memories will loosen their hold on you when you face them honestly with compassion and courage. Often the Eight of Swords will alert you to abandonment issues from the past. If we didn't receive all the love we needed in the past, we may be left with an insatiable hunger for a hero to swoop in and shower us with all the love we didn't get. Approaching relationships with this hungry, needy feeling usually ends the same way: feeling abandoned, powerless, and victimized...again. When the Eight of Swords appears, it reminds you that you don't have to wait for someone to rescue you. The Eight of Swords challenges you to repurpose your thoughts to cut the ropes that bind you, rip off the blindfold, and stand in your power. No one is coming to save you; however, you really don't need them to. You have the power to save yourself by making healthier choices. *You* are the hero you are looking for.

NINE OF SWORDS

The Nine of Swords represents circular obsessive thinking that agonizes for resolution. The crisis that triggered these thoughts could have happened last week, or a long time ago. In a love reading, the Nine of Swords can alert you if you're ruminating on *a person, thought, or episode* that keeps you stuck in sadness. This card can also reveal if you are turning your anger *inward* by excusing a person who hurt you and blaming yourself instead. The Nine of Swords has been called the worst card in the deck. However, it does not promise impending doom in your love life. It is called the worst because it uses negative past experiences as psychological bludgeons for self-harm. This card alerts you to the kind of self-destructive thinking that impairs decision-making. Sometimes the desire for closure can place you back in a destructive cycle with a person who hurt you … or an eerily similar situation. Free yourself from any self-sabotaging mental loops. Take control of your mind and you will reclaim your power.

In a Love Reading
New Relationship
The Nine of Swords can signify a relationship partner with an unresolved past. They may be experiencing the aftereffects of a major setback or disappointment. This person may not be ready to rush into a new phase. This card can also symbolize a new love interest who struggles with mental health issues.

Long-Term Partnership
The Nine of Swords can represent unresolved grief or sadness in a relationship. However, the grief in question does not always stem from a relationship issue. Sometimes it originates from a major disappointment, such as failing to achieve a goal. This card encourages open communication instead of isolating from one another.

Intimacy
The Nine of Swords can signify many unspoken problems with intimacy. At least one partner is stressed or anxious about sex. This problem is often made worse by isolating or avoiding it altogether. This card can also signify dysmorphia or unhappiness with one's body image.

Seeking Romance
If you are single, you may not feel emotionally ready to move beyond a past relationship. Allow yourself to come to terms with your loss. Tears can be immensely cleansing. Feeling your authentic feelings will loosen their hold on your heart. Take your time. Resolving the past will set you up for future success.

Desires

The Nine of Swords often signifies a desire for closure. It may seem like your current challenge will last forever, but this is simply not true. If you are feeling isolated, seek support from those you love or trust. There is still a vibrant life of unlimited possibility awaiting you. Don't allow past unresolved emotions to extinguish your hope.

Reversed
New Relationship

The person you are inquiring about has made a dramatic life change and is still on a shaky road toward recovery. While their life is improving, they're also plagued by uncertainty. This card can also signify an excessive fear of getting hurt, which may be clouding your perspective. Do not allow your mind to be overthrown by worst-case scenarios. Wait and see.

Long-Term Partnership

The Nine of Swords Reversed can represent a relationship partner who is slowly crawling out of depression. They may still need time to recover their motivation, but they are on the mend. This card can also signify someone who is still processing a personal loss.

Intimacy

The Nine of Swords Reversed can represent the breaking of a bad relationship cycle. Painful patterns that made you feel hurt or inadequate are being released. Sometimes, this card can signify a person who is the survivor of past sexual abuse or trauma. Although these issues may affect their approach to intimacy, they are ready and willing to work through past shadows.

Seeking Romance

You've decided to move on from a situation that has caused you an abundance of grief. Resist the urge to go back to the source of your unhappiness. The closure you seek will not come from ruminating on the past. Leave the nightmares of the past behind. It's time to start over.

Desires

The Nine of Swords Reversed can appear when you are waking up from the nightmare that you are less than you truly are. A desire to return to a brighter time has been rekindled. Upright or reversed, the Nine of Swords encourages you to walk away from anything toxic and to be true to your own path.

What the Nine of Swords May Be Teaching You

The Nine of Swords does not foretell doom for your love life; it uncovers unresolved grief that may fuel your fears. This card teaches that life rarely ever turns out as bad as our worst-case scenarios would have us believe. The Nine of Swords is a reminder to differentiate what you are temporarily experiencing mentally from your present reality. Old hurts may need to be felt and released before you are ready to move on. Take all the time you need. Until the shadows of the past are resolved, your perspective about your future happiness may be distorted. The Nine of Swords is the necessary journey through the Valley of Shadow before ascending to the mountaintop and witnessing the glorious possibilities of your future. You may be grieving through a challenging time. Be on your own side; don't allow negative thought spirals to fuel your inner saboteur. Allow your mind and spirit to reconcile with one another again. Remember, *it always seems darkest before the dawn.*

TEN OF SWORDS

Many of us would prefer to look away from the gruesome image of the Ten of Swords, just as we might wish to avoid facing our unresolved anguish and hurt. However, like the other dark cards in the tarot, the Ten of Swords presents an opportunity for profound healing. The Ten of Swords urges us to confront and accept when it's time to leave something painful behind. The ending is not *always* the end of a relationship. Sometimes, the ending is a self-sabotaging behavior that is keeping you ensnared in suffering. If you are stabbing yourself in the back by repeating a destructive cycle, the Ten of Swords compels you to acknowledge and change it. The Ten of Swords symbolizes emotional rites of passage that you didn't necessarily choose but must bravely pass through. It takes courage to honestly acknowledge your hurt and make the required change. Let go of whoever or whatever is torturing you. The Ten of Swords promises that the restorative light of truth will disperse any black clouds of despair.

In a Love Reading
New Relationship
The Ten of Swords can highlight a major ending that either you or your new love interest is still reeling from. Try not to rush forward if time is still required for healing or resolution. A healthy new relationship can only take root if past issues are confronted and resolved. This card can also alert you if you are falling into a self-sabotaging past cycle with a new relationship.

Long-Term Partnership
The Ten of Swords can represent a difficult issue you may feel more comfortable avoiding than talking about. Sometimes, this card signifies a painful breakup. You may feel stabbed in the back by the heartless behavior of someone you thought you could trust. Stop investing your entire self into an unsustainable relationship. It's time to leave betrayal behind.

Intimacy
The Ten of Swords can signify past trauma that is affecting your attitude toward sex. A trusted, qualified therapist may help you confront and heal the issues currently impeding your sex life. It's time to courageously confront old wounds. This card will also alert you if you are playing out past painful patterns with your intimate partner.

Seeking Romance
If you are single, you may be struggling to release expectations of disappointment or defeat. The storm has passed, and it's time to pick up the pieces. A positive new beginning will occur when you truly move on from the past. This card will also warn you to avoid committing to a partner who causes you pain.

Desires

The Ten of Swords often accompanies a desire to ignore red flags in your relationship. If you are asking about another person, you may be ignoring warning signs that are slapping you in the face. Do not be afraid of accepting the truth, even if it dispels your illusion. Walk away from any person or pattern that isn't worthy of you.

Reversed

New Relationship

The person you are asking about has been through a lot. Although there are signs of improvement, they are not out of the woods yet. Your intuition may warn you if they are promising to deliver more than they can truly give. You must be honest with yourself about their current limitations.

Long-Term Partnership

There is a far deeper rite of passage happening for you and your partner, even though past experiences brought much pain. *It wasn't all for nothing.* Sunlight is starting to peek through the dark clouds. The Ten of Swords Reversed can also signify healing after a devastating loss.

Intimacy

You or your partner are still recovering from the end of a past intimate relationship. Although the pain and grief have not entirely gone away, resolution is on the horizon. New opportunities for connecting are finding their way to you.

Seeking Romance

The sunlight is finally returning after what seemed an eternity of dark days. You have broken a destructive cycle and are putting yourself first again. Retain the lessons the past has taught you. Be brave and open your heart to new beginnings.

Desires

The light peeking through the black clouds of the Ten of Swords encapsulates the old saying, "Sunlight is the best disinfectant." It's time to shine a light on the shadowy areas you've been afraid to confront. By speaking your shadows into the light, they will cease to haunt you. Your heart is urging you toward truth. Follow its lead.

What the Ten of Swords May Be Teaching You

The Ten of Swords may be teaching you to accept an ending, even if you are resistant to accepting it. This could be the ending of a relationship or a destructive pattern you find yourself repeating. Humans are very skilled at rationalizing their discomfort away. If you feel a payoff for hanging on to a destructive pattern or person, your fear will continue to invent excuses for why you should cling to the very thing that's hurting you. The Ten of Swords appears when the immensity of your pain can no longer be denied. An uncomfortable ending is occurring, and it must be accepted with eyes wide open before you can progress to a happier place. The appearance of the Ten of Swords does not promise the destruction of your relationship or life. It symbolizes the inevitable destruction of rationalizations that are keeping you in a state of suffering. Honor yourself enough to end self-destructive patterns. *True love will never require your destruction.*

PAGE OF SWORDS

The Page of Swords can be the most delightful company, as long his cleverness is unquestionably appreciated and acknowledged. No one can match his biting sarcasm, for the Page of Swords is a master of snark. His ability to expose the hypocrisy of others diverts attention from the vulnerabilities he would rather people not see. In love, the Page of Swords is attracted to *appearances* with his partner and his relationship. In time, you may discover he is extremely concerned with how others see him. The Page of Swords prefers to retreat to the safe sanctuary of emotional detachment. Often, the Page of Swords manifests as a personality who displays intellectual genius, yet is emotionally underdeveloped and insecure. Although frequently charming, he struggles with acknowledging his imperfections. At his best, the Page of Swords is clever, brilliant, prodigious, eloquent, witty, and sharp. At his worst, he is petty, superficial, haughty, unaccountable, and deflective.

In a Love Reading
New Relationship
The Page of Swords can represent a love interest who is charming and funny, but who is also emotionally unavailable. They may be mercurial and sending out mixed signals. No matter how successful or intelligent the Page of Swords appears, there is also an element of insecurity. The Page of Swords can also represent a partner who is guarded or aloof.

Long-Term Partnership
The Page of Swords can signify a partner who is not taking responsibility for their own part to play in relationship challenges. There could be an opportunity for one or both partners to make a significant breakthrough if they can be vulnerable enough to admit when they're wrong and what needs to change.

Intimacy
It can be difficult to get close to the Page of Swords. His defensive nature is often on guard, with his sword upraised in a perpetually defensive stance. This card can also signify a partner who struggles with unrealistic expectations of body image perfectionism.

Seeking Romance
If you are single, the Page of Swords asks if you are sending mixed signals. Although you may say that you want to connect, your body language might come off as too guarded. The Page of Swords can highlight struggles with being more vulnerable. Be mindful of the signals you are sending.

Desires

The Page of Swords can represent a deep desire to connect, while also exhibiting body language that proclaims others should keep their distance. This card encourages self-awareness as to what signals are being sent. It's easier to catch flies with honey rather than vinegar. If desiring to connect, send out more inviting vibes through eye contact or smiling more.

Reversed
New Relationship

The Page of Swords Reversed warns of miscommunication. Either you or your new love interest may be misinterpreting the words or body language of the other. This card can signify a need for clarification if the communication you receive seems confusing. Avoid assumptions.

Long-Term Partnership

The Page of Swords Reversed warns of arguments, nonproductive communication, or passive-aggressive behavior. Communication goes far beyond merely speaking. If confronting immaturity from your partner, don't engage at a base level. Make sure your words are working to elevate the energy instead of polluting it further.

Intimacy

The Page of Swords Reversed can signify bitter arguments, grudges, or simmering conflicts that need resolution before intimacy can be restored. Either you or your partner may be deflecting blame onto the other. Seek resolution to problems by acting like an adult. For healthier communication, listening is just as important as speaking.

Seeking Romance

The Page of Swords Reversed can symbolize breaking bad relationship cycles as a mature adult. Avoid making excuses, deflecting blame onto others for what happened in the past, or relinquishing responsibility for the direction of your life. You are in the driver's seat. Take ownership of your life and its direction, and the ability to connect will be far easier.

Desires

The Page of Swords Reversed can represent a deep desire to deflect responsibility for one's life circumstances. There may be some very rational-sounding arguments for why a particular situation you suffered in the past was unfair. However, avoiding proactive steps to improve your life will only perpetuate feelings of disempowerment or resentment.

What the Page of Swords May Be Teaching You

The Page of Swords may be teaching you to take control of your life's direction by taking responsibility for it. The Page of Swords is famous for projecting his issues onto others. He will rationalize that he is unhappy because of what *someone else* did. He blames the past, his life situation, or other people's actions for his unhappiness. In this way, he doesn't have to be responsible for changing anything about himself. Deflecting personal issues really stunts his growth. Even though the Page of Swords is very intelligent, he is also very sensitive. He prefers not to face any discomfort that could result in personal growth. His appearance could be advising you that you need to be accountable for your own part to play in your life's direction. The Page of Swords teaches that *you alone* are responsible for your bliss. Nobody else has sole power to grant you happiness or to take it away. When you believe the illusion that others are responsible for your joy or misery, you surrender all power to change your life. The life your heart desires can only manifest if you take ownership of it.

KNIGHT OF SWORDS

The Knight of Swords is continually in fast pursuit of his desire. Whether he is chasing a love interest, a job, a deadline, or a personal goal, he gives 110 percent to achieve his objective. In love pursuits, the Knight of Swords will initially pour all his interest and energy on the object of his affection. However, his attention can be easily diverted toward the next conquest that captures his imagination.

It can come as a sudden shock when he abruptly switches gears toward a different pursuit. For the Knight of Swords, it's all or nothing. He is fiercely competitive, holding visions of glory for himself. The Knight of Swords wants to win, conquer, and vanquish anything standing in the way of *his* goal. His confidence gives him great sex appeal; however, he can lack the empathy to consider how his ruthlessness might hurt others. At his best, the Knight of Swords is dashing, intense, exciting, and attractive. At his worst, he is self-serving and ruthless and possesses an eerie ability to detach from compartmentalized emotions.

In a Love Reading
New Relationship
The Knight of Swords can represent a passionate and exciting paramour. However, it can be very difficult to maintain a hold on his attention for long. In a love reading, this card will advise you not to rush into commitments thoughtlessly. Time will tell if the intensity of this knight's initial passion finds the potential to be something more.

Long-Term Partnership
The Knight of Swords can represent a turbulent relationship. The pursuit of personal ambitions will often need to be weighed against the needs of the partnership. If both partners are engaged to the pursuit of a mutual goal, this union can succeed. A Knight of Swords relationship thrives when there are shared priorities. Clarify what those priorities are for both of you.

Intimacy
Intimately, the Knight of Swords can be a passionate lover … for a time. There is an element of thrilling darkness and taboo intensity that will keep you transfixed. However, the Knight of Swords lives in his head, and his mind is easily diverted. If he grows bored, he mentally detaches.

Seeking Romance
If you are single, the Knight of Swords can indicate that you are in the intense pursuit of your heart's desire. Be mindful of the path you are racing down, and who you may be running over. Your priority may be to get what you want at all costs. However, this can come at great expense to yourself.

Desires

The person you are inquiring about is obsessive and single-minded about his desires. It will be difficult to persuade him to choose a different course if his mind is made up. Once the desire for his new obsession is satiated, he often returns to what he previously abandoned. Like all knights, the Knight of Swords might cycle back regularly.

Reversed

New Relationship

The Knight of Swords Reversed can represent someone who has great difficulty making and keeping commitments. He requires absolute control over his own destiny and will rebel against anything that constrains him. His single-mindedness about his own desires can often leave others feeling hurt.

Long-Term Partnership

The Knight of Swords Reversed can also represent an on-again, off-again relationship that doesn't seem to grow. It may feel like you are running in circles and not progressing. Although the drama can feel thrilling and exciting, it often results in hurt feelings.

Intimacy

The Knight of Swords Reversed can also represent an individual who is overly stressed with external pressures, ambitions, and unfulfilled desires. This makes it very difficult to get close to him. Try to not personalize his actions; they are not about you. He simply has different priorities.

Seeking Romance

If the Knight of Swords Reversed represents you, he warns of obsessive thinking that can become self-destructive. Make sure what you are pursuing is healthy and worthy of you. Slow down and get a different perspective. You may not be seeing your current situation clearly.

Desires

The Knight of Swords Reversed can signify the feeling of being consumed by a desire. You may have to consider how your actions are affecting others at this time. In the pursuit of what you want, you may not be considering that others have different priorities.

What the Knight of Swords May Be Teaching You

The Knight of Swords is always racing forward. He can represent the cruel task-master within that drives you mercilessly toward what you think will bring you fulfillment. When you rush through life relentlessly pursuing an unmet need, you probably aren't making the best decisions. The Knight of Swords encourages you to slow down. The Knight of Swords is clearly stressed. His image is one of tightness and the unrelenting pursuit of his mental fixation, even if the price to pay is the health of his body, mind, or spirit. Feeling intensely about a fervent desire is normal. However, you may need to examine if the intense pursuit of your desire is hurting you. Reconnect with the calm, loving place within your heart buried far beneath the tension. Make peace with yourself and release strain and strife. Your well-being must come first. The fulfillment you seek is far more likely to find if your heart is kind, open, and relaxed. Take a deep breath and let your shoulders drop. Just allow.

QUEEN OF SWORDS

The Queen of Swords is powerful. She guards and maintains her personal authority without apology. In relationships, she can be a bit intimidating. The Queen of Swords has acquired a reputation for being a bit of an ice queen. However, this is only because she won't throw away her dignity for the acceptance of another. You won't see this queen submissively waiting by the phone or desperately stalking someone who obviously isn't interested in her. She would prefer to maintain her dignity than grovel at the feet of some lesser knave. The Queen of Swords is self-assured in her incalculable worth. She knows that *she* is a prize. If a suitor can't be bothered to put in the effort to give her the relationship that is truly worthy of her … well then, she's sensible enough to know that he obviously isn't worth her time. The Queen of Swords will never beg. At her best, the Queen of Swords is intellectually brilliant, witty, powerful, clever, beautiful, and balanced. At her worst, she can be rigid, haughty, detached, and uptight.

In a Love Reading
New Relationship
The Queen of Swords can represent a guarded personality. She has probably learned in the past how much love can sting. Be patient and pique her intellectual interest. Appeal to this person's mind, and you can begin to appeal to their heart. The Queen of Swords can represent an individual who is attracted to an intellectually mature partner without drama.

Long-Term Partnership
For an established relationship, the Queen of Swords can represent a power couple who shares mutual professional and life goals. However, physical intimacy can become neglected in this relationship. The Queen of Swords all too easily detaches from physical pleasure, and her partner may require physical intimacy more than she does. Honest communication can help.

Intimacy
The Queen of Swords can represent a partner who is a bit guarded. They can become a passionate lover but must first feel that trust is established. Secretly, the Queen of Swords personality desires relaxation, fun, and playfulness. However, she will likely test you before she opens her heart.

Seeking Romance
If you are single, the Queen of Swords encourages you to seize your power. Enjoy your unlimited freedom and opportunities leading toward your best life. Pursue all opportunities that lead toward personal success. The sky is the limit for what you will attain. The love you are looking for will likely find you when you find independent bliss and success.

Desires

The Queen of Swords can represent a deep desire to reclaim lost power. Be independent and clear in yourself. Remember your worth and value. Take charge and look at your situation logically and practically. It may also be a time to resolve anger. Channel past anger into self-improvement. It's time to reclaim your throne of dignity.

Reversed

New Relationship

The Queen of Swords Reversed is not the type of person you want to cross. She may keep score and try to catch others in every inconstancy to fuel her ever-raging righteous indignation. This person may have a chip on their shoulder and can be difficult to get close to.

Long-Term Partnership

The Queen of Swords Reversed alerts people to any harsh communication they are engaging in. This card can also represent arguments in relationships where bitter words are exchanged. This card warns not to eviscerate another to prove a point. This card can also advise you to find a healthy outlet for anger or irritation that can arise in relationships.

Intimacy

The Queen of Swords Reversed can represent the archetypal wronged woman. She encourages seeking closure for unresolved trauma before opening yourself to intimacy. This card may warn you not to overly identify with the ill treatment or victimization you may have experienced in the past.

Seeking Romance

If the Queen of Swords Reversed represents you, she warns you not to become too isolated from others. If you've been hurt or disappointed in the past, you may feel tempted to shut others out. Boundaries are important, but you need to allow for vulnerability and connection. Give others the benefit of the doubt before arriving at a conclusion.

Desires

Upright or reversed, the Queen of Swords can represent a desire to finally stand up for yourself and regain control over your mind and your life's direction. If you've been feeling victimized by the thoughtless behavior of another, the Queen of Swords places the steel in your spine to stand up and respect yourself again.

What the Queen of Swords May Be Teaching You

The Queen of Swords teaches you that you must have the courage to claim your independence and power. The Queen of Swords is unmatched in her ability to transform the energy from victimized to victorious. She brings order to the chaotic places within her life by facing them honestly and taking control. She wears the Cloak of Clouds. She is enfolded in the power of her brilliant mind. The Queen of Swords encourages you to let your head guide your heart at this time. If you are not sure what to do right now, she tells you the answer is simple: take the road that will replenish your personal power. The Queen of Swords motivates you to turn a critical eye toward your life and relationships. Nobody's acceptance is worth the price of your majesty and personal authority. Recognize that you are a prize. Use your sword to cut out any person, thought, or thing that diminishes your splendor. Embody your personal authority and retake control of your heart and mind.

KING OF SWORDS

The King of Swords is a fixed personality. Few people can match his immovable iron will. In a love reading, the King of Swords can represent someone who is stubborn and resistant to change. He will likely have a strong set of beliefs and values that he rarely deviates from. The King of Swords is also an authority figure, desiring absolute control. In relationships, he prefers to think of himself as wearing the pants. The King of Swords is old-fashioned, viewing the world in terms of black and white. He seeks unequivocal clarity. For him, people are either good or bad. Behavior is right or wrong. He is extremely uncomfortable with moral ambiguity and dislikes nuance. To maintain control over his life's direction, he arrives at conclusions with absolute certainty, even if he is wrong. At his best, the King of Swords can promise security and stability. He is a fierce protector of those he considers under his charge. At his worst, the King of Swords can be uncompromising, controlling, or judgmental.

In a Love Reading
New Relationship
The King of Swords can represent a cautious courtship. The person you are asking about will likely want to be sure you share the same values or worldview before making a commitment. Dating this person can feel a bit like an audition process. This king maintains his guard until his mind is settled. This card might also represent a conservative person.

Long-Term Partnership
The King of Swords represents a traditional relationship structure, providing safety and security. However, this card can also represent a partner who is entrenched in his systems and beliefs. A King of Swords will not deviate once his mind is made up; you may find yourself being the one who compromises more.

Intimacy
Intimately, the King of Swords is a very private person. He may struggle with expressing his vulnerabilities or emotions. Much like the other personalities in the swords court, he often appears guarded. You can only penetrate his emotional remoteness by gaining his absolute trust.

Seeking Romance
If you are single, the King of Swords could be telling you to stand your ground. If a person has proved to not be aligned with your values or moral code, it is okay to keep your distance. You may need to be careful and more discriminating in matters of love at this time.

Desires

The King of Swords desires to take the lead. Above all else, this person wants to feel strong and respected. The King of Swords expects others to bend since he is so often incapable of doing so. If relationships have been feeling unclear or messy, the King of Swords can signify bringing order to life once again.

Reversed

New Relationship

The King of Swords Reversed can represent a partner who desires to keep others at arm's length. This card can also symbolize an overly judgmental attitude that sabotages intimate connection. This is often a mask for fear. This individual finds it difficult to challenge their assumptions.

Long-Term Partnership

The King of Swords Reversed can represent a neurotic partner who insists on controlling everything. He may have established so many rules to follow that a relationship with him ends up feeling stifling. He believes his perspective is the only one that could possibly make reasonable sense.

Intimacy

The King of Swords can represent accumulated grievances concerning sex. One partner could be feeling neglected or resentful. This card can also symbolize a partner who keeps score of every sleight and holds on to toxic emotional baggage that interferes with intimacy. It may be time to address the elephant in the room to rebuild trust.

Seeking Romance

If you are single, the King of Swords Reversed might suggest that it is time to lower your guard. You could be coming across as remote or emotionally uninviting. You might also want to reexamine hardened beliefs about your prospects for an intimate relationship. Let go of rigidity. This card can also represent excessively finding faults in others.

Desires

The King of Swords Reversed can represent the desire to hold firm on an argument or dispute that you cannot win. Since both individuals don't agree on the same set of facts, their perspectives will be vastly different. You are unlikely to win a frontal assault on the King of Swords Reversed. It's probably best to retreat for now and devise a different tactic.

What the King of Swords May Be Teaching You

The King of Swords does not always play the role of the evil king. Sometimes, he will appear to encourage you to stand your ground. This is especially true if you are on the right side of an important issue. The King of Swords can motivate you to hold your ground when it comes to your values. All relationships need compromise, but there are limits. The King of Swords compels you to take a stand for the life you want for yourself. It may be time to stop conforming to what you think others need from you and establish a boundary for them to step up. The King of Swords can also represent detachment and clearing your head. It may be time to withdraw from an emotional experience that is just too intense to clear the air. Get clear on your values. Know what you stand for. The King of Swords may be telling you to step up and protect yourself from rationalizations, lies, and gaslighting. It's time to evaluate what is acceptable *for you* and hold to your convictions firmly. You know what feels right in your core. Adhere to your personal honor code.

CUPS IN A LOVE READING

Of all the suits in the tarot, cups are most associated with love. Cups reflect the element of water and the unconscious feelings that churn beneath the surface. Cups will not always reveal what is factually *happening* in relationships, but rather the *feelings and emotions* that are triggered by a person or issue. When many cup cards appear in a reading, strong emotions are influencing the situation. Cups can show you what emotional trajectory the relationship is on and what feelings are being experienced and expressed. Feelings and emotions can unconsciously distort your perception of reality. Cups can help you become more self-aware of the emotional undercurrents that are influencing your expectations and behavior. Understanding your feelings can help you channel them more constructively.

Cups can also reveal the *potential* for deeper connection in your relationships. The appearance of many positive cup cards in a love reading is a hopeful sign for positive relationship development. However, like the element of water, feelings are changeable. People do not stay in an unchanging permanent emotional state. They are constantly changing and evolving, and how they show up in their relationships can change over time as well. At the start of a relationship when first meeting an exciting new love interest, we are probably seeing the best of what *they* want us to see. As relationships deepen, you will begin to see other aspects of a person's character, which includes their shadows and vulnerabilities. In relationship readings, cups can grant clues into the emotional makeup of a person, which time will usually confirm.

When many joyous cup cards appear, keep your expectations in check. Sometimes tarot is marketed in a way that leads to unrealistic expectations of future certainty depending on which cards appear. Beware of preemptively proclaiming, "See here! He must be my soul mate; I got the Ace and Two of Cups! We are guaranteed to be together forever now!" This can set you up for a big disappointment if your reason is completely abandoned. The passion and attraction reflected in cup cards are wonderful for a relationship, but you must keep your expectations in check. Sometimes more time or information must bubble to the surface before a feeling can be confirmed as true. When reading cup cards, it is important to remember that *feels like* is not necessarily equivalent to *is like*.

ACE OF CUPS

The Ace of Cups is *the* quintessential love card of the tarot. It epitomizes the overflowing joy that love inspires. It activates the wellspring of happiness in one's heart. Like all aces, this card offers an opportunity to begin anew. The Ace of Cups is also a symbol for exciting romantic *firsts*. The first crush. The first date. The first kiss. The first time meeting the family, and so on. The Ace of

Cups reawakens the senses. Colors seem brighter. The whole world feels in perfect harmony. Infinite possibilities feel within reach. The Ace of Cups unleashes a surge of pleasure more intoxicating than the most potent drug. As such, the pleasure the Ace of Cups reflects is extremely addictive. It is important to keep one foot grounded in practical reality so you aren't swept away, trying to chase the next exhilarating high. Remember, the Ace of Cups symbolizes *beginnings*. It does not promise unchanging euphoria for all time. All the same, savor the energy of this card as it reawakens your heart to sweet bliss!

In a Love Reading
New Relationship
The Ace of Cups represents an auspicious start to any new partnership. A rebirth of romance is flowing through your life. Enjoy the present excitement, for the future is full of possibility. A word of caution, however. You are still experiencing the *beginning*. Keep your expectations in check as you enjoy this happy time. *Be present* with the burgeoning love that is developing.

Long-Term Partnership
The Ace of Cups symbolizes a positive new beginning in an existing relationship. The bonds of affection shared between you both are being renewed. This is an ideal time to reaffirm your commitment to one another. This card can also signify a birth, a rebirth, or an exciting new chapter in your life together. The Ace of Cups signifies a partnership based in true love.

Intimacy
Intimately, the Ace of Cups unleashes passion that brushes on the sacred. Sex is a transcendent experience that connects you and your partner at the soul level. The Ace of Cups has also been long associated with fertility. If you are biologically able to have children, this card places you on alert for a potential pregnancy (especially if the Empress also appears in your spread).

Seeking Romance
No matter what happened in the past, the Ace of Cups signifies that you are starting over. Your present rebirth is clearing away past unhappiness. Place yourself in new and supportive environments that activate your joy. Open yourself to new connections. Dare to be excited for all the happiness that still awaits you. Your true love will arrive at the right time. Trust it!

Desires

The Ace of Cups will signify *a desire to be desired!* Ask for the assistance of the love goddesses, such as Aphrodite, Oshun, Hathor, and Freya. They will increase your allure. Make your love wish to them. Cast a spell of glamour around you to attract attention. Adorn yourself in clothes and colors that flatter your figure and make you stand out. Make the extra effort.

Reversed

New Relationship

The Ace of Cups Reversed can signify a time when you need to invest more energy into yourself before giving to another. Upright or reversed, this card can signify a mutual attraction. However, this card can warn of one partner pouring more of their heart into the relationship than the other. Ensure this partnership is equally invested in before committing your whole heart.

Long-Term Partnership

The Ace of Cups Reversed can signify a relationship where one partner feels depleted. They may have sacrificed a great deal to ensure their partner's happiness or success. However, they may feel let down that they have not placed enough attention on their own goals. This partnership will thrive if the depleted partner feels supported in attaining their own desires.

Intimacy

The Ace of Cups Reversed can signify a need to be more nurturing in your intimate relationships. You may benefit from understanding your partner's desires before emphasizing your own. This card can also symbolize receptivity. Be open-minded and flexible when it comes to your partner's needs, even when they differ from yours.

Seeking Romance

When the chalice is upside down, all pours out. However, there is no bottom to the Ace of Cups. If you are experiencing a challenge where your love life seems turned upside down, take heart. Love is infinite. You may not see it in this moment, but there are boundless future opportunities for your love life to reawaken. Give your heart what it needs now to stay strong.

Desires

You may feel a strong desire to replenish your source. The Ace of Cups Reversed will appear when renewal is required. Flush out the stagnant waters that have been clogging your heart. Open yourself to experiences that bring pleasure again. If you invest love in yourself, you will have so much more to give. Tend to what your spirit needs to feel replenished.

What the Ace of Cups May Be Teaching You

The Ace of Cups gently reminds you to let love be the answer. By its nature, love is not afraid, controlling, tense, obsessive, or petty. Love is transcendent, healing, cleansing, calming, and kind. Love is all around you, and yet, it can seem elusive if you are hell-bent on *only* seeing it in a particular person or place. Love defies your expectations.

Love is in the air, the water, and the earth. It's found in your chosen family and your deepest friendships. In the Rider-Waite-Smith tarot, a dove descends from the heavens, forming a holy communion with the chalice below. Doves are associated with Aphrodite, the Greek goddess of love. The water depicted on the Ace of Cups endlessly overflows from the cup into the pond below. This reminds you that love is limitless. There is not a finite amount of love in the world. The Ace of Cups can teach you to release your fears surrounding love. More love is always being offered if you can let go of your fear of losing it. With love, there is no scarcity. You will attract the love you need when you clothe yourself in its limitlessness.

TWO OF CUPS

The Two of Cups mirrors the Lovers card in the Major Arcana. It represents attraction, love, affection, chemistry, immersive conversations, and partnerships that are meant to be. In a love reading, the Two of Cups emphasizes the importance of communication to deepen your most significant relationships. Although a Two of Cups relationship will likely feel destined, it is important not to assume that the partnership will be permanent or unchanging. Relationships, much like people, inevitably evolve. The Two of Cups also rules over making loving partnerships official through a declaration, commitment, promise, or ceremony. A Two of Cups partnership can only work if both people are fully invested in the relationship and meet one another as *equals*. For single people, the Two of Cups encourages an individual to become self-aware of what they are communicating to others, both verbally and nonverbally. These signals are likely at the root of their current experience.

In a Love Reading
New Relationship
Romance in the air! This card often appears when a significant bond is forming between two compatible people. The Two of Cups represents romantic messages, flirtation, deepening bonds, and all the excitement of falling in love. Communication, both verbal and nonverbal, is at the core of this connection. It will also be vital for this partnership to succeed long-term.

Long-Term Partnership
The Two of Cups represents a harmonious relationship based on shared values and respectful communication. Sometimes this card will herald the establishment of a lasting commitment to the partnership, a goal, or a positive change. This card reflects a complementary relationship of two equals that can withstand the tests of time.

Intimacy
The Two of Cups reflects significant sexual chemistry and the feeling of being swept away by mesmerizing desire. This card implies a complementary union between equally passionate partners. There is a great desire for both partners to deeply connect not only through the body, but through the heart, mind, and spirit as well.

Seeking Romance
If you are single, the Two of Cups can indicate the opportunity for a new relationship is more likely at this time. If you see someone you like, say something! For your love life to become revitalized, you may have to make the first move. Be courageous, take risks, and express yourself. This card governs the signals you are sending, both verbal and nonverbal.

Desires
The Two of Cups can signify a simple desire to connect. It can reflect a yearning for someone who truly meets you as an equal. The core message of the Two of Cups is communication. This card encourages you to become aware of what you are communicating to the world and to use your body language, voice, or manner to attract your desires.

Reversed
New Relationship
When the Two of Cups appears reversed, it can represent a potential partner who may be feeling misunderstood. This card rules all *indirect* forms of communication. Know that this person prefers to send unspoken signals rather than speaking clearly and directly about what they want. Applying more pressure will likely cause them to withdraw.

Long-Term Partnership
The Two of Cups Reversed can represent a loving partnership; however, a situation has arisen that is pulling both parties in opposite directions. You will have to choose whether to reconcile or compromise for the sake of the relationship or stay committed toward your individual courses. Facilitating a receptive conversation can help both people feel heard.

Intimacy
The Two of Cups Reversed may represent different approaches to intimacy between you and your partner. This can lead to a lot of misunderstandings. This card can also highlight an issue that is stoking one partner's jealousy. Both partners must try to not jump to conclusions. Delay your response to what you *think* you are seeing until you have all the facts.

Seeking Romance
It's time to examine what you are communicating about yourself when seeking relationships. Be self-aware of the body language, facial expressions, posture, and other unspoken signals when interacting with others. You should always feel you are meeting a potential partner as an equal.

Desires

The Two of Cups Reversed can represent a desire to clear up communication problems between you and another. What you are saying is either being misinterpreted or is striking something sensitive within your partner's heart. Work on clarifying what you are trying to say respectfully, which affirms both people's dignity.

What the Two of Cups May Be Teaching You

The Two of Cups teaches that the strength of any relationship hinges on what is communicated. Most importantly, this card highlights the messages you are telling *yourself*. Much like the Lovers card, the symbolism of the Two of Cups from the Rider-Waite-Smith deck shows three symbolic figures who must be brought into harmony with one another: the man, the woman, and the winged lion. The man represents your thoughts. The woman represents your feelings. The lion represents the pride you feel in yourself. All three aspects need to feel affirmed and internally harmonized to establish healthy self-esteem. The unity (or disunity) of these three internal elements is in the background of your consciousness and is responsible for what you nonverbally communicate to others. The Two of Cups encourages you to become aware of the messages you tell yourself and the signals you unconsciously send to others. When harmony is restored within, its grace is more easily reflected in your connections with others.

THREE OF CUPS

The Three of Cups features the famous Three Graces from Greek mythology. These goddesses were also called the Charities, where the English words *charm*, *character*, and *charisma* originate from. The Three Graces could help mortals sparkle and shine. Although some individuals seem to be born with more charisma than others, you can always increase your personal charm through your attitude. Ask yourself, "How are people feeling after they are done interacting with me?" If you are exercising your charm, people will inexplicably feel good after having spent time with you. When the Three of Cups appears, you may begin to feel more radiant, engaging, and attractive. This card encourages you to flirt, laugh, dance, and socialize. To increase your charisma, embrace what makes you shine. Pull out all the stops! Use your charms to the fullest, for they can magically attract your desires toward you. The Three Graces will always encourage you to smile more, express yourself, and *stand out*.

In a Love Reading
New Relationship
The Three of Cups signifies flirting, joy, and excitement. The person you are attracted to radiates charm and positive energy. Try not to impose too much seriousness on this union at this beginning stage. Establish a bond based on fun first. Keep it light. Enjoy laughter and freeness of spirit. This card can also signify a new love interest that is extremely physically attractive.

Long-Term Partnership
This card can indicate enjoyable activities that can rekindle fun and freedom in your relationship. You and your partner share a good sense of humor. The message of the Three of Cups is always to allow time for laughter and to have fun again. Involve yourselves in more activities where you can both let your hair down.

Intimacy
Intimately, there is a playful and flirtatious quality to this card. You are embracing your seductive charm, and it's time to cast aside perfectionism. Whenever the Three of Cups appears, it gives you permission to give yourself over to pleasure. This card can also signify an intense physical attraction to a strikingly beautiful lover.

Seeking Romance
If you are single, the Three of Cups encourages you to summon your charm. Smile, dance, flirt, laugh, socialize, and be free. Love is not likely to come knocking at your door. Stepping out into the world will increase your chances of finding meaningful connections. The Three of Cups can also encourage you to socialize more with friends. It's time to be seen.

Desires

The Three of Cups signifies a desire to express yourself. Lighten up and release expectations that are making you take life too seriously. You don't need to be constantly attached to someone to begin feeling good now. Allow others to see you shine. Socialize and reconnect with friends. Release self-limiting inhibitions.

Reversed

New Relationship

The Three of Cups Reversed can signify a person who may be great when times are good but struggles when unexpected challenges arise. This card can represent a flighty character who may find it difficult to commit when events become serious. Although you can share fun with this person, they may not be able to provide security during challenging times.

Long-Term Partnership

The goddesses that appear on this card are having fun. The Three of Cups Reversed reminds you that if you aren't feeling good in your relationship, change it! It's time to activate a more lighthearted, carefree, and positive vibe between you and your partner. Place yourself in environments where you can laugh more and enjoy yourselves.

Intimacy

Your partnership may be experiencing a lull in passion and enthusiasm. Upright or reversed, the Three of Cups hints at bonds established long ago through shared joy. If your partner is willing, it may be time to reconnect with what made you more carefree in the past.

Seeking Romance

If you are struggling with connecting, it could be because you are feeling insecure. Participate in low-pressure engagements with friends before dating again. Place your toe in the water before taking the plunge. Reestablish your confidence slowly. Smile and be gentle and understanding with yourself. Don't expect too much too soon.

Desires

When the Three of Cups appears reversed, you may be feeling out of touch with what makes you happy, carefree, and special. No one can feel happy all the time. Sometimes challenges are unavoidable. The appearance of this card encourages you to remember your source of joy.

What the Three of Cups May Be Teaching You

The Three of Cups may be teaching you that it's time to raise the energy around you by increasing your personal charisma. The Graces rule over glamour magic, which can help you enhance your attractiveness by raising your personal vibration. In my book *Fearless Tarot*, I wrote about how the gifts of the Graces can increase your opportunities for happiness. Each of the Three Graces has a name—Euphrosyne, Aglaea, and Thalia—and each goddess offers a gift to raise the energy in your environment. The Graces remind you that it's not just you who feels when a depressive gray rain cloud is looming above you—everyone else does, too!

Euphrosyne's name means to delight, cheer, and gladden. She can teach you how to raise the energy through humor and laughing at life instead of cursing its unfairness. Watch how much lighter your environment feels when you can smile at it, knowing that you can change the atmosphere with the vibes you bring to it. Aglaea's name means radiance, bright splendor, and light. Embracing your inner light creates a palpable positive force of energy around you that others will immediately perceive. When you wear your radiant light around you like a dazzling cloak of feathers, other will notice there is *something special* about you. Try it! Thalia's name means to warm, to foster, and to bloom. She teaches you to be gentle with yourself and others while you nurture your goals. She also brings your wishes to full harvest when you embody inviting, kind, and caring energy. Others feel attracted to environments that feel kind, warm, and supportive. When the Graces appear, it's time to embody your charismatic gifts instead of burying them beneath past heartache, grievance, or baggage.

FOUR OF CUPS

The Four of Cups can signify an intense attraction to someone who is emotionally unavailable. In a love reading, one partner may desire to deepen their connection, while the other holds back. This isn't because the love being offered holds no value. It's because the recipient isn't ready to receive it. This card can also signify an emotionally wounded person who simply isn't able to trust. The lesson of the Four of Cups is that one cannot make another person open their heart to the love being offered. As the old English proverb goes, "You can lead a horse to water, but you can't make him drink." For a relationship to work, *both* people must want it. Sometimes, the person who isn't accepting the current gift being offered is *you*. The Four of Cups can represent a fixed obsession for a particular outcome, which is thwarting your happiness. Ancestors and angels are guiding you toward a better future. Despite your disappointments, their loving hands are steering you through divine detours. Open your heart to their assistance.

In a Love Reading
New Relationship
The Four of Cups can represent a desire for an emotionally unavailable person. There is a mutual attraction, and yet you seem to be hitting a ceiling with how much this person can give you. Do not take their behavior personally and assume it reflects your quality as a partner. This card can also signify that *you* may be the one finding it difficult to be vulnerable.

Long-Term Partnership
One partner could be emotionally shutting down. It can be difficult to connect with them as they retreat behind their walls. This card can also signify a relationship partner who feels taken for granted, unacknowledged, or underappreciated. The trust in this relationship has likely experienced some damage. Both partners must be open to repairing it.

Intimacy
The Four of Cups can represent someone who may not attribute the same emotional significance to sex as their partner does. Try not to project your experience on another. This card can also signify a partner who has emotionally shut down and who finds it difficult to experience intimacy.

Seeking Romance
The Four of Cups can signify that negative thinking about relationships could be getting in the way of finding one. This card can also represent an admirer you are overlooking because they don't seem like your usual type. Open yourself to the possibilities for happiness right in front of your nose.

Desires

Stop casting your pearls before swine. If you are feeling disrespected, neglected, or consistently insulted, it's time to walk away. You can't make someone see your value. Your true love will not need to be convinced to desire you. A worthy partner will move heaven and earth to ensure you feel cherished. Anything less is an insult to your worth.

Reversed

New Relationship

Your new love interest is likely not in a position to grant you everything you desire at this time. There is likely some unfinished business emotionally that continues to hold them back. You may have to take a step back while they get clear on what they want. If the love is meant to be, they will come to you.

Long-Term Partnership

When the Four of Cups appears reversed, it can signify feeling depleted. Unlike the Ace of Cups Reversed, this upside-down cup has run dry. If you are constantly conforming to your partner's needs without the same respect, it's time to change. Relationships are about give-and-take. Be sure you are also getting what you need.

Intimacy

You may feel the need to retreat and sort out your feelings. There is likely an emotionally charged situation you are wrestling with. Until this issue is confronted honestly, it will continue to undermine your ability to authentically connect. Get your own feelings in order first.

Seeking Romance

The Four of Cups Reversed can encourage you to snap out of the illusion that you are alone or destined to be alone. Remove words like *never* and *always* from your vocabulary. Trust in divine timing. Be open to new people, places, and opportunities. Any loneliness you feel now will not last forever.

Desires

You may be feeling depressed or discouraged. This card will validate your disappointments while also encouraging you to recognize a new opportunity for happiness. Your needs and desires are changing. Open your heart to other forms of love available to you. The love being offered may not be what you *wanted*, but it is precisely what you *need*.

What the Four of Cups May Be Teaching You

The Four of Cups may be teaching you to stop repeating past traumatic rejection by pursuing emotionally unavailable partners. All fours in the tarot are governed by the supreme four: the Emperor. The Emperor is associated with the father archetype. As children, we are imprinted by our relationship (or lack thereof) with our caregivers. If you weren't validated or approved of or experienced the trauma of having the fatherly bond damaged, it can leave a hole in your heart that unconsciously aches to be filled. The desire for an emotionally distant partner is often driven by a hungry need to soothe this wound from the past. The fulfillment you seek will never be found with an emotionally distant individual who consistently abandons, rejects, or ignores you. You may have to take these healing matters into your own hands and seek authentic support. Even in the face of setbacks or disappointments, a gift is always being offered with the Four of Cups. The universe is constantly sending messages to lead you toward loving yourself more fully. Accept the gift being offered. Ask for divine assistance and you will receive it. You are not alone.

FIVE OF CUPS

The Five of Cups represents sadness from heartbreak or loss. The loss may be happening now, or it could have happened long ago. Although the Five of Cups signifies loss, *all* is not lost. It's difficult to recognize hope for future happiness when heartache is still fresh; and yet, hope does remain. The challenge of the Five of Cups is to mourn your past losses, but not to be consumed by them.

Some people get stuck in the negative trance of the Five of Cups for years. They become a ghost who mentally replays past heartache, over and over. Eventually their loss becomes their identity. Everyone will experience losses in love, and in life. Although the loss should be honored, absorbed, and felt, it must eventually be accepted and released. The Five of Cups encourages you to recognize what you will *gain* by releasing past pain and making room in your heart for joy. Seek the support you need. Instead of only focusing on the three spilled cups, remember that two still stand. The cups of *possibility* and *resilience* remain, even now.

In a Love Reading
New Relationship
The Five of Cups can symbolize a person who continually disappoints you. They may keep you waiting or not keep their word. People will usually show you their best at the beginning of a relationship. If you are feeling more sad than happy at the start of this partnership, it's not a good sign for the future. This card can also signify a person who suffers from depression.

Long-Term Partnership
The Five of Cups often indicates a disappointment. A loss for one or both partners must be accepted and grieved. This card can also represent two people who are stuck in an unhappy marriage. If this is the case, seek support from a trusted source to ascertain if the union can be salvaged. There may still be hope.

Intimacy
The Five of Cups can indicate dissatisfaction with your sex life. One partner's needs are not being met, which is leading to an emotional impasse. This card can also symbolize insecurity with one's physical appearance or body dysmorphia.

Seeking Romance
The Five of Cups can signify that you are still mourning a past relationship. Although you have experienced a sad loss, *all* is not lost. There are still many opportunities for joy in your future. Try not to unconsciously wallow in a past relationship. Engage in activities and friendships that encourage you to snap out of the trance of the past.

Desires

In a love reading, the Five of Cups can symbolize disappointment and heart-break. However, new opportunities for happiness remain *if* you can pull your attention away from past wreckage. You may be feeling depressed or apathetic about trying. Just know that you aren't doomed to feel discouraged or depressed forever. Follow your desire for happiness and move on.

Reversed

New Relationship

The Five of Cups Reversed can represent someone whose perspective is clouded by toxic emotions. Keep your energy clear of anyone who makes you consistently feel bad. New love is supposed to feel good! This card can also signify a lesson you've learned before but seems to be repeating with someone new. Don't get stuck in past ruts.

Long-Term Partnership

You and your partner are doing some major work on your relationship. You are releasing toxicity that has built up from the past. Everything you've experienced, including setbacks, have taught you something valuable. This card can also signify a mutual commitment to picking up the pieces together after a major storm in your relationship.

Intimacy

The Five of Cups Reversed can represent the breaking of a past relationship pattern that has proven unhealthy. You may be catching yourself before falling into the same weaknesses as before. This card will also advise you not to repeat a past mistake with an ex.

Seeking Romance

You've begun to snap out of the illusion that your unhappiness is permanent. You've given yourself space to cry, grieve, and truly accept a loss. Now joy will want its turn. Don't allow past attachments to ensnare your heart. You are strong enough to begin anew.

Desires

When the Five of Cups appears reversed, you are finally ready to recover from an unfair loss you didn't expect or deserve. Dare to dream once more. Aim for your next desire. Recast yourself as the victor in your story, not the victim. Your resilience will ensure happier times to come.

What the Five of Cups May Be Teaching You

The Five of Cups can appear when the sadness you are caught in begins to distort your perspective about the present and future. Although this card reveals the truth that you will periodically experience sadness and loss, your life isn't doomed to experience this for eternity. Even now, things are working themselves out. After the frustration, tears, and sadness, you must pull yourself away from viewing past wreckage. The losses from the past will change you for the better if you can learn and grow from them. Although there is a tangible loss depicted on this card, *all is not lost.* Two cups remain standing behind the figure that he cannot see. He is so focused on his disappointment he does not realize that, even now, much can be salvaged. It's true you can't get the spilled wine back in the cup. You can't re-create the way things were. You can, however, take the cups that haven't been spilled and cross the bridge toward your destiny. It may not feel like it now, but marvelous things await, *if* you can snap out of the trance of what came before.

SIX OF CUPS

The Six of Cups has long been associated with the past. It represents memory, shared history, and happier times gone by. Although this card can feel nostalgic, there is a danger of romanticizing the past and viewing it only through rose-colored glasses. In a love reading, this card can represent a resistance to letting go of a past relationship or identity, even when it's become unhealthy. The Six of Cups can also highlight issues from childhood that show up in your current relationships. Everything changes in time, including people, relationships, and yourself. This card becomes unhelpful when the querent's main objective is to resuscitate the past without accepting the realities of the present. The Six of Cups can entice you into mentally replaying a past fantasy instead of participating in your current life. Your power will not be found in the past long gone or in the future unformed, *it's here, now.* The Six of Cups encourages you to bring closure to any unresolved issues that have been holding you back.

In a Love Reading
New Relationship
It feels as if you've known your new love interest forever. There is a shared sense of familiarity between you. You can sense what the other is thinking or is about to say. You may share similar childhood experiences or even feel a past-life connection. The Six of Cups can also represent a partner with an eternally young, childlike spirit, especially when accompanied by pages.

Long-Term Partnership
The Six of Cups is a reminder of happy times gone by. If you and your partner haven't been feeling as enthusiastic about your current life, it may be time to revisit a place you found special in the past. If there are current relationship difficulties, they are likely rooted in an issue that was never fully resolved from the past. It's time to seek closure.

Intimacy
This card can represent a preoccupation with looking as you did in the past. Don't allow unrealistic expectations of past beauty to block you from enjoying physical pleasure in the present. You are beautiful now. Your future self will think you are crazy for judging yourself at your current age. Enjoy *this* moment and embrace your sensuality.

Seeking Romance
If you are single, this card may alert you to an old attachment that is unintentionally blocking you from experiencing new relationships. When your heart is occupied with a past love, you are unconsciously broadcasting to others, "Sorry, I already have a love. I don't have room for you." Perhaps it's time to do a cord-cutting ritual to finally let that past love go.

Desires

The Six of Cups can represent a person whose main desire is to re-create the past. One can hope for the past until they are old and gray, and it still won't come back. This card will always encourage you to surrender what *was* and redirect your attention to what *is*.

Reversed
New Relationship

The person you are inquiring about is mentally trapped in the past. Although it is time for them to let go of an old identity, expectation, or person, they feel resistant to surrendering it. Sometimes the challenge of the Six of Cups Reversed is looking for a relationship partner to fulfill unmet needs from childhood.

Long-Term Partnership

You (or a partner) are having trouble letting go of the past. Something significant has made its imprint and is indirectly playing out in your current relationship life. Avoid scorekeeping or nursing an old grievance. It's time to honestly communicate about what is bothering you and seek closure.

Intimacy

Abusive or traumatic experiences from the past are being processed and released. Bring closure to unresolved issues that negatively impact your openness with intimacy. Seek out a therapist or trusted counselor to pick up the pieces and create resolution. Be kind to yourself as you bravely face past shadows.

Seeking Romance

You might hear from a past love or get contacted by a former relationship partner. Don't be surprised if the past comes knocking. This could be an ideal time to bring closure to old issues. The past usually repeats itself, so try not to trick yourself into thinking that this time will be different. Learn from your personal history instead of repeating it.

Desires

You wish you could release the unresolved hurt in your heart. It's been dwelling in the background of your consciousness for too long. You are in a different place than before. You are also ready to close the book on your most difficult chapters. Your future love story is still unwritten. Take the first brave step away from the past. It's time for your breakthrough.

What the Six of Cups May Be Teaching You

The Six of Cups teaches one of the most difficult lessons in the search for love: *letting go of the past*. Our identities are forged by our personal history. And yet, we never remain exactly as we were, and neither do our relationship partners. The danger of the Six of Cups is assuming that the past is the ideal to strive for. This completely repels any possibility for new love, happiness, or joy in your current life. It's lovely to remember the thrilling blush of your first romance. Who wouldn't want that feeling again? However, the past path has been walked already. It's taught you what you needed to know at that time. Thrilling new experiences await if you can stop haunting the past like a ghost. Take all the time you need to feel the past. Enjoy its sweet memories and cherish your happiest times… but don't get stuck there. There is a new and important lesson that your heart is learning *now*. The breakthrough that eludes you is not going to result from the re-creation of an outgrown identity or relationship. It will come from letting go of what *was* and accepting what *is*.

SEVEN OF CUPS

The Seven of Cups symbolizes fantasies, dreams, and illusions. It can dazzle your imagination with visions of fairy-tale endings. Fantasies in relationships are not always destructive. Sometimes, they can excite passion and transform the mundane into magic. However, in a love reading, the Seven of Cups reminds us that our most fanciful dreams may not be accurately reflecting reality. This foggy card can cloud your wits with what you *want* to see, instead of what really is. The Seven of Cups warns against trusting beautiful illusions at the expense of your reason. When you want to believe something with your whole being, it's easy to trick yourself into ignoring glaring facts. This card can represent an imagination on overdrive as it struggles to fill in the gaps of what remains unknown. If you aren't careful, the Seven of Cups can leave you swinging back and forth like a pendulum from your greatest hopes to your worst fears. When the Seven of Cups appears, *trust your common sense* to guide you back to what's real.

In a Love Reading
New Relationship
The Seven of Cups can signify an element of fantasy that makes this union feel magical. However, this card frustratingly reveals that you don't have all the information yet. It may feel as if there is a confusing fog that is not allowing you to see clearly. Don't allow the *expectations* of what you want to see cloud reality. Stay tethered to your common sense as you proceed.

Long-Term Partnership
The Seven of Cups can represent a partner who escapes from reality. It may be difficult to confront serious issues. However, this card is also associated with intense creativity. One partner may dream big but may also struggle with manifesting their goals. They benefit from a relationship partner who creates structure and can see to the details.

Intimacy
The Seven of Cups represents magic and fantasy. Your sex could be spiced up by exploring your partner's fantasies. However, for a new relationship, this card warns of confusing sexual chemistry with *true love*. They are very different things!

Seeking Romance
You may not be perceiving reality clearly. Either your greatest hopes or deepest fears have distorted your perspective about love. Place your attention on the practical steps that can be taken to improve your current situation. This card can also warn you not to project the fantasy of what you want to see on someone you don't know that well.

Desires

You may desire to escape from a harsh reality. The facts of your situation may be poking holes in your beautiful dream. Don't accept imitations when it comes to true love. Although you may not be able to see the path ahead clearly, common sense can guide you through the fog.

Reversed

New Relationship

This card can represent a partner who succumbs to escapism to an excessive degree. They may have an addictive personality and be predisposed to abuse drugs or alcohol. The Seven of Cups Reversed can also warn of a person who gaslights or is unable to face facts.

Long-Term Partnership

If you are glimpsing an uncomfortable truth within yourself or your partner, don't continuously pretend it away. Avoiding relationship issues only makes them compound. Look at the reality of what is *happening*, not at what you are hoping or fearing to see. It's time to dispel illusions and face facts. This card can signify that you are waking up from an illusion you've bought into.

Intimacy

Your current relationship is experiencing a lull. It may feel as if your partner is lacking in romance or imagination. Communicate clearly and honestly about what you need. It may be time to rekindle passions that have been dulled by mundane concerns. Compassionate candor can make your partner aware of what you are longing for.

Seeking Romance

Although you've experienced the end of one dream, the future is still unwritten and brimming with possibility. Challenge any limitations you believe about yourself, especially if there are no facts to support them. This card will also encourage you to stop wishing for the life you want and to take action. You may need to make the first move to initiate romance.

Desires

You are waking up from a time that felt like a bad dream. Now you desire to take advantage of your newfound clarity. After feeling lost in a fog, you are once again regaining your wits. A deeper understanding of what eluded you for so long is now plain. You no longer need to cling to an attachment that was only an illusion. Accepting truth makes you powerful.

What the Seven of Cups May Be Teaching You

The Seven of Cups can represent your most beautiful dreams. It reflects the romantic childhood fairy tales of princes, princesses, and happily ever after. This desire for magic can draw us into delusions that blot out inconvenient facts. The challenge of this card is a difficult balancing act. On the one hand, you don't want to completely reject the wonder, magic, and romance within your heart. On the other hand, you don't want to delude yourself with wishes and fantasy at the expense of your common sense. The Seven of Cups represents the times in our lives that feel foggy, when it is difficult to decipher reality from fantasy. This card warns of applying wishful thinking to your decision-making process. It can be all too tempting to project your own hopes and dreams on someone you desire. However, if it looks like a frog, hops like a frog, croaks like a frog … it's probably a frog. Stop twisting yourself into pretzels to nurse the feeble belief that this frog is actually a heroic prince. The only way to prevent getting swept up in the fog of the Seven of Cups is to trust your instincts and common sense. This will always guide you when you are lost in the land of mists. If love is true, delusion will not be required to sustain it.

EIGHT OF CUPS

The Eight of Cups calls you home to your truth, even when it's difficult or inconvenient. Your inner self will always reveal the truth about yourself and your relationships, even if you initially feel resistant to hearing it. Buried suspicions can no longer be denied, numbed, or neglected. The Eight of Cups can initiate a time of soul-searching, of seeking what is *real* rather than maintaining a facade. This card can appear when navigating through confusing emotions or overcoming a period of depression. In a love reading, the Eight of Cups can represent the process of withdrawal that helps one reconnect with their *authentic self*. This card often accompanies amorphous feelings of anxiety, unluckiness, or feeling that your life has gone off target. Before proceeding with this situation, this card ensures you are clear within yourself and reconciled with the truth. Finally, the Eight of Cups will call you to trust your instincts and walk away from a duplicitous person you know has been gaslighting you.

In a Love Reading
New Relationship
One or both partners are undergoing a journey of emotional self-discovery. They may have just walked away from a relationship that failed to nurture their deepest needs. This person requires alone time and may periodically withdraw to regain clarity. Don't rush this individual if they are not ready. Trust your instincts and be patient as circumstances become clearer.

Long-Term Partnership
The Eight of Cups signifies a relationship that thrives when both partners can occasionally separate to restore clarity. This card does not necessarily foretell a breakup. It can reflect a midlife crisis or a desire to restore a piece of oneself that feels missing.

Intimacy
The Eight of Cups could indicate a partner who periodically retreats. Although you may fervently wish to connect, you must allow this person space. They will seek you when they are ready. This card can also signify a sexual relationship where one partner longs for a deeper, more substantive connection. Both partners benefit from clarifying their needs and expectations.

Seeking Romance
If you are single, you may be feeling sad or disappointed with your current options. You may think a new relationship is the cure, but you must first restore wholeness within. Be gentle as you reconnect with the part of you that felt missing. This will help you turn the corner with this frustrating time.

Desires

The Eight of Cups signifies a desire to clarify one's own needs separate from their relationship identity. You may also feel compelled to walk away from a situation that's no longer worthy of you. It is better to be single for a time than to deviate from your truth.

Reversed

New Relationship

The Eight of Cups Reversed can signify a distant person who keeps you waiting. You may feel ready for an authentic connection, but they may be self-absorbed. Establish a limit for how long it's healthy to wait before it's time to walk away. This card can also signify a person you are placing on a pedestal without their deserving it.

Long-Term Partnership

The Eight of Cups Reversed can represent a partner who is increasingly superficial, prizing image over substance. They may emphasize money, reputation, or external trappings over authenticity. These mental barriers can tune out the truth surrounding a deeper issue. Avoiding reality will result in feeling anxious, lonely, or depressed.

Intimacy

The Eight of Cups Reversed warns of placing another person on a pedestal at the expense of yourself. Admiration is one thing, but believing you are less than because you haven't captivated or impressed someone is just another way to hurt yourself. This card also urges you to trust your authentic instincts. If it feels like someone is gaslighting you, they probably are.

Seeking Romance

The Eight of Cups Reversed can also warn of getting wrapped up in appearances and not looking deeper. Try not to disregard a potential partner because of appearances. This card can warn of plastic people who lack empathy and heart. Money and attractive appearances do not necessarily equate to *quality*. All that glitters may not be gold.

Desires

You desire inner quiet and clarity. Take time to acknowledge what you *really* need to feel whole. It won't be a person, position, or thing. What you truly seek can always be found in the deep waters of your soul. Listen to the reassuring whisper within to get you back on track.

What the Eight of Cups May Be Teaching You

The Eight of Cups will appear when *soul work* is required. It's time to walk away from the needs of others to restore the trust that's been damaged within yourself. The Eight of Cups depicts an eclipse where the moon is blocking out the sun. The sun represents how we like others to see us, at our brightest and most radiant. The moon represents your authentic inner feelings, your deeper self. Sometimes the moon must take precedence over the sun. Your inner needs must come first now. Walk away from the need for validation. The Eight of Cups calls you to confront what you've authentically experienced and express it. Cry your tears and tend your wounds with loving kindness. Write in your journal or give yourself a tarot reading to identify what piece of you seeks repairing. In our search for love, it can be tempting to tuck away uncomfortable truths that influence events from beneath the surface. However, this image will always call you home. Listen to the whisper of your authentic self. This ageless wisdom will guide you back toward wholeness.

NINE OF CUPS

The Nine of Cups symbolizes pleasure in all its forms. It can refer to sex, sumptuous meals, luxurious gifts, and indulgences of every kind. This jovial symbol reminds you that life is a sumptuous banquet just waiting to be tasted. This card motivates you to release the perfectionism and inhibitions that block you from indulging in the pleasures spread before you. We can all come up with an excuse for why we can't experience pleasure. There's always more work to be done. Perhaps you think you need to be the perfect weight or have the perfect partner before you can begin to enjoy your life to the fullest. This card gives you permission to savor life's delights *now*. The Nine of Cups can also signify a wish you've been preparing for is about to come true. Lose your inhibitions and self-critical attitude and take the plunge. The Nine of Cups may also represent dinners, events, social engagements, and visiting places where laughter can be heard. Whenever this card appears, a good time is waiting to be had. Live a little!

In a Love Reading
New Relationship
The Nine of Cups represents intense sexual chemistry. Savor the excitement of this burgeoning passion. Leave your inner critic at the door and enjoy this new connection. Release your insecurities about your appearance or the gifts you bring. Be confident and take the plunge. You can plan for the future another day. For now, enjoy the pleasure *this* moment brings.

Long-Term Partnership
Make pleasure a priority in your relationship again. Stoke the fires of your partner's desire. Indulge in a bit of luxury. Schedule that vacation. Your relationship bond will be strengthened with shared experiences of laughter and delight. This card gives you both permission to connect through enjoyable pursuits. If life has gotten too serious, it's time to lighten up!

Intimacy
The Nine of Cups can signify indulging in the pleasures of sex. Its appearance can reflect an intense physical attraction between you and another. The chemistry you share is instinctual and will defy rationale. Experiencing passionate sexual chemistry does not necessarily equate to true love. This steamy connection might impair your common sense. Enjoy, but stay grounded.

Seeking Romance
If you are single, the Nine of Cups can represent opportunities to connect at social events, fine restaurants, clubs, or even bars. It may be time to have a night on the town. If you don't have a date, invite some friends out for some laughs. It's time to socialize and mingle. Don't be afraid to flirt, smile, and allure that attractive stranger with your eyes!

Desires
It's time to act on your desires and open yourself to pleasure. This is not solely limited to sex. Say yes to a dinner or social invitations and get out of the house! Perfection is not a prerequisite for pleasure. Lose the self-critical attitude and free yourself from self-doubt. Pamper yourself and indulge in the finer things. You deserve it!

Reversed

New Relationship
The Nine of Cups Reversed will advise that too much of a good thing can lead to imbalance. Love is the most intoxicating drug. If you have been without romance for a while, a new attraction can quickly overtake your reason. Beware of getting obsessive or addicted to a person you are physically attracted to. Stay grounded and maintain self-control.

Long-Term Partnership
The Nine of Cups Reversed can represent a partner who indulges too much in drinking, eating, or a particular substance. Although this isn't usually apparent at the beginning, it could be an issue that compounds over time. You may need to have a conversation about self-restraint or seek other support.

Intimacy
You may be experiencing physical relationships that fizzle out too quickly. The passion may be explosive at the beginning, only to burn out all too soon. When dating, try waiting a bit before sex to let the excitement slowly build. Don't be in a hurry to skip over the courtship phase. Sex can be even more profound when romance comes first.

Seeking Romance
You are excessively focused on one part of your life, such as work, school, or spirituality. This is distracting you from indulging in romance and pleasure. It is time to consciously reinvest in making yourself feel desirable again. You don't need a partner to begin feeling good in your own skin. Accept invitations for socializing and having fun with friends.

Desires

The Nine of Cups Reversed represents excess: excessive worry, obsessing, compulsive behavior, and a lack of self-restraint with the object of your desire. If you find you are falling into an obsessive mind frame, seek another perspective. A trusted friend or advisor can help you see your situation more rationally.

What the Nine of Cups May Be Teaching You

The Nine of Cups could be teaching you about self-acceptance. In the Rider-Waite-Smith tarot, we see a jovial merchant looking very pleased with himself. He is seated before a grand table. His red cap hints at a passionate and uninhibited mind. His table is meticulously set with nine golden cups he has taken care to arrange like trophies. The cups symbolize the pride he feels in all the gifts he has to offer. What he brings to the table is valuable. Notice how content he is *in himself.* We don't see another person in the image as being responsible for his happiness. We also don't perceive the merchant as having the perfect body or appearance. He feels good just as he is now. The self-acceptance of his gifts seems to attract the best luck. He's learned a valuable secret to making his wishes come true. Life doesn't need to be perfect before you can begin enjoying it. The Nine of Cups encourages you to accept yourself and say yes to pleasure again! Stop waiting for perfection. It doesn't exist! You are worthy of reveling in your beauty and sensuousness right now.

TEN OF CUPS

The Ten of Cups represents joyful resolution. It reminds you that there is always hope for future happiness. In a love reading, it symbolizes marriage, true love, intimacy, and a happy home life. The Ten of Cups mirrors events that play out in divine timing; that which is meant to be yours *will come to be*, at the appropriate time, and not before. Your own happily ever after may not follow the script of the storybooks, but this often proves to be for the best. No matter what personal trials, strife, or worries have plagued you before now, this card promises that happiness will eventually return. Just as the rainbow reappears after the storm, the Ten of Cups offers you the promise of renewed hope, beauty, love, and joy. Gratitude will enhance the many gifts you bring. Acknowledge the love that currently surrounds you. It's in all the colors and in every particle of light. Be present. Love is always attracted to those who already hold it in their heart. Open yourself to the bliss that seeks to find you. The best days are ahead.

In a Love Reading
New Relationship
The Ten of Cups promises an auspicious beginning. It is likely that both partners have endured some difficulties in their past relationships that make the sweetness of the present moment so enthralling. This card can also signify compatible long-term priorities. As with all idyllic cards in the tarot, keep your expectations in check as you get to know this person more... but enjoy!

Long-Term Partnership
The Ten of Cups represents a happy couple. This is not to say that you haven't endured your share of stormy skies. However, the core of this relationship is loving, compatible, and strong. This card often appears during a great relationship rite of passage, such as marriage, buying a home, or starting a family. The best of times awaits.

Intimacy
The Ten of Cups represents affection, harmony, and mutual attraction. You and your partner trust one another wholly. This allows you to share secrets and candidly talk about sex. This card can also signify the expansion of your family together, especially when accompanied by the Empress, any of the pages, or the Ace of Cups.

Seeking Romance
If you are single, the Ten of Cups advises you to keep the faith that you will meet that special someone. You may have endured your share of storms, but the rainbow of hope is delivering a promising message to you. The universe is bringing the right person at the right time, and not before. So, relax and enjoy *this* moment! A watched pot never boils.

Desires

The Ten of Cups can signify a desire to make a commitment to someone special. You might feel compelled to get engaged, get married, buy a house, move, or invest more fully in your partner's dreams. The Ten of Cups will also tell you to lighten up and engage in activities that lift your mood. Be grateful for the joy that is available to you now. Experience life's vibrancy and color!

Reversed

New Relationship

The rainbow is a messenger. Communication is at the foundation of any healthy relationship. If you are at the beginning of your relationship and you are not receiving responses to your calls or messages, this is unacceptable. Don't waste your time on someone who leaves you guessing. A true love will leave no doubt in your mind of their desire to connect with you.

Long-Term Partnership

The Ten of Cups Reversed depicts the rainbow at the foundation of the card. Rainbows are symbols for messages and signify the importance of direct communication to clear up any misunderstandings. Speak clearly about what you need rather than trying to drop hints. Express your truth to your partner with compassion.

Intimacy

Rainbows signify diversity. You may find that you're attracted to a person who isn't your physical type. Open your mind! If the definition of insanity is doing the same old thing over and over while expecting a different result, then someone completely different from your type may be just the medicine you need! Be adventurous and try new things.

Seeking Romance

The rainbow depicted on the Ten of Cups is also the emblem of Iris, the messenger goddess. Expect a call or message that will positively lift your mood. If you are invited to a wedding, attend it. If you are hoping to date again, perhaps you need to send the first message. You have nothing to lose! This card can also tell you to expect a message.

Desires

When the Ten of Cups appears reversed, you may want to brighten up your mood. One way to do this is through color. Add a pop of color to your wardrobe or appearance. Wear something that makes you feel vibrant and attractive. This can enhance your confidence and the attractiveness of your energy. Don't be afraid to stand out.

What the Ten of Cups May Be Teaching You

In the Rider-Waite-Smith tarot, a large rainbow appears in the sky overhead. Rainbows only appear after storms. This symbolizes that the most joyful times are often preceded by stormy weather. The trying times that life and love inevitably send must be endured. However, these storms don't last forever. To truly appreciate your happiest moments, you must also endure unpleasant times with courage and faith. The rainbow has long been a symbol for messages from the spiritual realm. You are being looked over by benevolent forces that seek to restore your faith in love. Many people look at the Ten of Cups and think, "Perfect! My relationship will *always* be blissful!" However, the Ten of Cups reveals that true love does not promise a life of perpetual idyllic fantasy. Even the greatest loves will inevitably endure troubling storms. The message of the Ten of Cups is that every storm life sends to your heart will eventually clear, and a rainbow will reappear. When you are experiencing the blissful moments that love brings, be present. Cherish these happy times and soak in their vibrancy and color! If you are undergoing a troubling time, take heart. There is a deeper meaning to be found in your current experience that is offering you great wisdom. The rainbow presents you with a message of hope: *If you've felt happy before, you will surely feel that happy again.* Keep your heart open to happiness.

PAGE of CUPS.

PAGE OF CUPS

The Page of Cups is sensitive, intuitive, and artistically brilliant. Although imaginative and talented, he can be naïve and immature when it comes to relationships. The Page of Cups loathes mundane concerns like keeping appointments, getting a practical job for health insurance, cleaning the house, or working within a budget. Embodying the Peter Pan archetype, he will always resist becoming a total grown-up. In relationships, this can seem charming at first, but it can become a trial if the other partner is left to tend to all the practical responsibilities. The Page of Cups will bring a sense of purity, playfulness, and fun to every encounter. The intense desires of others can often overwhelm him, and he will periodically detach and disappear to emotionally detox. At his best, the Page of Cups is artistic, sensitive, caring, compassionate, and authentic. At his worst, he is immature, childish, and susceptible to escapism through addictive tendencies or detachment into his own private magical world.

In a Love Reading
New Relationship
The appearance of the Page of Cups can signify a magical new connection. A feeling of safety and vulnerability arises when you are with your new love interest. Although this person is wise on many levels, there is also a part of them that has not yet matured. The Page of Cups may advise you to let go of all future relationship plans and just enjoy playing for now. Have fun!

Long-Term Partnership
The Page of Cups can symbolize a union that feels eternally young. It is important for you and your partner to play and create. If your relationship is becoming dull, playful humor is the antidote. The Page of Cups can also signify a time when you or your partner are more vulnerable than usual. Be sensitive and understanding when communicating.

Intimacy
The Page of Cups can represent a passionate yet somewhat inexperienced partner. However, this sensitive lover is also eager to learn. Lovemaking is experimental, imaginative, and fun. Be playful with one another and release your inhibitions. The Page of Cups can also represent someone who can be naïve when it comes to sex.

Seeking Romance
If you are single, the Page of Cups is leading you toward opportunities to connect with others through art, music, creativity, or play. Participate in activities where you can let go of self-criticism. Your playfulness and creativity will be your most attractive asset.

Desires

The Page of Cups personality desires to retain their youth and freedom. This person will likely seek a partner who shares their youthful enthusiasm and pure heart. However, the Page of Cups can also signify childishness, so they may not prioritize getting serious in relationships. Upright or reversed, the Page of Cups desires to escape reality.

Reversed
New Relationship

The Page of Cups Reversed can symbolize a person who is excessively immature. They will likely retreat to an inner world of dreams rather than confront reality. This card can represent an individual who needs a parent more than a partner. This card can also signify uneven levels of maturity between two people.

Long-Term Partnership

The Page of Cups Reversed can represent blocked communication or emotional intimacy in your relationship. The partnership may have temporarily lost its sense of magic. It may be time to detach from the drudging daily grind. Engage in activities that brought you both joy in the past. Allot time for playfulness, laughter, and relaxation.

Intimacy

The Page of Cups Reversed can represent a partner who retreats from intimacy. They may prefer to withdraw into their own fantasy world. They may have experienced disruption in early sexual development, which is now showing up in their adult relationships. A licensed counselor may facilitate the process of healing.

Seeking Romance

If you are single, the Page of Cups Reversed can represent a time when you feel excessively sensitive. Your heart may be healing. Be selective about who has access to your vulnerable heart. This card can also advise that you seek more mature relationships and turn away from a person who is acting like a child.

Desires

The Page of Cups Reversed can symbolize a person who desires to escape reality. They may not be facing their issues honestly, causing them to retreat. Although their sensitivity is a great asset, they struggle with confronting discomfort, anxiety, or conflict.

What the Page of Cups May Be Teaching You

The Page of Cups will sometimes appear when life has become too serious. He beckons you back toward the playful, mischievous part of your nature. This is the unrestrictive part of your nature. The Page of Cups asks you to free yourself from stifling energy that keeps you from connecting, playing, and experimenting in love. The Page of Cups encourages you to loosen up the tight, buttoned-up adult version of yourself. Get out of your head and back into your heart. Place yourself in environments where you're encouraged to let go and laugh. The Page of Cups whispers, "If it isn't fun, why are you still doing it?" Perhaps the child within is calling you back toward what you've lost touch with. Experience magic, playfulness, and wonder again. Let go of obsessively fixating on your desire and engage in activities that make you feel free. Laughter, friendships, creative pursuits, or travel could be just the medicine your heart currently needs. It's time to lighten up.

KNIGHT OF CUPS

The Knight of Cups is the archetypal knight in shining armor. Because of his beauty, he has been blessed with many unearned advantages in life. His dashing, romantic confidence can make you swoon, as past lovers fade into distant memory. The Knight of Cups fearlessly declares his heart with unmatched charm. It's easy to abandon all common sense when he sets his angel eyes on you. Although the chemical attraction to the Knight of Cups is irresistible, *he doesn't always translate into a substantive partner*. The thrilling pleasure of his presence is also laced with the danger of possibly losing him. The Knight of Cups will quickly gallop off if he senses desperation from a lover, preferring to idealize a romance that is just out of reach. This Knight secretly desires that rare person who is out of **his** league. At his best, the Knight of Cups is expressive, romantic, confident, charming, and devastatingly sexy. At his worst, he can be unfaithful, changeable, conceited, and emotionally unavailable.

In a Love Reading
New Relationship
The Knight of Cups signifies intense attraction. The pheromones swirling in the air around him can cause you to forego all common sense. Try to remain grounded amid the romantic messages, electric glances, and sexual chemistry. Time will tell if the relationship is viable. This knight quickly loses interest with a lover who is too starstruck.

Long-Term Partnership
For a long-term relationship, the Knight of Cups can represent that rare love where passion and attraction remain strong even after many years with one another. You probably played your cards expertly to keep this knight engaged! This is likely a great love for the ages.

Intimacy
The appearance of the Knight of Cups signifies *AMAZING sex*. Enough said.

Seeking Romance
If you are single, the appearance of the Knight of Cups could foretell exciting romantic possibilities. You might also develop a crush on someone new. The Knight of Cups can also signify a time when you feel bolder and more confident in expressing yourself. Flirt, smile, and be less inhibited…what do you have to lose?

Desires
You may strongly desire someone who is sexy and knows it. Although your heart races with thrill and danger around this person, you can't resist getting another look. The attraction isn't just emotional, but chemical as well. Try to

stay tethered to common sense. You will know the love of this knight is authentic if he doesn't keep you guessing.

Reversed
New Relationship
The Knight of Cups Reversed is a notorious breaker of hearts. Once he achieves his conquest, he gallops into the sunset, leaving many a bewildered damsel to wonder what went wrong. The appearance of this card does not always guarantee heartbreak. However, you must be strong, independent, and confident enough in yourself to retain this knight's interest.

Long-Term Partnership
The Knight of Cups Reversed can represent a partner who avoids difficult conversations. He may keep his deepest desires secret. This card signifies the necessity for a candid conversation. This card can also signify a partner whose eye is beginning to wander. Again, direct communication is key to maintaining trust.

Intimacy
The Knight of Cups Reversed can represent a partner who is often in pursuit of his own pleasure and may not consider how his actions impact the feelings of others. Often this knight is an emotionally immature individual who lacks wisdom and empathy.

Seeking Romance
If the Knight of Cups Reversed represents you, then he tells you to express your most ardent emotions rather than concealing them. Instead of waiting for romance, speak up. It's time to reconnect with the feeling of being sexy and powerful. Act with confidence.

Desires
The Knight of Cups Reversed can represent a fervent desire to declare a feeling that has remained unsaid. Express what you really want to say. You have nothing to lose if the person hearing your feelings authentically cares. If this person cannot handle your truth, then you can move on knowing that someone better is still on the way.

What the Knight of Cups May Be Teaching You

The Knight of Cups is an example of bravery in something so many of us find so hard to do: *expressing our true feelings*. Often the fear of driving another person away or being misunderstood can cause us to bottle up what we really have to say. The Knight of Cups challenges you to stand up to your anxiety and stop letting fear run the show when it comes to communication. It can be terrifying to express what is in your heart. This is especially true if you've been wounded by a deep betrayal or loss in the past. The Knight of Cups teaches that the heart mends when it is brave and open, allowing new experiences to take the place of past hurts. Whether you are single or with a partner, the Knight of Cups asks if you are being courageous and communicating your true feelings. Communication includes your words, body language, facial expressions, and energy. To gain what your heart most desires, you must first declare it into being. The Knight of Cups encourages you to be brave, even with the most difficult conversations. Honest communication will only drive away love that isn't real. True love can handle what is true. Be brave and speak your heart. Honestly expressing your feelings can clear the pathway toward your bliss.

QUEEN OF CUPS

The Queen of Cups feels every emotion with greater intensity than the average individual. Not just pleasurable feelings like joy, excitement, and love, but also the stinging emotions like heartbreak, grief, and sorrow. She loves and deeply desires to be loved. People who exhibit the queen's sensitive qualities make wonderful partners who shower their beloved with their whole being. The

Queen of Cups prioritizes her feelings in making all her decisions. She doesn't always make the rational or empowering choice, often choosing to follow her heart instead. This inevitably leads her through many stormy seas on her quest to find the safe harbor of true love. And yet, she wouldn't have it any other way. Once the Queen of Cups is in love, she's in it for the long haul. At her best, the Queen of Cups is empathetic, faithful, loving, patient, nurturing, and wise. At her worst, she is codependent, irrational, needy, insecure, and smothering.

In a Love Reading
New Relationship
The appearance of the Queen of Cups represents an exhilarating time when every moment seems to create a meaningful new memory. Although the relationship is still in its beginning phase, your heart feels compelled to dive in. The Queen of Cups can also represent a partner who authentically cares and acts with empathy in relationships.

Long-Term Partnership
The Queen of Cups can represent a union that has withstood the test of time. The journey was not always easy, but the love shared is legendary. You and your partner have a strong sense of loyalty to each other because of your shared history. The Queen of Cups can also appear when you need added compassion and empathy to address your partner's needs.

Intimacy
The Queen of Cups can represent a partner who appears modest in public, but who is privately very sensual. Lovemaking is equal parts physical and spiritual. Although she privately reveals her whole heart to her partner, she never loses her mystique.

Seeking Romance
If you are single, the Queen of Cups encourages you to be vulnerable, even if it feels scary. It is time to connect. Experience your life rather than hiding from it. Your sensitive heart is your greatest asset in your quest to find love. Allow it to remain open and curious.

Desires

The Queen of Cups can represent the desire to follow your heart rather than your head. You may be caught in a sea of emotions. Although this is a very sensitive time, your intuitive gifts are also heightened. Your deeper instincts will guide you through if you can listen beyond the crashing waves of your emotions. Listen for the inner calm that makes you feel clear, not anxious.

Reversed

New Relationship

The Queen of Cups Reversed can represent someone who repeatedly dives into tempestuous relationships, floundering in her desperate desire to be loved. She avoids learning how to swim, hoping instead for a strong savior to rescue her. By presenting herself as a victim needing rescue, she is continually victimized. Her life can change when she chooses to be empowered.

Long-Term Partnership

When the Queen of Cups is reversed, she represents someone who is often overwhelmed by their great sensitivity and may need assistance in dealing with feelings. She can also represent a smothering or needy partner in personal relationships. She may need to channel more of the attentive devotion she shows her partner toward herself.

Intimacy

The Queen of Cups Reversed can represent toxic emotions and disappointments. It may be time for a good cry. Tears release toxins from the body and can heal the heart. This card can also encourage you to address what issues need to be brought to the surface and released concerning intimacy.

Seeking Romance

Sometimes the Queen of Cups appears reversed when your heart has become numb or you aren't allowing emotional experiences to sink in. To begin the process of opening your heart, start in environments where you feel safe and protected. It may be time to reconnect with nature, meditate, or allow quiet time to listen within to what will heal old wounds.

Desires

The Queen of Cups Reversed can represent a person who desires to be heard. An unresolved emotion is likely dominating her perspective. She yearns for someone to listen to, rather than solve, her problem. Once the feeling is spoken and heard, she may find closure.

What the Queen of Cups May Be Teaching You

The Queen of Cups teaches the importance of feeling your life, even when it hurts. It may be difficult for you to keep your heart open when you've endured so much. The Queen of Cups asks you to never give up on love by numbing your heart or losing hope. If the Queen of Cups appears as your guide, you are likely extremely sensitive and may be trying to make sense of turbulent emotions. She reminds you that even challenging emotional moments are valuable teachers. The Queen of Cups is wise enough to know that when you love, you will also inevitably feel pain. Opening yourself to the full experience of love means opening yourself to unparalleled bliss, but also to the potential for disappointment and loss. She gently guides you through the turbulent seas of your own love story. The Queen of Cups compassionately guides you toward opening your heart with loving kindness. If you must pass through a layer of tears on the way to your center, allow them to flow. The Queen grants you safe harbor as you find your way back home. You heart will always be welcomed and protected on the calming shores of the gentle Queen of Cups.

KING OF CUPS

The King of Cups is loyal, kind, stable, and emotionally mature. Although he is strong, he is also extremely sensitive. When the King of Cups steps into a room, he immediately perceives the vibes of everyone in it. He looks people straight in the eye and isn't afraid of feelings or sensitivity. Although he is both compassionate and expressive, the King of Cups rarely gets swept to sea by tumultuous feelings. He is exceptionally self-controlled. The King of Cups keeps his cards close to his sleeve and will only reveal his greatest vulnerabilities with those he absolutely trusts. Once the King of Cups establishes trust with someone, he will be loyal to them unless *they* break that trust. If this sensitive king is ever wounded, he'll remember the slight. He may forgive, but he'll never forget. At his best, the King of Cups provides emotional security, kindness, and loyalty. He is fiercely protective of his partner, family, and loved ones. At his worst, he is moody, miserly, and brooding, and he will chew on a grudge forever.

In a Love Reading
New Relationship
The King of Cups can represent the archetypal good guy who is both sensitive and sweet. Be careful with his emotions. Nice guys often tend to finish last when dating, but don't underestimate this individual. He may not be as outwardly attractive as flashier personalities, but his heart is true. If you are looking for long-term security, you may have just struck gold.

Long-Term Partnership
The King of Cups can represent a partner who is a stable anchor for his home or family. He tends to get very comfortable in his home and may need some encouragement to exercise or get more active. The King of Cups can also represent a partner who serves as a compassionate sounding board. His wise counsel comes straight from the heart.

Intimacy
The King of Cups is a very sensitive lover. However, he can be a bit insecure, relying on his partner to validate his prowess in the bedroom. In the past, he's likely been passed over for sexier personalities, feeding even further into his inferiority complex. If you make him feel like a king, he will spare no effort in pleasing you.

Seeking Romance
If you are single, this card can signal a possibility of meeting a partner who is close to home. In fact, there could be a potential relationship with someone sweet right in front of your nose. Try to look outside your physical attraction type. You may be surprised.

Desires
The way to the heart of the King of Cups is through his stomach. Sharing food is his way of strengthening bonds. Inviting restaurants, gourmet meals lovingly prepared, and good company are some ways he expresses care. He desires a partner who either cooks or loves to be cooked for. The King of Cups can also represent a person who is most comfortable at home.

Reversed
New Relationship
The King of Cups Reversed can represent someone who appears adrift in life. He is not anchored to a particular person, purpose, or place. This can be difficult because the King of Cups (upright or reversed) can connect powerfully with others without even trying. You may want to rescue this person, but he will only swim to shore when he is ready.

Long-Term Partnership
The King of Cups Reversed can represent an emotionally brooding partner. He may keep replaying a past slight in his head over and over, constantly surrendering himself to the raging storms of his past. Time may not heal all wounds, but it will lessen their sting. The King of Cups Reversed has a hard time letting the past go.

Intimacy
Sometimes the King of Cups Reversed can also represent someone who has spent years building protective walls around their vulnerabilities. This armor can feel impenetrable. Your intuition may tell you that this person has a tender heart, and that may be true. However, it is currently encased in ice. He may not be emotionally available to connect.

Seeking Romance
If you are single, the King of Cups Reversed advises you to remain anchored during emotionally tempestuous times. Shelter your heart in environments that feel safest and most supported. Although you may *feel like* your heart may never open again, this is an illusion. The storm will pass, and the seas will be calm once more.

Desires

The King of Cups Reversed can represent a desire for someone from the past. It is time to stop trying to get the approval of a partner who's proven to be emotionally unavailable. Your kind heart and loyalty make you excellent relationship material; however, you cannot progress by moving backward. Learn from the past rather than harming yourself to replicate it.

What the King of Cups May Be Teaching You

The King of Cups may be guiding you to stay steady during emotionally turbulent times. Emotions are powerful things. They can buoy or sink us. The voyage across their unpredictable waters can be full of surprises; some pleasant, and others devastating. The King of Cups teaches you how to master the churning waves of your emotions so you aren't swept out to sea by them. The King of Cups doesn't have to fight against or control the waves, and neither do you. Sometimes, the universe intercedes on our journey to steer us away from the sharp rocks beneath the waves. The King of Cups cooperates with nature and with the natural flow of things. Go with the flow, even if it is guiding you through turbulent waters. Trust that these magical waters will guide you to the safe embrace that is meant for you. You must learn that love is intrinsically linked with *trust*.

PENTACLES IN A LOVE READING

The pentacles suit governs your relationship's values, practical matters, family, finances, and, most importantly, sense of *worth and value*. Associated with the element of earth, pentacle cards can quickly reveal if your relationship is built upon solid ground or an impractical foundation. Although you may want to avoid the practical realities of the pentacles suit in the first blush of a romance, they can grant invaluable insight into issues that could interfere with the security of the relationship down the road.

Pentacles are also concerned with realism. You won't find fanciful promises that don't amount to anything tangible in this suit! When many pentacles cards appear in a love reading, they draw your attention away from what people say, think, or feel, but rather toward what they **do.** Of all the cards in the tarot, the pentacles suit can give you the most concrete answers to how *realistic* a relationship is. Most importantly of all, the pentacles suit will reveal if the relationship is based on an even exchange of energy, or if one partner is benefiting more than the other. The pentacles suit emphasizes value and equity. The work you put in should reflect in the benefits you take out. This not only concerns your job, but also your relationships. Pentacle cards will quickly reveal if you are becoming emotionally impoverished in an unhealthy partnership.

One issue that many couples disagree about is money. The pentacles suit can also reveal current financial issues that may surface in the relationship. They will also refer to work stresses and their impact on the relationship. Long-term investments or expenditures, such as property, commodities, vehicles, and appliances, will also be reflected in this suit. If you are asking about the best way to confront a financial issue the partnership is facing, pay attention to whatever pentacle cards appear.

Pentacle cards are concerned with long-term success in all its forms, and this includes long-term relationship success. If you are wondering if your romance can last for the long haul, don't write off the pentacles suit as you scan your spread for gushing cups! It may not be the sexiest suit, but it will likely lead you toward someone stable. However, if a reading is just inundated with pentacle cards, it could indicate that there is a lack of passion, romance, intimacy, or spontaneity. Although they are considered safe cards, too many pentacles can signify a relationship that needs to be spiced up more. Romance requires a lot more than money and safety. No one wants to be the couple that dines out in a gorgeous restaurant and yet can't make eye contact or discuss anything past the flavor of the soup. As with any healthy relationship, a blending of the other elements is essential for happiness. Pentacle cards will also reveal if one partner needs to have a better work-life balance. For any partnership to thrive, there should always be a sense of fun where work, stress, and struggles can be set aside for a time.

Pentacles can also reveal romantic opportunities after establishing your profession. If you are asking your cards about romance and continue to receive pentacle cards, it could indicate that it is time to prioritize your career. By creating success in your life, you develop self-esteem, which is the most intoxicating aphrodisiac you can place in your arsenal. Successful people are often romantically attracted to other successful people. By going for your best opportunities, you are proclaiming to others that you expect nothing but the best. Sometimes true love waits to find you until after you've established yourself so that you are ready for the best sort of partner. It pays to invest in the pentacles!

ACE OF PENTACLES

The Ace of Pentacles represents positive new beginnings that lead to *tangible* results. It governs serendipitous events that are opening doorways and can manifest your heart's desire. Initially, the pentacles suit may not appear to lead toward love, but don't be fooled! Being at your best and realizing your goals is extraordinarily attractive. Investing in yourself will telegraph to others the values you exemplify and what you feel you are worth. This can serve to attract a mate who holds similar values and also possesses healthy self-esteem. Traditionally, the Ace of Pentacles is associated with constructive energy, which draws success toward you. When the Ace of Pentacles appears, it is time to take full advantage of the opportunities presenting themselves to you now. By realizing your potential, you will experience a renewed sense of your own worth. The Ace of Pentacles can also signify starting over. Establishing self-empowering goals will lead toward the life you most desire. If you invest in your own success, your patience will pay off.

In a Love Reading
New Relationship
The Ace of Pentacles promises a successful beginning. There is likely an intense physical attraction. Your new love interest is likely self-motivated and driven. Career will be a huge priority for this individual and may prove to be their top priority. This card can also signify a romance that blooms in a work environment.

Long-Term Partnership
A new opportunity is arriving that will positively affect your relationship. Although it will be challenging and will require hard work, success is assured. The Ace of Pentacles can reflect a new job, a new home, or a new financial prospect that will make your lives together more secure and abundant. A golden doorway is opening for you both; walk through it!

Intimacy
When the Ace of Pentacles appears, it's time to indulge in the pleasures of the senses. This card can also signify a new approach toward physical lovemaking. Both partners will enjoy each other more if they get out of their heads and back into their bodies. Money is well spent on luxuries that can stimulate your sensuality.

Seeking Romance
If you are single, the Ace of Pentacles gently redirects your attention away from relationship anxiety and toward tangible goals you can achieve for yourself. You will set yourself up for the right partner if you work on becoming the best version of yourself first. This card also advises that if you invest in your career first, love will naturally follow.

Desires

It's time to walk through the doorway of opportunity that is opening before you. This path is leading you toward a new and improved life. You are finally basking in the self-esteem that accompanies success. If you are considering what you need to do, choose the path that leads to your personal growth. The manifestation of your wishes will follow.

Reversed

New Relationship

The person you are focused on is not taking advantage of the opportunity presented. They may be impractical or they don't feel a desire to establish a firm commitment toward a stable future. You must choose the path that sets *you* up for success. If that road leads you away from a second-best opportunity, be assured that something even better is on the horizon.

Long-Term Partnership

You and your partner have been having trouble adapting to the new reality you find yourself in. It may feel like the mountain you've both been reclimbing has become too much to endure. Career troubles may also be negatively impacting the relationship. You (or your partner) need to be more sensible about your current challenges.

Intimacy

The person you are asking about is feeling out of touch with their body. They may lack confidence in their appearance or sexual prowess. This card can also signify a partner who prioritizes their career over intimacy. Do not allow their issues to erode your own self-esteem.

Seeking Romance

You are reexamining issues surrounding your sense of worth or worthiness. You may have been hitting a wall, over and over, only to finally get the message, "Invest in yourself!" Stop fruitlessly expending your energy on those who don't truly value you. Move on from any person, job, or environment that undercuts your sense of self-worth.

Desires

The Ace of Pentacles Reversed can represent procrastinating when it comes to a new opportunity that you would benefit from. There is an unconscious urge to put yourself on hold as you wait for others to act. Resist the impulse to remain stagnant. Your priorities are shifting. Allow the positive changes leading toward your success to begin.

What the Ace of Pentacles May Be Teaching You

The Ace of Pentacles asks you to stop obsessing about what you feel you lack and instead reengage with your opportunities. It may not feel like the work you do on your personal goals is the most direct path toward improving your love life, but you may be surprised. The Ace of Pentacles symbolizes the part of your life where you have witnessed tangible success. By investing more in that place and taking full advantage of the opportunities before you, you will cultivate boundless opportunities that will pool into other aspects of your life. People who feel successful within seem to attract other confident successful people. Success is not just restricted to money. Success can be described as embodying the *best possible version of yourself.* On its surface, the Ace of Pentacles may not appear to lead toward love. However, the opportunity presented may indirectly lead you to the right person or circumstances for your love life to flourish. Divine synchronicities are opening all the right doorways for you now. It's time to walk through them to manifest your best life.

TWO OF PENTACLES

The Two of Pentacles represents unpredictable energy. In a love reading, it symbolizes fluid events that are still changing and evolving. This card can also represent a love interest who acts erratically or unpredictably. The Two of Pentacles encourages you to keep your sense of humor when the unexpected occurs. People who harbor rigid expectations for how their love life *should* unfold often have a problem with this card. The Two of Pentacles doesn't necessarily signify good or bad events, just unexpected ones. You have a choice. You can either get bent out of shape because life is not unfolding according to your expectations, or you can adapt to where the energy *is* flowing. In nature, that which cannot evolve goes extinct. It's the same for relationships. Life doesn't adhere to a preordained script. People are changeable and will likely evolve beyond the person you first met. The elastic quality to this card challenges you to stretch yourself and adapt. If you remain rigidly resistant, your expectations can snap in two.

In a Love Reading
New Relationship
The Two of Pentacles symbolizes someone who is a lot of fun, but extremely unpredictable. This person may not return your messages one day, and then unexpectedly show up with flowers the next. If you seek consistency and stability, this juggler may disappoint you. This humorous personality is unconventional and seeks an easygoing partner who doesn't apply pressure.

Long-Term Partnership
For couples, the Two of Pentacles can represent changing priorities, values, or needs. This card requires *both* partners to compromise and adapt to the changing needs of the other for the partnership to progress. Issues surrounding financial or career instability could also take center stage. Do not fight the waves of change; ride them.

Intimacy
The Two of Pentacles signifies a lighthearted and fun approach to lovemaking. However, this card is very unpredictable. Be less serious and more playful. If you are concerned about an unwanted pregnancy or any other undesirable result from sex, take a hint from the juggler's hat and take your necessary precautions!

Seeking Romance
If you are single, the juggler tells you to expect the unexpected. Have a bit more fun with life and start mingling. Play, flirt, express your sense of humor, and lighten up. If you haven't found true love yet, lighten up! What will be, will be, *at the right time*. Life rarely goes according to plan, so have fun with where the unpredictable waves might speed you toward.

Desires
You may wish for certainty, but the person you are thinking about is sending mixed signals. First they blow hot, then cold. Although your random meetings can feel exhilarating, there is also an element of inconsistency that can be very frustrating. If your current situation is not in alignment with your deepest desires, you may need to evolve beyond it.

Reversed
New Relationship
The person you are asking about is acting thoughtlessly, immaturely, and erratically. Although you may be struggling with your own disappointments, you may need to reevaluate if this is what you truly want. The Two of Pentacles Reversed represents inconsistency at an extreme degree. You are responsible for establishing your boundaries and sticking to them.

Long-Term Partnership
The Two of Pentacles Reversed can represent unexpected financial stresses that are negatively impacting your relationship life. Either you or a partner are experiencing anxiety about where your financial path is leading. Practical responsibilities need to take precedence now. Once you are on surer footing, all other issues that have arisen can be addressed.

Intimacy
You are feeling dominated by emotional extremes. An intimate relationship causes your moods to shift like the waves—one moment soaring skyward before plunging into the depths. Try not to let the highs get too high or the lows, too low. Although diving into the drama is hard to resist, self-care and responsible choices are needed now to regain your footing.

Seeking Romance
It may feel as if everything is up in the air. It's time to adjust to change instead of fighting it. If your heart is not able to bend, it may break. Try to retain your sense of humor and don't take temporary experiences too seriously. Seek out laughter. This will help you ride out the waves with grace and ease instead of making war with them.

Desires

The Two of Pentacles Reversed can represent stubborn resistance to change. You may feel overwhelmed by the shifting tides. Although it may feel counterintuitive to adapt to what is happening, rigidity will cause more suffering. Seek out support if you are feeling lost at sea and ask for help. Reclaiming your sense of humor could provide the resilience you need.

What the Two of Pentacles May Be Teaching You

The Two of Pentacles encourages you to remain flexible and adaptable. Everything in life changes. People, relationships, physical appearances, priorities—everything is constantly shifting with time. You may be on a collision course with reality if you can't stretch beyond stubborn insistence. The Two of Pentacles encourages you to accept change, even when it makes you stretch beyond your comfort zone. Whatever you are facing, your situation is teaching you how to evolve. The Two of Pentacles shows you how to meet the unpredictable moments. Keep your sense of humor and accept the changing reality. Life will be far less of a struggle if you can learn to laugh at its absurdity and adapt to its shifting landscape. Resisting change is as fruitless as fighting the ocean. The Two of Pentacles can appear when you have been taking yourself and your situation too seriously. *Allow* the change you are stubbornly resisting and watch the magic unfold. It's time to ride the waves instead of fruitlessly swinging punches at them. These same waves will carry you toward a safer harbor.

THREE OF PENTACLES

The Three of Pentacles governs the process of learning and self-improvement. In a love reading, it will advise you to learn from the repeated scenarios you continually encounter in your relationships. Although the characters or environment may change, the plot remains eerily repetitive. Instead of trying to understand what is happening in the mind of the other person, the Three of

Pentacles redirects your focus back onto *you*. Repeated lessons reveal something important that must be repaired within. This card encourages you to know yourself, including your past weaknesses or tendencies. This will give you the power to initiate a huge personal breakthrough. The Three of Pentacles is associated with manifestation. If you want to see a change, it may be time to draw up a plan for what you desire and get to work. By focusing on self-improvement, you will witness a positive shift in your energy. Finally, the Three of Pentacles can signify a romantic attraction to someone in an academic environment.

In a Love Reading
New Relationship
The Three of Pentacles symbolizes a connection between two people who are still engaged in a learning process. In the beginning of a relationship, this card will advise you to be patient and gather more data before completely diving in. This card can also highlight a relationship at school or an attraction to someone in a teaching profession.

Long-Term Partnership
Your connection with your partner has taught you some of the most important lessons you are on this planet to learn. This card may also advise you to engage in mentally stimulating pursuits that interest you both. Support your partner's long-term goals if they are considering an education or training process that will positively impact their career.

Intimacy
This card always encourages you to learn more. If you feel like you are in the dark about what your partner is feeling, be more inquisitive. This card can also indicate that you are discovering more about what excites your love. Part of the fun of learning is experimentation!

Seeking Romance
If you are single, this card can signify that you must invest in yourself at this time. This process will not last forever, so take heart. You may feel the desire to get lost in another, but you cannot skip over your own self-development. This card could also be telling you that romance is more likely to occur after completing your education or manifesting a major goal.

Desires

The Three of Pentacles can signify a desire to invest in some form of self-improvement. Staying committed to your long-term goals will positively impact your relationship life. This card can also represent a relationship partner who can break through their present impasse when they invest in education or training.

Reversed
New Relationship

The person you are inquiring about is stuck on their own repeated life lesson. They appear to have learned nothing from their past experience. It is not your job to teach this person or to perpetually wait for them to grow up. This card can also advise you to stop repeating a habitual relationship cycle that's been causing you heartache.

Long-Term Partnership

The Three of Pentacles Reversed can illuminate hard relationship lessons that you and your partner have been repeating for too long. The past must be learned from, and destructive cycles must be broken. Conditions can only improve through *mutual* effort. If one partner is not committed, the past will continue to repeat itself.

Intimacy

The Three of Pentacles Reversed can signify a partner who is naïve or awkward when it comes to sex. Be patient and understanding as you teach your lover what you desire. This card can also signify feeling ignorant of your own desires. It's time to get back in your body and out of your head.

Seeking Romance

You are ready to try a different approach when it comes to dating. Instead of chasing after another person to feel comfortable in your own skin, it's time to invest in yourself. Upright or reversed, the Three of Pentacles encourages you toward self-improvement. By achieving your own success, you are more likely to attract someone who also has their life in order.

Desires

The Three of Pentacles Reversed can represent impatience with what life seems to be teaching you now. Be kind to yourself now, for you are still learning something very important about your values. You may need to release perfectionist tendencies. Know that what you desire will come to you when you understand yourself better. Learn from your past.

What the Three of Pentacles May Be Teaching You

The Three of Pentacles may be teaching you to have patience with your learning process, especially when it comes to love. With every experience you share with another, you gain more insight into yourself. Whether a relationship is healthy or unhealthy, realistic or unrealistic, all relationships have important lessons to teach you. Learning about yourself isn't always easy and takes time. There are no shortcuts. You can't just grab the fairy tale off the shelf and skip to the *happily ever after* part when it comes to your own learning process. There is a whole plot that will unfold before finding your pathway to true love's kiss. There are many lessons to learn, trials to overcome, and insights to be gained before you can enjoy the next chapter. Nothing you have learned was a waste of time or a mistake. Everything you've experienced is offering you the opportunity to become a better version of yourself. The Three of Pentacles asks you to have patience with your unfolding story and the lessons it is teaching you. You can't skip over your lessons. The wisdom they bring cannot be learned from a book. What you are currently learning must be *experienced*.

FOUR OF PENTACLES

The Four of Pentacles represents the compulsion to cling tightly to something external that is mistakenly believed to provide security. In actuality, the act of grasping for security is rooted in fear, which inevitably keeps the grasper in a state of suffering. In a love reading, the Four of Pentacles can reflect a needy partner who constantly clings to the very person who repeatedly leaves them feeling insecure or abandoned. So much of their identity and self-worth is dependent on this other person's affection; and yet, they just can't seem to let go. Their heart tells them to cling to the source of their happiness, and yet the joy in their life has long since gone, leaving them in denial that anything is broken. The Four of Pentacles represents the desire for an authentic sense of *value and worth*, which can never be found outside of oneself. The person this card signifies struggles to let go. Counterintuitively, their insatiable desire to cling to love has also become the greatest barrier to receiving it.

In a Love Reading
New Relationship
The Four of Pentacles can represent a person who places a lot of value in the external trappings of success or power. This card can also represent a needy or clingy partner who is insecure. At its most innocent, the Four of Pentacles can represent a tightwad, or someone who begrudges paying for things. You can tell by their response to the first restaurant check!

Long-Term Partnership
The Four of Pentacles encourages you and your partner to focus on goals for future security. Sometimes this card places an emphasis on pinching your pennies or saving up for a major expenditure. Try not to take needless financial risks or splurge on extravagances. This card can also signify a possessive person who has trouble sharing their partner's attention with others.

Intimacy
You may be holding on to a past love that is blocking you from connecting intimately. Let go of any heavy emotions that are keeping you weighed down with worry. This card can also signify a partner who is career obsessed, which makes them neglect their lover. Healthy parameters should be discussed concerning the balance between career and personal life.

Seeking Romance
If you are single, you may be realizing that your desire to keep yourself safe is blocking you from making meaningful connections. The Four of Pentacles can also signify that you are focusing too much on career or the acquisition of wealth. Restore balance between work and play and make more time for socializing.

Desires

The Four of Pentacles can represent a desire to cling to something that is no longer healthy for you. It's time to stop grasping for the person or belief that is consistently making you miserable. Although this fixation may have provided a sense of security in the past, you have long outgrown it. It sounds counterintuitive, but *letting go* will lead to your happiness.

Reversed

New Relationship

The person you are asking about is releasing old burdens. They are beginning anew and uneasy with taking on more pressure from another person. They may need to place themselves first; this is not entirely a bad thing (for either of you). The Four of Pentacles Reversed encourages patience as events are still in motion.

Long-Term Partnership

The Four of Pentacles Reversed signals a time when you and your partner are finally removing the external barriers that have kept you from connecting. This card can also signify a positive career change, where one partner is leaving a profession that brought them more misery than happiness. This will positively affect their mood and the relationship.

Intimacy

You are seeing through the facades that others use to mask what is really happening. Your perception is sharp, and you can no longer be gaslit. Trust in the grounded reality you see. You know the truth of this situation and how you feel. Your common sense holds the answer.

Seeking Romance

It is time to be more giving, open, and vulnerable. This will transform your energy from shutting down to allowing good things to naturally find their way to you instead. You are beginning to recognize that what is yours will always come to you. You are also learning to let go of a past relationship that once seemed impossible to get over.

Desires

The Four of Pentacles Reversed can signify a desire to let go of a relationship that has been weighing you down. Although it may have provided security in the past, it no longer seems to hold any magic. This card can also signify a realization that when you marry for money, you earn every cent! You don't need to sell out your soul to lovelessness for security.

What the Four of Pentacles May Be Teaching You

The Four of Pentacles can represent the hollowness we feel whenever we make another person the sole foundation for our sense of security. In the search for love, people who embody the clingy energy of the Four of Pentacles are confused as to why they can't seem to attain a happy relationship. The blunt truth is that most people don't want to be conscripted into the role of caretaker for a person who is clearly out of power, nor does a healthy mate want to feel their lives highjacked by another person's *need*. In the Rider-Waite-Smith tarot, we witness a miser, firmly clutching four golden coins. He believes with his whole heart that these coins are the source of his security. Without them, he believes he would be nothing. In the image, the coins have become barriers. Look at the miser's face. In his obsession to hold on to this security, he's making himself miserable. In a love reading, the coins can symbolize the security that a relationship partner is believed to provide. The towers in the distance remind us of the Tower card, which can keep you imprisoned in a state of denial. The artificial belief that another person will be the foundation for your happiness and security will only serve to cause love and security to further elude you. By letting go of what you most feel the need to cling to, love will have a chance to bring your heart what is authentically yours. Letting go opens you to even better things.

FIVE OF PENTACLES

The Five of Pentacles has traditionally been called the poverty card. Poverty has less to do with a dollar amount and more to do with your sense of self-worth. In a love reading, the Five of Pentacles can highlight unhealthy relationships or beliefs that keep you in a state of emotional impoverishment. This card will also alert you to partnerships that leave you feeling emotionally depleted. You may be giving everything of yourself to another but receiving little to nothing in return. *Poverty consciousness tricks you into believing that the scraps of a broken relationship are all you'll be able to get.* These kinds of partnerships often leave one feeling emotionally starved for more. The Five of Pentacles can also appear in a love reading when a relationship is subsisting on starvation rations. This drought is not sustainable. Something must change, or the bonds will inevitably fray. Even if one partner is heroically pouring in all their effort, one person can't do it alone; two people, equally invested, must work together to ensure a healthy relationship's survival.

In a Love Reading
New Relationship
The Five of Pentacles warns of one partner not being completely self-sufficient, financially or emotionally. This can manifest into a needy relationship dynamic where one partner uses guilt or head games to secure their emotional needs. This card will also warn you not to approach a new relationship like a starving dog, needy for affection. Maintain your dignity and know your worth!

Long-Term Partnership
The Five of Pentacles can indicate a relationship subsisting on starvation rations. It's time for both partners to recommit equal love and effort if the union is to survive. This card can also highlight a major financial problem that is negatively impacting the health of the relationship. Identify the energy wasters in your partnership and eliminate them.

Intimacy
Intimately, the Five of Pentacles represents an absence of physical affection in relationships. One partner may be too tired, depleted, or struggling with a health issue that has been stifling their passion. This person will need self-care before the ice can melt. This card has also been long associated with a fear of rejection.

Seeking Romance
If you are single, the Five of Pentacles advises you to raise your standards and keep them high. Don't listen to people who tell you you're being too picky. Wasting your time with someone who is not meeting your standards is just that: a waste of time. Second best will never be enough. Raise the bar.

Desires

You feel a desire to stop expending your energy on people who drain you. After your interactions, it is important to check within. Do you feel drained, depleted, guilty, anxious, or unappreciated? These are big red flags. Raise your standards and insist on the life you desire without settling for less.

Reversed

New Relationship

The Five of Pentacles Reversed warns you to steer clear of people who don't have their life together. Users, energy vampires, or people who play head games will always try to latch on to someone whose energy, money, or resources they can drain. You do not have to sacrifice yourself in payment for a manipulative person to stay.

Long-Term Partnership

Your partner either struggles financially or is emotionally depleted. They may not have the resources physically, mentally, or emotionally to give you the life you deserve. If you are getting less investment than you are giving, you must make them aware. If they still can't get you what you need, you may have to make the difficult choice to choose yourself first.

Intimacy

There's a difference between high quality and low quality. It is the same for who you decide to open yourself up to in intimate relationships. The Five of Pentacles Reversed tells you to stop taking low quality home. The honest voice within will whisper warnings when you know you are ignoring your values.

Seeking Romance

The Five of Pentacles Reversed also appears when it is time to toss out the beliefs that make you feel like garbage. This card tells you to take out the trash. No matter what happened in the past, today is a new day to start fresh. It's time to restore your confidence and self-esteem. Engage in fulfilling connections and activities that reaffirm your worth.

Desires

When the Five of Pentacles appears reversed, it's time to stop depleting yourself with experiences that feel hollow or unfulfilling. The definition of insanity is doing the same thing over and over while expecting a different result. It's time to turn off the spigot to the biggest energy wasters that have been draining your life force.

What the Five of Pentacles May Be Teaching You

The Five of Pentacles teaches you to avoid succumbing to poverty consciousness in love. A healthy, thriving, loving partnership will have joy and love at its center, not guilt, head games, or desperation. The Five of Pentacles encourages you to cast out any thought, person, or belief that is draining more than it gives. If you've allowed the belief into your heart that you aren't worthy of the best, it's time to throw that garbage out! Love yourself enough to stop begging for scraps. In the Rider-Waite-Smith tarot, we see two sickly figures limping through the snow. They've lost everything. They feel unworthy of entering the warm church they pass, glowing with security. The sick figures on the Five of Pentacles can represent a sick situation you've remained in way longer than it is healthy. This card encourages you to walk away from any unhealthy situation that drains more from you than it gives. No matter how you're currently feeling, you deserve a place by the warm fire, living your best life. Insist on the life and love that are truly worthy of you. You deserve nothing less.

SIX OF PENTACLES

Traditionally, the Six of Pentacles is associated with generosity and giving. However, in a love reading, it's a bit more complicated. The Six of Pentacles will usually highlight an unequal power dynamic in a relationship. One partner may play the role of the giver in the relationship, occasionally tossing a pittance to their out-of-power partner. The giving partner might have significantly more resources or may be more confident in their own worth; however, it's clear that they hold all the chips in the partnership. The powerless partner plays the role of the beggar. Having forgotten their own value, they desperately plead for whatever scraps they can get. They are so used to being unfulfilled they don't even realize they are begging. The Six of Pentacles can alert you if both partners aren't meeting each other as emotionally secure *equals*. Whenever this card appears in a love reading, it asks you to consider the role you are acting out in your relationships. Are you showing up as an *equal*, a *giver*, or a *beggar*?

In a Love Reading
New Relationship
The person you are interested in appears to have it all. Make sure you are not placing their perceived value on a pedestal at the expense of your own. Embrace what makes you powerful and meet this person as an equal. The Six of Pentacles can also signify a new relationship with someone who holds a higher position or has secured more wealth than you.

Long-Term Partnership
For a *healthy* relationship, the Six of Pentacles can be a secure card. A balance has likely been struck in your union. Your partnership is complementary. Although one partner may wield more worldly power, they are complemented by their beloved's inner strengths. This card can also signify a time when your partner needs your selfless help and support through difficulties.

Intimacy
Intimately, the Six of Pentacles highlights preferred sex roles, where one partner is naturally more dominant, and the other is more submissive. When this card appears, the dominant-submissive dynamic will often be linked to your partner's sexual desires. This card can also signify a sexual relationship where one lover seems to hold all the power.

Seeking Romance
If you are single, the Six of Pentacles asks you to be mindful of the role you are embodying: the equal partner, the giver, or the beggar. You don't need to beg for someone to love you. Likewise, you don't need to constantly give in to disempowered people. Seek equity in your relationships and enter them with your power intact.

Desires
You may wish to be more mindful of the role you are donning when you show up in your relationships. Your words and body language are broadcasting to others what you truly feel about yourself. Remember that no one is better than you. Their love is not worth more than yours. Embrace your personal power and never resort to begging for scraps.

Reversed
New Relationship
When the Six of Pentacles appears reversed, it warns of extremes. Both partners aren't sharing their responsibilities equally. One partner may be excessively giving while the other takes, attempting to remain unchanged. Don't settle for less than the best.

Long-Term Partnership
The Six of Pentacles Reversed can highlight a relationship dynamic where one partner enables the other's bad habits, addictions, or self-destructive tendencies. Healing can happen, but first you must face the problem, create boundaries, and be willing to change. Professional support may be helpful. Insist on accountability.

Intimacy
The Six of Pentacles Reversed can signify an intimate relationship where one partner places the other on a pedestal, feeling their entire worth hinges on their continued attention or approval. They may not believe in their own beauty and may struggle with sexual confidence.

Seeking Romance
This card may also appear when you are lacking confidence in your own abilities. You might find yourself excessively placing others on a pedestal at the expense of yourself. Belittling yourself to gain another's favor is also a form of devaluing who you are. Enter your relationships as an equal.

Desires
The Six of Pentacles Reversed encourages you to restore balance with whatever feels lopsided in your head or in your heart. Do not look to others to take control of whether you feel harmony within yourself. This card can also signify a

desire to restore harmony and self-esteem within your own heart. Value what you bring to the table and know your worth.

What the Six of Pentacles May Be Teaching You

The scales that appear on the Six of Pentacles can also be interpreted as a symbol for the universal law of karma. This concept pervades most every culture but is basically understood as "what goes around, comes around." The energy you invest in your life is the energy that will eventually come out, even when you don't see immediate results. Life inevitably holds its share of disappointments for everyone. All people deal with a loss, upheaval, or situations they perceive to be unfair. The Six of Pentacles reminds you that everything in the universe eventually balances out. If you feel unresolved about something that happened in the past, the Six of Pentacles reassures you that *all will be made right* in time. However, *you* are responsible for restoring balance within your own heart. Your current situation may be teaching you how to let go and allow karma to do its thing. The love that you invest in your life will always return in unexpected and often mysterious ways. All will be made right in time. Give yourself the loving kindness you wish to receive. Be your own benefactor. That which currently feels off-kilter will rebalance in time.

SEVEN OF PENTACLES

The Seven of Pentacles will often appear when you are still waiting for your future hopes to manifest. Although this card can test your patience, it also carries an encouraging message: *You are on the right track, keep going!* In a love reading, the Seven of Pentacles symbolizes the concept of divine timing. That which you hope for will materialize, but only when you're ready for it, and not before. Everything has its season, and our most momentous events occur exactly when they are meant to. The Seven of Pentacles will appear when you've been working on yourself. Unlike the Seven of Cups, which signifies hoping, wishing, and fantasizing about your dreams coming true, the Seven of Pentacles affirms the actionable steps you've taken toward manifesting your desires. Everything is growing just as it should. The Seven of Pentacles reminds you to chillax and simply allow your dream to manifest at its right time. It's time to focus on another source of excitement while you are waiting. A watched pot never boils.

In a Love Reading
New Relationship
The Seven of Pentacles emphasizes a clear message: "Take your time!" You are on the right track, but events are still changing, growing, and developing. Take it slow. Be present and enjoy the moments you are creating with your new love interest, rather than getting too far ahead of yourself with future fears or plans. Stay present.

Long-Term Partnership
Your relationship has matured slowly and steadily over the years. You can count on your partner to remain consistent and to seek the most practical route toward future security. You've both arrived at a stage in your life where there will be fewer surprises. Long-term investments, both personal and financial, are finally paying off.

Intimacy
The Seven of Pentacles can signify it's better to move slowly when it comes to sex. Savor the moment. Let the excitement build. There is no need to rush. This card can also signify a time of waiting between intimate encounters. One partner may have many external demands that must be seen to.

Seeking Romance
If you are single, rest assured that everything is growing and developing as it should. There is nothing you need to do to expedite the appearance of the relationship you want. It simply isn't time yet. Stay busy with what *is* working out in your life. Your heart's desire is still on its way.

Desires

It's time to step back from what you have been so fixated on. Fervently desiring something can cause you to feel that it will never arrive. This may not be the most exciting period, but all will manifest in its proper time. Find something constructive to engage your mind with while you are waiting for your harvest. This card often signifies a need for patience.

Reversed

New Relationship

The person you are asking about is steady, pragmatic, and averse to risks. Sometimes, the Seven of Pentacles appears reversed when the person you are inquiring about continuously keeps you waiting. You may need to identify if they are just being overcautious or simply aren't ready to give the relationship what it needs.

Long-Term Partnership

The Seven of Pentacles Reversed can appear if you or your partner is trying to artificially speed up the natural flow of events to get what they want before it's time. Try not to breeze through the work that must be currently done. This card can also represent a partner who rushes you into making decisions before you are ready.

Intimacy

The Seven of Pentacles appears reversed when you are feeling bored in your relationship life. If things have become too dull or predictable, change up the energy. Boringness is romance repellent! Create your own excitement instead of waiting for another to take the initiative. You can still experience a more passionate life, but it starts with you.

Seeking Romance

When the Seven of Pentacles appears reversed, it signifies that you may be feeling impatient. It may seem like you have been waiting to connect with someone special *forever*. This is likely because you have been transfixed by this issue. A watched pot never boils.

Desires

The Seven of Pentacles Reversed represents a desire to see a goal manifest faster. You are taking all the right steps toward your dream. The prep work has been done. The stage is set. Now all that is required is patience. Find something to do while you're waiting to keep your anxiety in check. The work done on yourself will ensure a great harvest.

What the Seven of Pentacles May Be Teaching You

The Seven of Pentacles may be teaching you to relax with the part of your life that still feels incomplete. You don't have to wait for all your goals to manifest before you start enjoying your life. Sometimes the intense desiring of something actually drives it away. The Seven of Pentacles encourages you to *simply be* and allow yourself to feel joy for your daily improvement. Wherever you are seeing good results is where you want to open yourself to the joy in your life. Joy attracts good energy. Pessimism is easier, but it will keep you stuck if it is your go-to reaction. You aren't on the wrong track, and you didn't take a wrong turn. You didn't miss anything… you are exactly where you are meant to be. Hindsight will eventually reveal why you had to take a little more time. Enjoy your life just as it is now and watch as it gets even better.

EIGHT OF PENTACLES

The Eight of Pentacles is traditionally associated with hard work, consistency, and effort that eventually pays off. In a love reading, its meaning is similar. The energy you invest in yourself is never a waste of time. Whether you are single or in a relationship, the Eight of Pentacles advises that you make the extra effort and invest in your best. This card encourages you to continue to work through the part of your life that feels most challenging. Investing in your best life will produce the conditions for love to flourish. Sometimes, this card advises that *both* partners in a relationship must invest *equal* effort. The Eight of Pentacles can also signify a romantic attraction that can occur at work or through social engagements with coworkers. Surprisingly, your job may be what places you in the crosshairs of Cupid's arrow! The Eight of Pentacles encourages you not to give up, even when your search for love requires *even more* effort. As the old saying goes, "If at first you don't succeed, try, try again."

In a Love Reading
New Relationship
Your love interest will likely prioritize their career goals ahead of love and romance. This isn't necessarily a reflection of their feelings for you. This individual will be naturally self-motivated and driven to succeed. Their heart is in their work. This card can also signify an attraction to someone in the workplace.

Long-Term Partnership
You and your partner are not afraid of hard work. This card can signify a period where a long-term investment must be made to produce the results you are both looking for. Sometimes, this card can also signify the possibility of working together professionally. If you and your partner have a business idea, this card will encourage you to move forward with it.

Intimacy
Sex may take a backseat to your career or responsibilities. Stress, exhaustion, or simply having opposite work schedules could also be interfering with the connection between you and your partner. Create some time for play! The Eight of Pentacles can also represent a sex life that has become monotonous. Break up your current routine with some spontaneity.

Seeking Romance
If you are single, the Eight of Pentacles could indicate opportunities to meet people through your career. If your friends and colleagues invite you out, say yes! There might also be an opportunity to meaningfully connect with others through the work you are passionate about. If you are loving your life and career, romance has a much better chance of finding you.

Desires
The Eight of Pentacles can signify a desire for self-improvement. *Are you show-ing up as your best in the world?* Self-care, working out, updating your style, attending school, improving your career, self-sufficiency—investment in your-self elevates your self-esteem! When you love who you have become, your confi-dence will draw what you desire to you.

Reversed

New Relationship
The Eight of Pentacles Reversed can represent an impractical relationship. Although there is an intense attraction, both parties are entering the union with a lot of unfinished business. One or both partners may need to bring closure to what they have recently abandoned before beginning something new. This card can also represent a lot of effort with few results.

Long-Term Partnership
You or your partner may be experiencing trouble at work or may need to change careers. An unfulfilling job can really depress a relationship. This card can also appear when one partner is not putting enough effort into the relation-ship. Improvements can only happen if both people are equally committed to the partnership. Focus your efforts into creating positive change.

Intimacy
Upright or reversed, the Eight of Pentacles can indicate you have been working too hard. You may need to schedule more time to socialize or relax. If you are looking for a way to increase romance, you may need to break away from your routines. Avoid predictability and make time to play!

Seeking Romance
The Eight of Pentacles Reversed calls you to confront the uncomfortable part of your life. The self-work you've habitually avoided must begin to move beyond your present impasse. This card will also advise you not to mix love with your work life. Maintain your common sense. Avoid acting impulsively no matter how strong an attraction may feel.

Desires

You may be *trying* too hard to get what you want right now. If you are consistently putting effort into something that is not producing a positive result, it's time to stop the insanity. This card will also encourage you to infuse some more *fun* into what you are doing. Working toward your best life should feel pleasing and not seem like a joyless hamster wheel.

What the Eight of Pentacles May Be Teaching You

The Eight of Pentacles could be teaching you to remain consistent with improvements you are making in your life. In the Rider-Waite-Smith tarot, we see a craftsman busy in his workshop. The hammer blows must strike repeatedly for him to complete the job. This symbolizes the concept of consistent, gradual, continued effort. Whether working on yourself or a relationship, it isn't just "one and done." Many people fail at achieving their goals because they simply give up too soon. They get frustrated when they don't see an immediate result for their efforts. The Eight of Pentacles could also be teaching you to be mindful of the energy you are infusing your tasks with while you are out in the world. Whether it is work, engaging with friends, or dating, ask yourself what expression you have on your face. *Is your energy open, warm, inviting, or loving?* If you show up in the world with the negative belief that something isn't going to work or will probably be a big waste of time anyway, you are setting yourself up for disappointment. Whatever it is that you are doing, working on, or improving, infuse it with love. Romance can spark just about anywhere. Every time you step into the world, smile, and allow the goddess of love to walk beside you.

NINE OF PENTACLES

The Nine of Pentacles symbolizes wealth, security, and all the pleasures money can buy. It governs luxurious gifts that are expressions of love, such as velvety roses, sumptuous dinners, sparkling jewels, or lavish vacations. The appearance of this card could signify a wealthy suitor or a love interest from an affluent background. On a personal level, the Nine of Pentacles will encourage you to maintain *high standards*. Not every partnership is equal, and not every person will treat you in a manner that is worthy of you. By insisting on getting the best, you telegraph to the world what you feel you are worth. The Nine of Pentacles advises that you not accept conditions that are clearly beneath you. Many people experience unhappiness in their relationships because they settle for less, feeling they should just be happy with whatever scraps they can get. The Nine of Pentacles assures you that there is nothing wrong with turning your nose up at any substandard condition beneath your dignity.

In a Love Reading
New Relationship
The Nine of Pentacles can signify a love interest who is wealthy or who is destined to be financially successful. They have extremely high standards and are looking for a partner who also knows their worth. The message of this card is to maintain high standards and to not accept treatment from a lover that is less than what you deserve.

Long-Term Partnership
The Nine of Pentacles signifies long-term security and prosperity for your relationship. Opportunities for increasing wealth arise whenever this card appears. Any investments you make will eventually pay off. This card could also give permission to splurge on something you both can enjoy. Investing money in pleasurable pursuits can awaken slumbering passion.

Intimacy
The Nine of Pentacles encourages luxuriating in the senses and treating yourself to the finer things in life. Spoil yourself and enjoy the pleasures money can buy, even if it seems a frivolous expense. Like the Empress, this card can also indicate increased fertility. Last, this card will encourage you to express your passion through luxurious gifts.

Seeking Romance
If you are single, the Nine of Pentacles advises you to always keep your standards high. Don't doubt yourself or your value. You deserve to be courted by someone who not only appreciates you, but also respects your worth. Don't accept a partner who doesn't check every box on your list. This card also signifies a need for patience as you await the best person for you.

Desires

It's time to insist on the best. This is the only life where you get to be the current version of yourself. Don't settle for any behaviors that are beneath your dignity. No person's acceptance or approval is worth more than your integrity. If someone is not giving you everything you require with a generous heart, then it is better to be on your own for a time. The best is yet to come.

Reversed
New Relationship

The Nine of Pentacles Reversed may be alerting you to a messy relationship that you are settling with. It's time to clear your heart of anyone who makes you feel less than you're worth. Stop casting your pearls before swine.

Long-Term Partnership

This card can indicate financial or career concerns that may be causing an amorphous sense of unfulfillment that affects your relationship. Compromise may be needed to support your partner in finding a position they feel truly fulfilled in. Sacrifices made now will pay dividends well into the future. Support happiness above fruitless obligation.

Intimacy

This card can represent an intimate partner you are projecting a fantasy of stability onto. Although the sex is great, you may be ignoring the fact that they are unwilling to commit to you. You may have accepted subpar conditions for so long that you've become numb to them. This should not be your new normal! You deserve someone who is of substance.

Seeking Romance

The Nine of Pentacles can also appear reversed when you are feeling unclear about what your standards truly should be. You may feel so embroiled in a messy situation that you've lost perspective. Seek out the support of a trusted counselor or friend to identify what your list of non-negotiables in love should include. It takes self-discipline, but *adhere to your list!*

Desires

You may be getting impatient as you are waiting to see results. As frustrating as it is, this is not the time for quick movement. Gentle growth and improvement are happening in the garden of your life, even if this isn't outwardly perceptible. Refocus your attention on the part of your life that shows signs of flourishing.

What the Nine of Pentacles May Be Teaching You

The Nine of Pentacles may be teaching you to restore your highest standards and reclaim your dignity. If you've been enduring a messy situation long enough, your senses may have become dull to it. The Nine of Pentacles gives you permission to be selective about what you allow in the sacred garden of your heart. It should not be wide open for some moronic brute to trample over! In the Rider-Waite-Smith tarot, a noble lady wears a glove on her left hand to protect herself from the sharp talons of the falcon. The left hand is symbolically the hand of receptivity. You must be protective of what you are allowing yourself to receive. The Nine of Pentacles assures you that no matter what your current situation is, all can be made right again when you decide to take out the trash in your love life. It's time to clear out the stagnant smells and allow a fresh spring breeze to waft through. Once you start smelling the fragrant blossoms of your best life, you'll wonder how you tolerated the squalor of the substandard past for so long.

TEN OF PENTACLES

The Ten of Pentacles symbolizes family, security, and shared values. In a love reading, it can refer to a relationship that is stable enough to grow into the next natural stage of development. The Ten of Pentacles also governs our responsibility to others that may transcend our personal desires. It emphasizes the virtues of *duty*, *honor*, *loyalty*, and *respect*. This card can also refer to long-term investments in home, family, or career. If you are wondering what choice to make, this card will advise you to take the most *practical* path and to avoid acting recklessly. It may be time to make a plan or establish some structure to manifest your long-term goals. This card also reminds you that the way we show up in relationships is often shaped through how relationships were modeled for us through family. Understanding the past can grant valuable insight into the present. Finally, the Ten of Pentacles can refer to a significant age difference between two people who are in love.

In a Love Reading
New Relationship
The Ten of Pentacles represents a growing bond with a person who shares your values. The person you are seeing will likely have a strong sense of duty to their family. They are likely looking for someone who shares their long-term goals. This person is repelled by drama and will want events to unfold securely and predictably. Impulsivity makes them nervous.

Long-Term Partnership
The Ten of Pentacles can signify an investment in your future security together. Issues of financial planning, buying property, and investments in education all come to the fore when this card appears. The needs of extended family may also become a major priority. If you are considering any changes, make sure they are practical; avoid taking unnecessary risks.

Intimacy
The obligations to family, friends, or work may be interfering with your sex life. You might be feeling bored or unfulfilled when this card appears, since responsibilities are taking precedence. However, this card can be a welcome sign if you are hoping for children or are looking to expand your family.

Seeking Romance
If you are single, this card urges you to reconnect with your community or chosen family. Family events or outings with loyal friends may lead to romantic opportunities. Say yes to more social invitations. Reconnect with your community. The Ten of Pentacles also advises that you not waste your time with flighty partners who don't share your values.

Desires

You may feel a desire to grow beyond relationships that don't share your values. Choose to invest only in those who have proven themselves reliable and honorable. You may be maturing beyond past connections that didn't bring happiness or security. The Ten of Pentacles promises future stability if you allow yourself to grow.

Reversed

New Relationship

This card can represent a well-meaning but unstable partner. Although they have many excellent qualities, they may lack personal security and therefore cannot offer it to another. If you are confused, take the most practical course of action to ensure your own security. This card can also signify family drama that is interfering with this relationship.

Long-Term Partnership

The Ten of Pentacles Reversed can signify a relationship that feels habitually insecure. If you are wondering how events will likely transpire in the future, look to past patterns. This card can also signify intrusions from meddlesome family members who wish to create drama. Stronger boundaries are needed between your relationship and external interference.

Intimacy

Your partner may be prioritizing duty to their long-term goals over love. This card can also represent a time when intimacy grinds to a halt. External obligations are stifling the magic you once felt. This card advises that you both occasionally unplug from extraneous responsibilities and focus on each other. A little getaway may help.

Seeking Romance

When the Ten of Pentacles appears reversed, the qualities you once prized in relationships could be changing. You may be establishing a higher standard and insisting on authenticity. Although you may endure a temporary period of discomfort, inner growth is happening. This will lead you toward more meaningful connections with people who share your values.

Desires

The Ten of Pentacles Reversed can highlight generational cycles you wish to break. Call on the support of loving ancestors who've passed on. Learn from their experiences so you don't repeat their mistakes. It's time to grow beyond learned behaviors that have resulted in instability. Be intentional about the life you want and avoid unconsciously repeating old patterns.

What the Ten of Pentacles May Be Teaching You

The Ten of Pentacles may be teaching you to reconnect with *familial love*. Your family is not limited to the people you are genetically linked to. You get to choose who you consider family. Put simply, *family* is your supportive community and your anchor of support when all else feels awash in stormy seas. Family means different things to different people. They may be living people or wise ancestors that are ever near in your heart. Although you may have been focused on romantic love, the Ten of Pentacles lovingly offers the support of those who love you without conditions. All too often, the love and support available to us get taken for granted. You don't have to wait for the perfect relationship to feel loved and understood. Although it may not be the love you *want,* it just may be the love that's needed to meet this moment. If you are feeling unsure, insecure, or lost, listen to the whisper of your spirit and *come home.*

PAGE OF PENTACLES

The Page of Pentacles can talk to just about anybody. He is a jack-of-all-trades. This makes him relatable to people from a variety of backgrounds. The Page of Pentacles seeks a partner with whom he can share his interests. He will tire very quickly of a person who is not intellectually curious. The Page of Pentacles has a gift for bringing abstract concepts down to earth and putting them in layman's terms. People who exhibit his qualities make excellent students, teachers, scholars, and detail-oriented workers. This page also considers himself an introvert; however, once he feels welcome and in good company, his gift for gab is irrepressible. In relationships, the Page of Pentacles has extremely particular tastes. He is a bit of a perfectionist and takes his time before finally making up his mind. At his best, the Page of Pentacles is amiable, friendly, dependable, interesting, and loaded with potential. At his worst, he is nitpicky and exacting and may come across as an aloof know-it-all.

In a Love Reading
New Relationship
The Page of Pentacles represents a fresh union overflowing with possibility. This card can also represent a partner who shares similar interests. This relationship is at its best when engaged in shared activities that stimulate the mind.

Long-Term Partnership
This card can describe a partner who lives in their head. This relationship thrives when there is a meeting of the minds on something both partners can grow toward. The relationship will likely last because of mutual interests or a passion for working toward the same goal.

Intimacy
Intimately, the Page of Pentacles is eager to learn what you like. He may be a bit awkward at first, but if you teach him, he will exceed your expectations. Like all figures from the pentacles suit, he is physical, earthy, and sensuous.

Seeking Romance
The Page of Pentacles may call you toward academic environments or places of shared interests. Take a class, join a membership club, follow where the passion of your interests leads you. Romance may reawaken when you place your focus on self-improvement and learning.

Desires
The Page of Pentacles desires a partner who speaks enthusiastically about their interests. He loves to identify shared pursuits. The Page of Pentacles will be fascinated by the activities you excitedly rattle off facts about. Don't worry if you look like a nerd; he will likely find you all the more endearing.

Reversed
New Relationship
Every reversed page can signify a level of immaturity. The Page of Pentacles Reversed can highlight juvenile behavior or someone who is very bright but struggles to take full responsibility for their choices. The above-average intelligence of this person can make them extremely adept at rationalizing away what needs to grow.

Long-Term Partnership
The Page of Pentacles Reversed can represent a person who upholds unrealistic standards of perfection in himself and in his potential partners. He may also come across as overly critical. He may seem a bit off when trying to connect in relationships. This card can also signify a partnership where one partner is extremely difficult to satisfy.

Intimacy
The Page of Pentacles Reversed can represent a dysmorphic idea of how one appears to others. This can greatly interfere with developing intimacy with a partner. This card can encourage you to work on developing self-esteem and confront any issues related to body shame. Beauty is never skin-deep. Embrace what makes you beautiful, inside, and out, and let yourself shine.

Seeking Romance
If you are single, the Page of Pentacles Reversed will highlight a lesson you seem to be relearning. Until this lesson is learned, you may feel your plans for romance keep getting derailed. *What issue do you seem to be relearning again and again in your relationships?*

Desires
The Page of Pentacles Reversed can represent a desire to be perfect. You may be holding yourself to an impossible expectation of being flawless. This can erode your sense of self. In actuality, your imperfections make you more approachable and relatable. You may be learning to be more vulnerable with revealing your true heart.

What the Page of Pentacles May Be Teaching You

The Page of Pentacles also reveals how your interests can aid in your healing process after a turbulent time. Focus on education, self-improvement, school, working out, business, or your profession or talent. Refine yourself and watch how your life improves. Pages often appear when you are still within a beginning phase. The seeds have been planted, but your growth is not yet complete. Just as you wouldn't endlessly stare at a plant and berate it for not growing fast enough, you also shouldn't bully yourself with your own growth process. Find somewhere constructive to focus your mental energy. *What are you passionate about?* That quality is what people are attracted to. It's okay to be in a learning cycle… everyone is! Place your interests and self-development *first* at this time. You are currently growing into a better version of yourself. The best is yet to come if you can allow yourself to grow at your own pace.

KNIGHT OF PENTACLES

The Knight of Pentacles can captivate you with his potential. He exudes an aura of self-confidence and all the external trappings of success. The problem is, the Knight of Pentacles hasn't quite *reached* his full potential yet. In a love reading, the Knight of Pentacles can represent a person who attracts you with his *possibilities*. However, the Knight of Pentacles is usually slow to grow. The Knight of Pentacles will often step on the brakes before making a big commitment. He also harbors a secret frustration for not quite attaining the success he aspires to. The appearance of the Knight of Pentacles will often advise you to keep your expectations in check. Beware of projecting your wants and desires on a person who is currently unable to deliver the total package. At his best, the Knight of Pentacles is attractive and charming, exudes confidence, and has great plans and aspirations for the future. At his worst, he can be stagnant and slow to grow, and he will constantly keep you waiting.

In a Love Reading
New Relationship
The Knight of Pentacles can symbolize a partnership where the reality does not always match hopes or expectations. This card can also represent a relationship where one person is constantly stepping on the brakes. You may have to decide if you are willing to repeatedly wait for this person to express their intentions for the future.

Long-Term Partnership
There may be a financial decision or a major commitment that affects the partnership and should be placed on hold as you learn more. See to the details and gather more information before rushing ahead. This card can also represent a partner who is at an impasse in their personal or professional life. This person will resist feeling rushed.

Intimacy
Intimately, the Knight of Pentacles can represent a very sensual lover. He feels at home in the realm of physical pleasure. The lovemaking may be so good it may affect your perspective about other aspects of the relationship that actually need work.

Seeking Romance
If you are single, this card can represent feeling frustrated with the slow pace of your love life. Although it may not look like it now, growth is happening beneath the surface. The knight's horse may have stopped because there is something important you are learning about *yourself* now. Don't be in a hurry to attain every dream. There is much to be enjoyed in the present.

Desires

The Knight of Pentacles can represent a desire for a person or relationship that seems just out of reach. The situation you are inquiring about has loads of potential. However, watch out for using their possibilities as substitutes for their present reality. This card can also signify desire for a person who feels stuck with their personal development.

Reversed

New Relationship

The Knight of Pentacles Reversed can represent a person who sends mixed signals. They may assure you they want a deeper connection and then not follow through. This card can also represent someone who struggles with making a commitment. If you are confused, focus on actions to reveal the truth more than the words you hear.

Long-Term Partnership

The Knight of Pentacles Reversed can represent a time when a relationship feels at an impasse. The horse can start moving when both partners truly understand one another. One partner may be feeling nitpicked, constantly interrogated, or unable to live up to the other person's exacting expectations. Respect needs to be reaffirmed for bonds to be repaired.

Intimacy

This card can symbolize a person who has difficulty articulating or asking for what they want. Waiting for issues to resolve themselves isn't a practical solution. The Knight of Pentacles Reversed is often anxious about opening up. Creating a safe space where secret desires can be heard and respected may bring both people closer together.

Seeking Romance

The Knight of Pentacles Reversed can represent times when life has been feeling barren for too long. This might be because you have been waiting for other people to make the decisions. You have the power to get events moving again, but first you must leave fruitless fields behind.

274 The Minor Arcana in Love

Desires

The Knight of Pentacles Reversed can represent a strong desire to get over something unpleasant and get things moving again. However, there are times when life progresses slowly for a reason. Healing takes time. This card encourages patience with a healing process that is progressing slowly, yet effectively.

What the Knight of Pentacles May Be Teaching You

The Knight of Pentacles may be teaching you to manage the expectations you place on yourself. If you are struggling with understanding your current situation, it could be because you are choosing to rationalize away something that needs to heal or grow within you. The Knight of Pentacles rules people and situations that are works in progress. Accept that your current life isn't meant to be a perfectly finished product. Something important needs time to strengthen, heal, and grow at the crossroads you find yourself at before you can progress. Although it may feel as if no growth is happening, this is an illusion. Be patient with yourself, your process, and the big picture your current situation is teaching you. The Knight of Pentacles reassures you that when the season is right, the heart will open.

QUEEN OF PENTACLES

The ever-patient Queen of Pentacles remains focused on the long game. She seeks relationships that promise long-term security, both emotionally and financially. An unrelenting workaholic, the Queen of Pentacles benefits from occasionally stopping to smell the roses. She revels in the earthy pleasures of the senses, and her anxiety is significantly reduced when she can indulge in the simpler delights of life. The Queen of Pentacles is ambitious yet modest, accommodating but firm. She is a master at balancing external obligations with the needs of her loved ones. The Queen of Pentacles is also self-motivated, requiring time away from her relationship to invest in her career, education, or personal projects. Because she expects so much from herself, she has extremely high standards when it comes to finding the right relationship partner. At her best, the Queen of Pentacles is prosperous, stable, dependable, and sensual. At her worst, she can be stubborn, anxious, materialistic, and an extreme perfectionist.

In a Love Reading
New Relationship
The rabbit that accompanies the Queen of Pentacles can signify an intense physical attraction accompanied by nervous anxiety. Be present in the moment rather than projecting too far into the future. The foundation you are establishing must be cultivated slowly and steadily, with time and patience. All is blossoming in the queen's garden.

Long-Term Partnership
The Queen of Pentacles governs long-term security and well-established relationships. Bonds are reaffirmed by investing in shared goals for the future. This couple can benefit from spending a bit more money on leisure and relaxation, making pleasure more of a priority. This card can also signify a couple that is patiently accumulating wealth over time.

Intimacy
The Queen of Pentacles encourages you to get out of your head and into your body. If you have been feeling uncomfortable in your own skin, this card can herald a time when you are healing issues centering on body image. If you are hoping to have a family, the arrival of the Queen of Pentacles can also signify fertility, especially when accompanied by the Empress.

Seeking Romance
If you are single, the Queen of Pentacles reassures you that all is growing in its appropriate time. Be patient with the process. Redirect your attention to where successes are occurring in your life. This is where the magic is pooling. The seeds have already been planted for your future happiness. Focus on the work before you as the garden steadily comes into full bloom.

Desires

The Queen of Pentacles can signify someone who desires a partner who is financially stable, patient, and practical. She is not swayed by passion alone, but rather by tangible results. This card can also signify a desire to raise standards in relationships so that they accurately reflect one's self-worth.

Reversed

New Relationship

The Queen of Pentacles Reversed can represent anxiety triggered by mixed signals. If you are receiving mixed signals, it's likely the person you are inquiring about isn't quite ready for a relationship. When a person wants to be with you, it will be made very clear by both their words *and actions*. Find a constructive outlet for anxiety instead of ruminating in it.

Long-Term Partnership

The Queen of Pentacles Reversed can signify a person who places too much emphasis on appearances. This card can represent a partner who is content with how things look rather than addressing their bottled-up feelings. This card can also signify an overly anxious or neurotic partner who would benefit from seeking support for their anxiety.

Intimacy

The Queen of Pentacles Reversed can signify a partner who is neglecting intimacy by prioritizing work or external duties over their relationship. Responsibilities have been compounding and the stress is intensifying. Although it is convenient to use external obligations as an excuse, this issue must be addressed so that it doesn't result in resentment.

Seeking Romance

When the Queen of Pentacles is reversed, her jittery rabbit rises to the top of the card. You may be experiencing unsubstantiated anxiety about your future possibilities for love or what a potential partner might be feeling about you. Seek out activities that reenforce your self-confidence. Know your worth.

Desires

If the Queen of Pentacles Reversed represents you, then she can represent a time when you feel impatient, anxious, or frustrated with an unfulfilled desire.

Upright or reversed, this queen reassures you that your best life will grow when you redirect your focus toward what is growing in your life. Return to what makes you smile, and the world will smile at you.

What the Queen of Pentacles May Be Teaching You

The Queen Pentacles symbolizes all works in progress, be they goals, relationships, or aspects of yourself. She may be teaching you to be patient with your life as it is now, and to grow from what this moment is teaching you about yourself. She reminds you to keep investing in your best life, and to apply the gentle wisdom of patience to your particular situation. Although the Queen of Pentacles is seated in a garden that is not yet in full bloom, she is at peace with the pace of its growth. In love, the Queen emphasizes the importance of self-investment and of planting the seeds that will make your own life flourish. She knows that everything has its season, and she doesn't push her plants to grow before they are ready. Let go of the tension you are carrying and inhale the peace of truly being *present*. There is no need to feel anxious about the future when the Queen of Pentacles appears. With love, time, and patience, all will flourish in its proper season.

KING OF PENTACLES

The King of Pentacles radiates success and stability. He is diligently committed to a life of financial wealth, security, and comfort. Of all the personality types in the tarot courts, the King of Pentacles is the most likely to see his ambitions materialize. In a love reading, the King of Pentacles represents a seasoned and experienced lover who knows his worth and what he has to offer. He is sober and repelled by immature games. He will be married to his career just as much as his eventual spouse. Because the King of Pentacles endeavors to secure the finest life, he will also strive to attain the best partner. Although the King of Pentacles may not be the most physically attractive or charismatic personality, he will unrelentingly pursue a partner *who is*. This king likes a challenge, and nothing but the best will do. At his best, the King of Pentacles is successful, secure in himself, protective, patient, and a capable leader in all his affairs. At his worst, he can be extremely stubborn, shallow, greedy, and ruthlessly ambitious.

In a Love Reading
New Relationship
The King of Pentacles is attracted to self-motivated people who are also going places. This card can also represent a union that is getting off to a secure start. As with all pentacles, take it slow. The King of Pentacles is looking for a mature relationship with someone who can not only envision their future success, but attain it.

Long-Term Partnership
The King of Pentacles represents a partner who is a leader, providing comfort and safety for those he loves. This king seems destined for personal or financial success; however, patience is needed. This card also governs long-term investments. If both partners are considering a shared investment in business or property, go for it!

Intimacy
The King of Pentacles can indicate that lovemaking may be taking a back seat to external responsibilities. Although this card signifies a person who is overworked, he is also very sensual. Invest more time or money into pleasurable pursuits. There is always more work waiting to be done … why not return to it in a good mood?

Seeking Romance
If you are single, the King of Pentacles could signify a time when you are focusing more on your long-term goals for success. Don't worry about the future. Love will follow your successful accomplishments. Don't settle for less and keep your standards high.

Desires

The King of Pentacles can signify a desire to become more financially stable before beginning a relationship or taking it to the next level. Although this card governs long-term security, it also requires a lot of patience. You might even find yourself waiting on a particular person. Establish practical perimeters around how long it's reasonable to wait.

Reversed

New Relationship

The King of Pentacles Reversed can represent a potential relationship partner you are increasingly impatient with. Perhaps you aren't receiving a commitment within a reasonable amount of time. Sometimes a situation will become increasingly uncomfortable to motivate you toward something better.

Long-Term Partnership

The King of Pentacles Reversed can represent a partner who is financially successful but emotionally unavailable. He might also be content with how things appear on the surface and not address the deeper needs of the relationship. This card can also signify an unhappy relationship that has come to feel more like a business.

Intimacy

The King of Pentacles Reversed can represent a relationship that has become too mundane. Although many practical concerns have been prioritized, they've come at the expense of intimacy. Try to diverge from daily routines. A little spicy spontaneity can go a long way.

Seeking Romance

If the King of Pentacles Reversed represents you, there is likely some unfinished emotional business that is thwarting your new beginning. You cannot rush through this process. Until you bring complete closure to the past, you may feel your new chapter is continuously out of reach.

Desires

The King of Pentacles Reversed can signify a desire to receive a concrete answer as to where a relationship is heading. Your patience may be wearing thin with a situation that has gone on too long without changing. Instead of hoping and waiting, you may need to be more assertive and ask for clarity. Insist on tangible results rather than effusive future promises.

What the King of Pentacles May Be Teaching You

Of all the court cards in the tarot, the King of Pentacles alone is entrusted with the armor of the Emperor *and* the scepter of the Empress. The Emperor's armor allows him to speak up for himself and to protect his boundaries. The scepter of the Empress enables him to patiently listen to the needs of others with nurturing compassion so that established bonds can thrive. The King of Pentacles may be teaching you to bring the lopsided archetype within your own psyche into balance. It's totally showing up in your relationships! Too much Emperor can make you too guarded, pushy, or angry. Too much Empress can make you overaccommodating, passive, and depleted. Energize the part of your psyche that feels diminished to restore inner balance. Speak up if you need to or be more assertive. If your heart has become too hardened, soften up, and be more receptive instead of continually trying to force your will on others. The King of Pentacles patiently tills the soil of his inner and outer environment so that only the sweetest grapes can grow.

WANDS IN A LOVE READING

The wands suit is associated with the element of fire. In a relationship reading, wands govern sex, passion, self-esteem, ambition, desire, and personal development. Often, wands reveal what is currently *growing* in your relationship life. In love, each individual has their own priorities, ambitions, and desires. Wands can quickly reveal if the aspirations between two people are conflicting or in alignment.

In many decks, wands are depicted as long staves that look like tree branches. Sprouting out of the tops of the wands are little leaves. Everything in nature must evolve; this includes relationships. For a partnership to grow strong, it must be allowed to develop organically, as it branches into new and unexpected directions. Wands can help you set healthy goals for yourself. Improving yourself most often has the added benefit of enhancing your relationships.

The appearance of many wands in a reading can indicate that events are speeding up and change is in the air. Wands bring the fire of transformation with them. Each card can show you how best to improve yourself and your partnership. Wands will advise you when to move forward boldly and when to hold your ground. They will also reveal if the issue you are in conflict about is a battle worth fighting. Whenever wands appear, know that what is being experienced is likely temporary. Fire is unsustainable unless more fuel is added. Wands can represent those times in our lives that force us to develop through trials by fire.

Above all else, wands illuminate your *presence* and what your personal energy is proclaiming to others. Wands expose whether you are embracing your light or are burying it beneath past heartaches and grievances. They can show how to increase your personal charisma to confidently stand out. In relationship readings, wands are often associated with self-esteem and self-respect. More than how you feel about another, wands reveal your level of confidence in yourself.

ACE OF WANDS

The Ace of Wands will signify a fiery spark that ignites a blaze of passion. In a love reading, it can refer to a new attraction or renewed excitement within an existing relationship. The Ace of Wands is associated with sexual chemistry, especially with a new love interest. All aces embody great *potential*; however, time will tell if the passion burns out or smolders into something more significant.

The Ace of Wands is also associated with magic. When this card appears, serendipitous events occur, chance meetings happen, and life begins to shimmer with renewed possibility. You may witness a wish that finally comes true or see an ordinary night transformed into an enchanted evening. However, the magic of the Ace of Wands *is only as good as your ability to act.* Magic is useless without initiative and passion. If your intuition nudges you toward a specific place, go to that place! If you see someone you are attracted to, confidently introduce yourself. If you act with passion, the mundane can be transformed into magic!

In a Love Reading
New Relationship
The appearance of the Ace of Wands signals the exciting potential of a new romance. Events are still developing, but you definitely share a passionate spark. Let this connection grow organically. The spark can be smothered by needy, obsessive energy. This card can also signify serendipitous romantic encounters in settings that foster creativity or entertainment.

Long-Term Partnership
You and your partner still have that magical spark even after much time together. You are likely passionate about the same interests. This card encourages you to rekindle passion by attending to intimacy, travel, or exciting mutual goals. Remain spontaneous to keep the spark ignited.

Intimacy
The Ace of Wands often represents a spark that can ignite a blaze of passion. A hot breeze is reinvigorating your sex life. Instead of hoping your partner will make the first move, be spontaneous and initiate. This card will always signify intense sexual chemistry. Break away from ruts and routines and make time for more play!

Seeking Romance
If you are single, the Ace of Wands inspires serendipitous meetings, new passion, and new relationships. Be bold. A fresh breeze of possibility is blowing. Follow where your inspiration seems to be leading you. Listen to your instincts and *act* on them.

Desires
The person you are inquiring about feels a burning desire for you. Passion often blazes brightest in the beginning. Time will tell if sexual chemistry develops into something even more substantive. This card can also signify a new infatuation. Instead of just imagining talking to the person you have a crush on, take a chance and do it!

Reversed
New Relationship
The connection with the person is intense and passionate. However, they may not be interested in a long-term relationship. Keep your expectations in check and observe the facts of where the union is heading before committing your whole heart to it. Although there is still *potential* for more, time will reveal if this can last.

Long-Term Partnership
You and your partner may feel inspired to start anew; however, you may also still feel stuck on a past issue that hasn't been fully resolved. This card motivates you to try a different approach to addressing whatever has plagued you in the past. Upright or reversed, the Ace of Wands still holds the potential for future happiness.

Intimacy
Upright or reversed, the Ace of Wands can signify a passionate relationship that blazes brightly. Be careful of confusing great sex with love. A fire that blazes too hot can burn out too soon. Try to exert a bit of self-control so that the flame fueling your love affair isn't extinguished too quickly. This card often points toward intense sexual chemistry.

Seeking Romance
The Ace of Wands Reversed encourages you to stop wishing and start doing. Don't passively hope for the new beginning you're considering. Make your move! Whether it is a new relationship, a new attitude, or a new passion you want to cultivate, it's time to make it happen. Be aware of the magical momentum that is propelling you toward your best life.

Desires

You may be feeling inspired to make a change that defies the status quo. Follow that desire! Your happiness is no longer found in the old ways. This is a magical time to reinvent yourself. Follow your bliss. When you act on your inspiration, magic starts to happen!

What the Ace of Wands May Be Teaching You

The Ace of Wands may be teaching you to stop looking backward. The Rider-Waite-Smith tarot depicts a hand emerging from a cloud, holding a shining wand. Like all wands, the Ace of Wands is illustrated as a tree branch with fresh, springy green leaves sprouting from it. This symbolizes that your life is sprouting into new and unpredictable directions. Rest assured; you are branching out into a new reality that will benefit your life … *if* you have the courage to follow your heart. An old, ruined castle crumbles in the distance. If you've been living in the castle of the past, it can feel stagnant and depressing. The Ace of Wands teaches that your happy new beginning won't be found in the old, ruined structures of your former life. You can never rekindle a better yesterday. It is gone. The future is still unmade. A fresh warm breeze is blowing through your life. Following its momentum can lead you to your heart's desire.

TWO OF WANDS

The Two of Wands symbolizes that aching longing to obtain your heart's desire. In a love reading, the Two of Wands can signify the mistaken belief that another person or the perfect relationship will magically grant you happiness. This insatiable *need* might compel you to seek love or wholeness in all the places they won't be found. However, the Two of Wands can also motivate positive change.

When this card appears, you may feel a nagging desire to improve your current life. The Two of Wands can motivate you to get in shape, elevate your career, travel, improve an existing relationship, or seek more compatible companionship. Nevertheless, the Two of Wands has an *insatiable* quality to it. No matter how many improvements are made or how much success is achieved, it still doesn't seem to soothe that aching need. The lesson of the Two of Wands is that the attainment of a relationship or objective will not miraculously satisfy an already unsatisfied heart. Be the love you seek.

In a Love Reading
New Relationship
The person you are inquiring about is restless and ambitious. They may long for unfettered freedom to explore all their options. The Two of Wands can also signify a love interest who is still striving to achieve their best life and may not be interested in settling down.

Long-Term Partnership
One or both partners may be feeling unfulfilled with their current life. No relationship can satisfy every interest. This card may encourage you to seek friendships or activities out in the world that your partner can't provide. The Two of Wands can also symbolize a partner who is consumed by their career goals or personal ambitions.

Intimacy
The Two of Wands can indicate that one or both partners is not feeling currently fulfilled with their sex life. Have the courage to initiate a compassionate conversation and be open to hearing what your partner feels they are missing. This card can also signify a desire to break out of a sexual slump.

Seeking Romance
If you are single, the Two of Wands beckons you to get out into the world. It's time to travel, strive for your next success, or grow. You may have forgotten that the world is a big place … far bigger than the bubble you've been residing in. Explore more of its possibilities. This card can also signify the opportunity for romance in a distant place.

Desires

The Two of Wands often represents someone who is restlessly searching outwardly for fulfillment. They may not feel settled with their current life and are still weighing their options for the future. This card can also represent a desire to find fulfillment outside of a relationship through a personal ambition or career goal.

Reversed
New Relationship

The Two of Wands Reversed can signify an obsession with a future that has not happened yet. It can represent a desire to control events that are still unfolding and that seem to resist your best efforts to shape them. Sometimes this card warns you not to project best-case or worst-case scenarios on a situation that is unfolding. Stay present to remain grounded in reality.

Long-Term Partnership

The Two of Wands Reversed can represent a relationship partner who isn't satisfied with their current life. They may harbor a feeling of malcontent with their present options. Upright or reversed, the Two of Wands can signify a person who is still striving to attain a sense of accomplishment. You may have to accept that you cannot make this person feel fulfilled.

Intimacy

It's time to look inward and ask yourself if you are truly happy. It may be time to seek wholeness in yourself before reaching out for someone or something to complete you. Exciting romantic opportunities may be happening in your world; however, you must remain anchored in your self-worth.

Seeking Romance

You may be worrying too much. If you are spending too much time in your head, it may be time to get out into the world again. If you are seeking inspiration, reach for the friends and places that make you smile. Leave your isolation. If you have been feeling anxious, scared, worried, or powerless, go out again and seek some fun!

Desires

You may feel blinded by an insatiable desire. Getting what you desire can feel good for a time, but if you gain it without feeling your own worth, the victory will soon feel hollow. You can't skip over the lesson of loving yourself by looking to another person to distract you from yourself.

What the Two of Wands May Be Teaching You

The Two of Wands may be teaching you that reaching for any external person or ideal to bring your life validation won't allow you to bypass the vital lesson of self-love and acceptance. The endless outward longing completely misses the point of what's been neglected within. In a love reading, the Two of Wands can symbolize not feeling satisfied with *yourself.* You may desire some amorphous person or thing "out there" to grant the peace in your heart that has been eluding you. Turn your gaze inward. Truly see and acknowledge your gifts. *Smile* at who you are and how far you've come without breaking. Too many people breeze through their successes on the endless marathon to get over the next mountaintop. All their lives they look to the horizon to attain a fabled magic spring that will finally make them feel at peace within themselves. The future does not hide your happiness. *It is already here, in this space with you.* Validate the gift that is you. Look inward and honor the light you find there. Watch how this simple magic can change the energy.

THREE OF WANDS

The message of the Three of Wands is clear; your future is *still* brimming with limitless possibility. The world remains wide open and waiting. Despite your worst fears, your life isn't irrevocably screwed up. It is a blank canvas. You have the power to paint whatever you aspire to see. In a love reading, the Three of Wands represents rebooting your relationship perspective. No matter what happened in the past, each new day offers the opportunity to reset your mindset. The Three of Wands can beckon you to distant locations, different company, or other exciting adventures. However, you must have the courage to leave your small pond of past limitations. Although this card promises possibility and potential, it does not guarantee a particular outcome. The Three of Wands pulls you out of the minutia of thinking you are somehow limited by the past. *The future is unmade and remains up to you.* Your present choices are where your power resides. Whether you choose to grow or stagnate is wholly up to you.

In a Love Reading
New Relationship
The future is full of possibility for your new partnership. The success of the relationship is left to the choices you currently make. You are both entering this union during a pivotal time of personal growth. This card can also signify exciting adventures abroad.

Long-Term Partnership
The Three of Wands beckons you and your partner to start making plans for the future. You are both feeling free to make decisions that are in alignment with your mutual desires. A major transition is happening, clearing the horizon for unlimited possibilities. This card can also signify excitement about an upcoming trip or change of residence.

Intimacy
The Three of Wands can indicate open-mindedness in matters of sex and sexuality. This may be a time to experiment and try new things. This card can also indicate a romantic passion that is kindled from afar. Although there may be distance, there is also intense chemistry.

Seeking Romance
If you are single, the Three of Wands reminds you that the world is wide open and waiting for you. You may need to leave the security of your deserted island to explore what is out there. Be open to the potential for happiness when this card appears. Your future remains a blank slate.

Desires

You are feeling a desire to broaden your horizons. If you have been repeatedly confronting the same issue over and over, it may be a sign that you are ready to grow. Leave any situation that keeps you feeling small, stuck, or limited. Open yourself to new people and possibilities. When the Three of Wands appears, the sky is the limit!

Reversed

New Relationship

The person you are asking about is flighty, scattered, or ungrounded. There is a sense that they do not stay tethered to anything for long. Where the wind blows, they follow. The Three of Wands Reversed can warn of impulsivity. Try not to project your desire for commitment on a person who is showing you they still want their freedom.

Long-Term Partnership

You and you partner may be worrying about your potential for future happiness or security. Don't borrow trouble. Often, this card will remind you to stop unhelpfully projecting your thoughts into the future and deal with what is right in front of you. You both may need a break from a stressful situation to regain perspective.

Intimacy

The Three of Wands Reversed can signify restlessness in an intimate relationship. One partner may be feeling unfulfilled or even bored. This card can also signify a partner who is close-minded or limited when it comes to sex.

Seeking Romance

This card can symbolize the feeling of being lost. The future is wide open and waiting, but its possibilities might feel overwhelming. This is a good problem to have! Start wherever you are. Take small steps instead of trying to overhaul your entire life at this time. With each step you take forward, the future will come into sharper focus. You are on your way.

Desires

The Three of Wands Reversed can remind you that *new* does not always translate into *better*. This card can leave you with a yearning desire to connect with new people, places, and opportunities. However, you may be failing to recognize the love that can be found in front of you.

What the Three of Wands May Be Teaching You

The Three of Wands may be teaching you that the future is still undetermined and full of possibility. Sometimes we find ourselves stuck in a rut. Life loses its vibrancy, excitement, and joy. Old cycles are rinsed and repeated, and our imagination feels diminished. This unfulfilled feeling is an important inflection point. The universe makes the current situation so untenable that it forces you to *grow*. The Three of Wands reminds you that there is a whole world waiting out there for you. It still holds adventure, opportunity, and wonderful people you haven't even had the pleasure of meeting yet. However, to fully take advantage of the future possibilities, you must leave the unfulfilling past behind. Never believe the lie that you are a victim, that you are stuck, that you have no choice in how your future plays out. Bad things can happen to us, without warning…but so can good things! Even the most devastating episodes in life will not last forever. Be wise enough to grow. Embark on your next adventure and leave the past behind.

FOUR OF WANDS

The Four of Wands represents celebrations, excitement, socializing, laughter, and, most importantly, *fun*! It encourages you to give yourself over to uninhibited joy. In a love reading, the Four of Wands can indicate exhilarating social events, dating, parties, mingling, dancing, and music. Although the Four of Wands can indicate an easygoing chemistry between you and another, it lacks expectations for the future. Whether a relationship is old or new, this card signifies play, entertainment, and enjoyment. The Four of Wands also represents celebrations and rites of passage. This card could appear when a relationship is reaching an anniversary or a milestone. The Four of Wands breaks up the monotony of life with pleasure and enjoyment. It calls you toward the joyful spaces where you can let your hair down. If you've been getting too serious, the Four of Wands urges you to abandon monotony and reclaim your sense of fun. It's time to leave inhibitions behind and be seen!

In a Love Reading
New Relationship
The Four of Wands can signify the courtship phase of a relationship. If you are just beginning to see someone, don't skip over this part! Let go of expectations and plans for the future. Be pursued. Enjoy the flirtation and fun. Dance, laugh, kiss, eat great food, and enjoy the moment! Save the seriousness, gravity, and heavy expectations for a later day.

Long-Term Partnership
You both maintain a great deal of lighthearted fun in your relationship. The Four of Wands could signify an upcoming celebration or social event. Make sure that you are marking your important rites of passage. As a couple, you may also want to give yourselves over to pleasurable pursuits or socializing. This card is also associated with hosting or attending parties.

Intimacy
The Four of Wands signifies a playful attitude toward sex. Encourage your partner to release their inhibitions. Heavy expectations or too much pressure will kill the mood for this person. They prefer spontaneity, mischief, and fun.

Seeking Romance
If you are single, the Four of Wands encourages you to socialize. If you are invited to a wedding, event, or party... go! When you are out socially, abandon your self-consciousness. Seek out company that allows you to feel safe being yourself. Go where you can laugh, smile, flirt, and play.

Desires

The Four of Wands reflects a desire to give yourself over to joy. It's time to allow yourself to feel happy again. You may have been trying too hard to do all the correct things to attract the love you seek. However, love is desperately attracted to joy. If you can reclaim your joy, you can lure love's magic toward you.

Reversed

New Relationship

This card can signify a fair-weather friendship or relationship. When times are good, all goes well. There is laughter, joy, and fun. However, when a challenge arises, one partner lacks the maturity to face the challenge. This can lead to confusion since the connection feels so vibrant when all is going well. This card can also represent a person who struggles with escapism.

Long-Term Partnership

The Four of Wands Reversed can indicate a major difference of maturity levels between two people. One partner may act irresponsibly while the other remains the adult in the room. This card can also signify a toxic social environment that is negatively impacting one or both partners.

Intimacy

The Four of Wands Reversed can also signify immature relationship drama. One or both people may be acting out immaturely and abandoning all self-control. There is an unaccountable quality to this card, where a person acts more on impulse and less on reason. The Four of Wands Reversed will likely promise more drama. Do what you know is right to grow.

Seeking Romance

The Four of Wands Reversed can warn you of the current company you are keeping. Do the people you socialize with make you feel drained, depleted, or depressed after your encounters? It's time to gravitate toward an environment that feels more supportive. Letting go of toxic people is never a mistake.

Desires

When the Four of Wands appears reversed, you may be experiencing a desire to change your social scene. The same old places and people no longer bring you the joy they once did. This is totally normal and signifies you are growing. The qualities you are attracted to in a partner are also evolving. It's time to evolve socially.

What the Four of Wands May Be Teaching You

The Four of Wands beckons you toward gaiety, laughter, music, and the abandonment of stress. Release your addiction to obsessing about what might happen later. The Four of Wands motivates you to celebrate the moment. It frees you from toxic conformity that makes you stuff down your authentic joy to seem more acceptable to others. The Four of Wands urges you to abandon what you *should act like* or who you *should be* to attract the "right people." Joy is all you need. Whether you are dancing alone or with a partner, if *you* feel the music, that's what counts. In your quest to find love, this card encourages you to find your own joy first. Much like the Fool, the Four of Wands asks you to abandon the anxieties of other people's reactions that prevent you from connecting with others. When the Four of Wands appears, it's time to take a chance on having some fun!

FIVE OF WANDS

The Five of Wands is associated with conflict, arguments, competition, and reactivity. Every relationship experiences conflict at some point. How the conflict is resolved will usually reveal the maturity level of both partners. The Five of Wands is a fiery card that can swiftly activate the ego. This card can warn you not to sink to lower vibrations to resolve your conflicts. Letting your ego take the lead in a dispute is like pouring gasoline on an already raging fire. In a love reading, the Five of Wands triggers raw, prideful emotions that a person will rush to defend. More often, this card refers to simmering resentments, verbal swipes, or other bad vibes that can accumulate in a relationship over time. The Five of Wands can also highlight differences in maturity levels, emotional skill sets, or relationship values. However, this card does not always refer to conflict with others. More often than not, the Five of Wands can signify an *inner conflict* between your rationality and competing desires.

In a Love Reading
New Relationship
The Five of Wands can warn of childishness, immaturity, or incompatible values in a new relationship. Just because you prize certain qualities or expectations, that does not promise the person you feel strongly about feels the same. This card can also signify an internal conflict about whether you should proceed with this person. Let your maturity lead the way.

Long-Term Partnership
The Five of Wands can highlight a simmering conflict that habitually boils over. This can come in the form of bickering, squabbling, or scorekeeping insignificant infractions. The point trying to be proved has nothing to do with the underlying source of tension.

Intimacy
The Five of Wands can signify the neutralization of anger through passionate sex. Ares, the god of raging conflict, was often tamed by his lover Aphrodite, goddess of love, after retreating to their golden couch. Renewing the bonds of love through passion can de-escalate simmering resentments or conflict.

Seeking Romance
If you are single, you may still be feeling conflicted about a past love. Although you may feel hurt and angry, there is a strange attraction to revisiting the past. Before attempting a new relationship, seek closure for unresolved feelings first. This card can also signify unresolved anger that is frustrating your search for love.

Desires

The Five of Wands can represent conflicting desires in a relationship. One partner wants one thing, while the other prioritizes something completely different. Although you may want to project your own expectations on this person, you may be disregarding that they simply don't want the same things.

Reversed
New Relationship

The Five of Wands Reversed can reveal a relationship dynamic where one partner feels they are in competition with the other. The competitive person may try to diminish their companion to feed their own weakened ego. This sort of behavior only reveals their underdevelopment. This card can also signify a new partner with an easily triggered, volatile temper.

Long-Term Partnership

The Five of Wands Reversed can signify a partner who is extremely insecure. They may act petty or behave thoughtlessly. This card can also represent a nitpicker who always insists on being right. They may use passive-aggressive behavior and guilt to get their way. Avoid engaging in any toxicity that perpetuates conflict.

Intimacy

The Five of Wands Reversed can represent the breakdown of intimacy. However, it takes two to tango. It isn't easy to admit our own shortcomings, especially when it's so easy to point at what the other person hasn't done. This card can also highlight *your own* part to play in the struggles that seem to revisit your relationship like clockwork.

Seeking Romance

The Five of Wands Reversed can appear if you are excessively comparing yourself to others. Other people's appearance, successes, relationship status, or accomplishments… none of these things have anything to do with you. Keep your eyes on your own paper. You cannot shine if your life is lived in another's shadow.

Desires
This card signifies a desire to move on from a person who is unwilling to take responsibility and resolve their own issues. Engaging in perpetual conflict ensures no one wins. Be a class act and maintain your dignity. The Five of Wands Reversed can also advise you to stop rushing to defend your ego.

What the Five of Wands May Be Teaching You
The Five of Wands highlights conflict, competition, and struggle. The friction this card refers to could be manifesting in your relationships or could be happening within. The Five of Wands teaches that your anger could be a mask for an even deeper fear: Fear of being alone. Fear of humiliation. Fear of being abandoned. Fear of being hurt again. The ego will always rush to the defense of the raw spots that expose our hidden fear. The lesson of the Five of Wands is to face our own fears with self-love and compassion before rushing to defend them. Fear is like an insecure child who just wants to hear *everything will be okay*. Allow the wise adult who resides within to comfort the childish fears that habitually lash out. If you give the hurting place within the love it needs, you will not need to struggle for another person to take care of it. Allow your maturity and wisdom to take the lead, and *everything truly will be okay*.

SIX OF WANDS

The Six of Wands represents confidence, dignity, and personal excellence. In a love reading, this card inspires you to rise above anything that is eroding your self-esteem. When seeking love, there is nothing more appealing than someone who knows their own worth and doesn't *need* a relationship partner to appease their insecurity. Sometimes this card comes as a gentle warning not to place another person on a pedestal at the expense of yourself. The Six of Wands encourages you to fully embrace what makes you shine. It is nearly impossible to be stuck in a toxic relationship dynamic when you are aligned with your inherent self-worth. Like all cards in the wands suit, the Six of Wands implies growing pains on the journey toward achieving self-confidence. You may be confronting a situation that continually challenges you to raise your standards. When you truly know your self-worth, you will attract the right people and repel those who aren't on your level. This card can also encourage you to attract more attention.

In a Love Reading
New Relationship
The Six of Wands can signify an engaging and charismatic partner. Your new love interest shines brightly and is likely attracted to the confidence you also exhibit. Avoid acting overly apologetic with this person. Lack of confidence is a huge turnoff. Occasionally take the initiative and make the first move. Be radiant, dazzle, and shine.

Long-Term Partnership
The Six of Wands can signify an extroverted partner who likes to take the spotlight. This relationship works well because the other partner doesn't mind playing the role of the supporting cast. In many ways, this relationship is on full display. Ensure that there is occasionally time for just the two of you.

Intimacy
Intimately, the Six of Wands represents a partner who is sexy and knows it! This card challenges you to be more confident and embrace what makes you exciting and attractive. The lover you are inquiring about is easily turned on by flattery, compliments, and ego stroking. Be vocal.

Seeking Romance
If you are single, the Six of Wands encourages you to keep increasing your self-esteem by engaging in whatever makes you shine. If you step into the spotlight, the arrow of love will find its mark. This card can also signify better relationship opportunities after the achievement of a personal accomplishment.

Desires
The Six of Wands can symbolize a desire to attract attention and shine. It's time to restore your confidence and self-esteem. If your energy has been too self-effacing or diminished, then you are making yourself appear small. Stop worrying how others will react and *be radiant*.

Reversed
New Relationship
The Six of Wands Reversed can appear if you are trying too hard to shine. Watch out for overly adapting yourself to what *you think* your new love interest wants to see. This card can also warn of a relationship dynamic where your whole self-confidence hinges on another person's approval.

Long-Term Partnership
One partner in this relationship struggles with being clear and assertive. They may avoid saying no to avoid hurting the other's feelings. If you are trying to reach this person and not getting a response, they may be struggling to communicate something they are afraid you won't want to hear.

Intimacy
The person you are asking about feels most at ease when you are confident in yourself. Try not to be obsessively worried about doing or saying the wrong thing. Upright or reversed, the Six of Wands encourages you to feel confident in yourself before connecting intimately with another.

Seeking Romance
When the Six of Wands appears reversed, you may be experiencing an erosion of your self-confidence. A difficult breakup, habitual disappointments, or some other form of letdown has taken the wind out of your sails. No matter where you find yourself, you can always take small steps to restore your confidence. Engage in activities that set your sprit free!

Desires
The Six of Wands Reversed can represent feeling depleted or depressed, even after securing a major success. What may be missing is a *goal* to strive for. If you are feeling lost, find a goal that will support the development of your confidence. The fulfillment of a desire (that isn't a person) will bolster your spirits.

What the Six of Wands May Be Teaching You

The Six of Wands may be teaching you to restore your dignity and self-esteem. Sometimes this card will appear if you are trapped in the illusion that another person is more special, important, or significant than you are—that somehow you *need them* to validate you. Existing in the shadow of another person's approval cheats you out of living your best life. This shadow covers a fear that if this person leaves, your life's value will fly away with them. This anxiety keeps so many people stuck in relationships that perpetually deplete and disempower them. The Six of Wands can highlight if you are desperately seeking your light to be reflected in the eyes of another, at the expense of yourself. Remember that you are continuously telegraphing to others what you think of yourself. It's time to hold your head high and command the respect you desire by embodying it. Know your worth.

SEVEN OF WANDS

The Seven of Wands symbolizes taking the high road and standing up for what you know is right. This card teaches the importance of maintaining your highest values. The high road isn't always easy to take. Sometimes this card requires you to create healthy boundaries so you don't continue to get hurt. This card might also encourage you to walk away from a situation you've set your hopes on because in truth, it's become toxic. In a love reading, the Seven of Wands governs your non-negotiables. These are the core values you hold that cannot be compromised. An example of core values could include requiring honesty in your relationships, or not allowing yourself to be habitually disrespected, abused, or disregarded. If your standards have slowly eroded by holding on to a situation that is no longer healthy, this card urges you to stand up for yourself. The Seven of Wands governs the tough calls you must make to ensure that your life is on course for future happiness.

In a Love Reading
New Relationship
The Seven of Wands advises you to know your values when walking into a new partnership. Follow your highest ideals and embody them. This will show your new partner how to treat you. Don't compromise your standards to please people. Stand in your integrity.

Long-Term Partnership
The Seven of Wands can compel you to communicate about an elephant in the room. You are likely avoiding a difficult discussion to keep the peace, but remaining silent is only depleting your power. Be clear and honest about an issue that must be addressed. If the issue can be talked about and confronted honestly, it can be resolved.

Intimacy
The Rider-Waite-Smith tarot depicts a man wearing two different shoes. The mismatched shoes can represent differing approaches to intimacy that may be leading to conflict. This card can also represent a partner who is overly defensive and difficult to get close to.

Seeking Romance
If you are single, the Seven of Wands encourages you to maintain your standards, even if that means you aren't in a relationship for now. The right person will be worth the wait. You could easily attain a second-best relationship now, but it wouldn't fulfill your needs. Stay strong and preserve your values.

Desires

The Seven of Wands can represent a desire to stand up for yourself. If you have been meekly acquiescing to a situation that is not respecting your standards or boundaries, it is time to take the high road. Walk your talk, even if it requires you to walk away. Stand up for the truth and for what you know is right.

Reversed
New Relationship

The person you are asking about is hard to get close to. They may also be erecting barriers because they aren't ready to connect. This person doesn't follow a type and is likely very sensitive. If you want to get close to them, you may have to wait for them to come to you.

Long-Term Partnership

The Seven of Wands Reversed can represent a relationship conflict that is at an impasse. Both partners are dug into their positions. You may need to ask yourself if your viewpoint is aligned with your values or if you are just being stubborn. If your core values aren't being violated, then don't sweat the small stuff, and resolve the conflict.

Intimacy

Intimately, the Seven of Wands Reversed can represent a partner who is extremely defensive. When it comes to intimacy, you will have to respect this person's boundaries and be patient. This card can also signify escalating tension around an unmet sexual desire.

Seeking Romance

The Seven of Wands Reversed could suggest that you are currently difficult to get close to. Allow yourself to be more open to others, especially if you desire a connection. If a relationship is what you desire most, you must lower any unnecessary defenses and take a risk.

Desires

When the Seven of Wands appears reversed, the message is to stop pushing so hard to make your life be what you want. If you approach each day gearing up for battle and anticipating conflict, you are setting yourself up for a struggle.

When reversed, this card can encourage you to let go of the tension and allow your desires to manifest naturally.

What the Seven of Wands May Be Teaching You

The Seven of Wands could be teaching you to align with your integrity. Whatever struggle you have been engaged in, internally or externally, has been keeping you from connecting with your highest values. The Seven of Wands calls you home, to where truth dwells in harmony with your highest aspirations. If you have been lingering in the valleys of shadow for too long, you may have forgotten how to listen for your spirit's gentle voice of guidance. You may need to stop looking to others for direction and find the way forward for yourself. The Seven of Wands appears when it's time to ascend. Choose to take the high road in your relationships. Don't engage in a battle with reality. Allow the changes that are occurring. A soaring breeze is propelling you toward higher ground. Take a stand for the truth and for what is right.

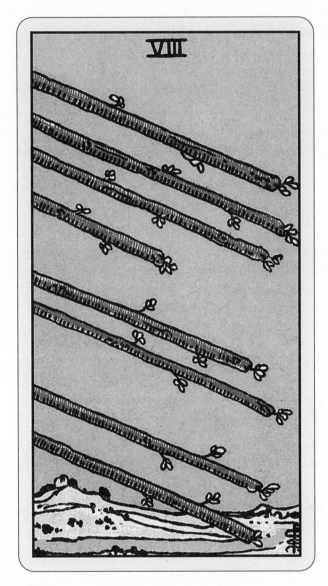

EIGHT OF WANDS

The Eight of Wands is associated with activity, progress, movement, and messages. When this card appears, events will start to speed up. Answers to questions become available. Stuck issues will become unstuck. If you have been waiting to receive communication from someone special or you've been in a romantic lull, this card foretells forward progress. This card can also refer to communication over the internet. If you've been seeking to connect with someone special, you just might find that opportunity in an unconventional or online setting. The appearance of the Eight of Wands often signifies increased communication through social media, text message, or good old-fashioned phone calls. This card can also signify long-distance relationships or a deep connection with someone who isn't necessarily within close physical proximity. The Eight of Wands advises you to not allow anxiety to impede your progress and take action. Whenever this card appears, expect news, answers, and excitement!

In a Love Reading
New Relationship
The Eight of Wands can represent an exciting, fast-progressing partnership. The person you are inquiring about is thrilling, offering endless opportunities for exciting experiences. Your ability to communicate is unmatched. Expect engaging conversations, shared interests, and ideas. This card can also represent a close connection to someone who is separated by a long distance.

Long-Term Partnership
The Eight of Wands can signify sweeping changes that are providing new opportunities for either you or your partner. This card can also represent increased passion and communication after a period of quiet and distance. A fresh breeze of exciting momentum is blowing through your life together. When this card appears, go with the flow.

Intimacy
The Eight of Wands can represent flirtation through notes, texts, or written messages. This card may indicate a physical distance that is preventing you from connecting with another. No matter what the obstacle is, the attraction and excitement are undiminished. If you are looking to spice up your sex life, flirtatious notes and messages could do the trick.

Seeking Romance
If you are single, this card encourages you to act instead of overthinking. Avoid analysis paralysis. If you see someone you like, say something. Socializing online can also give you a safe opportunity to put your toe in the water before taking the deep dive with dating.

Desires
The Eight of Wands represents the desire to get moving, express yourself, and take action. If you are feeling excitement building toward a specific place or person, follow the energy's lead. Participate in all that life is offering you now. Increased momentum is urging you forward.

Reversed
New Relationship
When reversed, the Eight of Wands can represent inconsistent communication. You might experience a flurry of messages one week, only to receive silence the next. Upright or reversed, there is an impersonal quality to this card. The inconsistency you are experiencing is not because of something you did. Don't personalize another person's issues.

Long-Term Partnership
Your partner is experiencing increased demands on their time and energy. They may be spread too thin. Instead of taking their distance personally, understand that there are too many irons on the fire at this time. This card can also represent a partner who is scattered or forgetful about issues you find important.

Intimacy
Often, this card advises that you increase your physical activity. Get moving, exercise, socialize, and find ways to express yourself without being trapped in neuroticism. Whether your personal energy feels good or bad, it's time to release it through movement. This card can also advise that bottled up tension or anxiety may find beneficial release through sex.

Seeking Romance
The Eight of Wands Reversed can represent a heightened sense of anxiety. It's time to keep calm and carry on. There is likely a situation that is triggering some nervous tension and interfering with your ability to think clearly about your current prospects. You will connect with others more effectively if you restore inner calm.

Desires

The Eight of Wands Reversed signifies feeling unfocused. This scattered energy may be interfering with achieving your desires. Get organized in your thinking, and the achievement of your desires will again be within your reach.

What the Eight of Wands May Be Teaching You

The Eight of Wands could be teaching you to identify what feels stuck in your life to get it moving again. If you've been dwelling on the past or are anxious about the future, it's time to find a healthy outlet for your anxiety. Sometimes, physical activity or working toward a goal is all that's needed to get the energy moving again. Whatever you do, the Eight of Wands motivates you to *try*. Add the extra effort. Create change instead of waiting for it to find you. Like attracts like. If you want life to bring you more exciting opportunities, be more exciting! The impersonal quality that accompanies the Eight of Wands could be telling you to proceed without personalizing your current situation or overthinking. It's time to find a constructive release for any remaining apprehension within your head and heart. Set your intentions toward improving your situation, and then act! You can hit your mark, but you must first aim at your target.

NINE OF WANDS

The Nine of Wands encourages *healthy boundaries*. This card can appear when you need to take a stand for yourself, especially if you have been habitually dishonored or disrespected by someone who claims to care for you. Although establishing boundaries may trigger a fear of losing love, they are necessary to break abusive cycles. The Nine of Wands can also represent a person with a chip on their shoulder. Nursing old grudges and resentments may cause them to avoid getting close to others. Although the lessons illuminated by this card can be painful, the Nine of Wands also grants invaluable wisdom and resiliency. The Rider-Waite-Smith deck depicts an individual with a bandage on his head. In a love reading, this can represent old wounds that one must learn from. Learning from past pain is the first step in ensuring that it is not repeated. The Nine of Wands reminds you that *you show others how to treat you, by how you treat yourself.*

In a Love Reading
New Relationship
The Nine of Wands can symbolize a new love interest who carries emotional baggage from the past. This person is likely recovering from an emotional injury that shattered their old reality. It may be difficult to truly get close to this person if they haven't made peace with a past heartbreak or betrayal. It will take time to gain their trust.

Long-Term Partnership
The Nine of Wands can symbolize old grievances that have accumulated over time in a relationship. One partner may use passive-aggressive communication to mask hidden pain. Open a dialogue without rushing to defend your own vulnerabilities. This card can also signify a resilient relationship that has weathered many storms.

Intimacy
Intimately, the Nine of Wands can symbolize someone who harbors resentment about a sexual issue. One partner may be feeling undesirable, embarrassed, or rejected in some way. Understanding and addressing their underlying wound can facilitate healing. Although this person may defensively push away, they really want to feel heard.

Seeking Romance
If you are single, the Nine of Wands can indicate that you are still healing from an old relationship wound. You may be giving off the impression that you are uninterested or that people should keep their distance. Watch out for coming across as jaded, unhappy, or overly sarcastic. Toxic vibes are love repellent.

Desires

The Nine of Wands represents a desire to protect your vulnerabilities. Learn from what has hurt you in the past and take steps to ensure that it isn't repeated. This card also warns of emotionally shutting down. Place yourself in environments that support your strength and resilience. Seek support from those who have proven to have your back.

Reversed
New Relationship

When reversed, the Nine of Wands can represent a person who seems to have a huge chip on their shoulder. Although a painful experience from the past can explain why this person is disgruntled, it does not give them license to be unkind or rude. This card can also represent a person who habitually repeats an unhealthy relationship dynamic.

Long-Term Partnership

Sometimes this card is associated with passive-aggressive behavior that is masking one partner's annoyance or anger. Try to lower the temperature and have an honest conversation without blaming or attacking. A long-standing resentment can be resolved, but only if an honest and compassionate dialogue is initiated.

Intimacy

This card can signify a sexual attraction to someone who repeatedly hurts you. You must stay strong and maintain your boundaries, even if you have let them falter in the past. Be selective about who you are most vulnerable with. Don't place yourself in a situation that will compromise you. Know your weaknesses and be prepared.

Seeking Romance

The Nine of Wands can highlight unexpressed anger or resentment that is coloring your current attitude. Don't allow past grievances to harden your heart toward future possibilities. You've been through the worst of it, and now it is time to create some optimism.

Desires

The Nine of Wands Reversed can represent a desire to overcome grievance. It's time to stop nursing your anger about an unfair past relationship. No more whining, making excuses, or blaming others for your present conditions. You aren't being fair to yourself if you keep clinging to the past. Give yourself some resilient tough love. Get back up and dust yourself off.

What the Nine of Wands May Be Teaching You

The Nine of Wands may be teaching you to bounce back from the adversities life inevitably sends. No one gets a free pass in love, and eventually we will all confront our own portion of unfair treatment, disappointment, heartache, or grief. This card carries a theme of resiliency despite the hardships. The Nine of Wands can alert you if your heart has become so hardened by disappointment that it's difficult to open. You may be receiving a gentle reminder to allow yourself to connect to new people and opportunities, even if past people and past circumstances have left a painful mark. Take time to feel the hurt, anger, unfairness, and betrayal, but know that eventually they must be set aside. The more you exist in your grievances, the more you push away the potential for happiness. For your heart to feel renewed, it must allow the wisdom of the past to remain, while also letting go of the hurt. Perhaps it is time to seek support with issues that crave resolution. Your heart is on the mend. You will persevere if you don't lose hope.

TEN OF WANDS

The Ten of Wands is associated with feeling burdened. In a love reading, it can represent carrying the full weight of a relationship's hardships or disappointments on your shoulders. This card can represent a period when life simply isn't easy. At its core, the Ten of Wands is associated with service. Sometimes in relationships you will be required to help bear the burdens of the person you love.

Not every day is laden with cooing doves and glittering rainbows. Relationships take work and effort. However, this card can also provide a wake-up call if you are habitually shouldering the burdens of another person who isn't taking responsibility for their own actions or for the health of the relationship. The Ten of Wands can also represent trudging through a barren time in your relationship life when love seems absent. The hidden positive message of the Ten of Wands is that you are entering the final phase of struggle before the harvest. Take heart and remain determined. You are just about to cross the finish line.

In a Love Reading
New Relationship
The Ten of Wands can indicate a connection that seems beset with struggles and challenges from the beginning. One or both partners may be carrying a lot of baggage. Other cards will reveal if those challenges are something that can be overcome or if they will prevent the partnership from progressing.

Long-Term Partnership
The Ten of Wands can represent a challenging time when your partner needs support. You both feel tested by external demands, and it is a struggle to find quality time for one another. This card can also represent a partner who struggles with chronic pain or tension. Hang in there. You will both persevere.

Intimacy
Intimately, the Ten of Wands can represent extraneous burdens that are placing a damper on your sex life. This card can symbolize exhaustion from too many external demands that are interfering with your ability to connect. You might have to consciously partition time for romance and pleasure. This card can also signify a serious need for a vacation.

Seeking Romance
If you are single, the Ten of Wands can symbolize a period of frustration when it feels like you are trudging through an endless romantic wasteland. This is an illusion. The work you are doing on yourself right now will lead you toward your harvest. The investments in self-improvement will pay off. Take heart; happier times are on the horizon.

Desires
Although the Ten of Wands requires a heavy lift, it can also represent an approaching harvest you've been striving toward. The message of this card is to keep going toward your desire. You are on the last lap of this challenge. Focus on resolving your present challenge. Don't give up.

Reversed
New Relationship
You may be doing all the work at the beginning of this partnership. You cannot be the only one investing effort. It's time to stop people pleasing at the expense of yourself. If your love interest is not prioritizing the relationship equally, it may be time to move on.

Long-Term Partnership
The relationship burdens you've been carrying in your heart have become too heavy. They are beginning to weigh down your spirit and are stifling your ability to connect with your partner. It's time to remember what fun felt like. Inviting in more lighthearted activities can help turn the tide for you both. Take a break!

Intimacy
The person you are asking about is still carrying heavy burdens from a painful past or a previous relationship. Try not to push against or ignore the reality of their situation. Their last chapter must be completed before they can open their heart. Time is needed for closure. This card encourages patience when it comes to intimacy.

Seeking Romance
When the Ten of Wands appears reversed, it can indicate that it's time to take a break from trying too hard. If you've been struggling with a relationship that does not bear fruit, it's time to invest your energy elsewhere. You may need to redirect your attention to what is showing evidence for growth now, instead of struggling for a future harvest.

Desires
The Ten of Wands can also appear reversed when you've begun the process of crossing the finish line. It's time to commit to doing the work on yourself, even if the path doesn't currently feel easy. If you endure this temporary discomfort,

you will eventually attain your heart's desire. Do the right thing for yourself, even when it's difficult.

What the Ten of Wands May Be Teaching You

The Ten of Wands may be teaching you that you've been carrying too many burdens. If you've been accustomed to bearing heavy feelings, you may have become numb to how crushing these feelings can be. The determined figure on the Ten of Wands is focusing on his goal without considering the punishing weight on his shoulders. The Ten of Wands teaches you to be conscious of the ordeal you are putting your heart and spirit through at this time. Working to attain a happy life is important. However, when the work replaces all the joy in your life, it's not sustainable. The Ten of Wands gently asks you to be kinder to yourself and let your spirit rest from its burdens. You can pick them up again in the future, but for now it's time to lighten the emotional load. One way to relieve emotions is to have a good cry. Tears do help. They release toxins from the body and can alleviate the heaviness of the storm clouds on your heart. Be kinder to what your heart is experiencing. You are the one who must be supported now. Allow spirit to take the burdens from your shoulders that have become too heavy to bear.

PAGE OF WANDS

The Page of Wands has many talents. He has an irrepressible optimism and aspires to do great things. People are magnetically drawn to his unpretentious warmth and charisma. Although he is funny, likable, and charming, he can also be evasive when it comes to serious commitments. In love, the Page of Wands is repelled by overbearing types who want to smother him. He has a notoriously

short attention span and can be very impulsive. This often results in him promising more than he can reasonably offer. He is famous for sending mixed signals
and might even play games. His evasiveness doesn't stem from him being a bad
person; he just wants to remain likable and tries to avoid directly disappointing
people. The Page of Wands can prove to be a passionate lover but still requires
time and space to grow and mature. At his best, the Page of Wands is passionate, talented, humorous, enthusiastic, attractive, and engaging. At his worst, he
is immature, restless, procrastinating, and indirect, and he avoids commitment.

In a Love Reading
New Relationship
The Page of Wands symbolizes a lighthearted beginning. Your new partner is
enthusiastic and never boring. He gets along best with a person who isn't overly
serious and has a good sense of humor. At this stage, he is probably not ready
for a serious commitment. Try not to be smothering, for you can never cage
this page.

Long-Term Partnership
The Page of Wands signifies a relationship that flourishes when it is fun. This
partnership requires enjoyment, play, adventure, and travel to thrive. You both
also benefit from an eclectic social circle. One partner may require a more active
social life that can create conflict if the other partner is prone to possessiveness
or jealousy.

Intimacy
The Page of Wands wants sex to feel liberating. He is wonderful when he knows
his partner is happy but struggles when there is a serious issue to overcome. If
he feels intimacy is becoming too emotionally ensnaring, he'll want to bolt.

Seeking Romance
If you are single, the Page of Wands can signify a growing process. You are
likely undergoing a major developmental stage in your personal evolution. It
may feel difficult to find a serious relationship at this time, but for good reason.
Although it may not feel like it, the best days are yet to come. Don't lose your
optimism about the future.

Desires
The Page of Wands desires *freedom*. Much like the Fool, he is fun, open-minded, and ready to try new things. His eye darts to the newest shiny object as he flies toward independence. He is resistant to commitments, both consciously and unconsciously. This page also desires fun and benefits from a partner who is equally carefree.

Reversed
New Relationship
The Page of Wands Reversed can represent a person who caves into pressure of stronger personalities around him. Although he has a potential for leadership one day, he still comes across as a follower. His self-esteem requires the approval of those he looks up to or admires. This tends to lead to bad decisions. The Page of Wands Reversed remains a bit "green."

Long-Term Partnership
The Page of Wands Reversed can signify a partner who has a bit of a temper. Although he is quick to anger, he is also swift to forgive and forget. He will often need space to cool down when he is upset. If you are engaged in a conflict with him, give him some time to simmer down. This card can also represent an overly impulsive partner who acts now and thinks later.

Intimacy
When the Page of Wands is reversed, he will ferociously guard his freedom and resist being stifled by another person's needs. The more pressure applied to him, the more he will resist. The best advice is to let him come to you. The Page of Wands can also represent someone who rushes into sex without considering the other person's feelings.

Seeking Romance
If the Page of Wands Reversed represents you, he provides a gentle warning to not rush into relationships or commitments without thinking. Slow down, take a deep breath, and think. This card urges you to work through your present issue instead of using another person to avoid it. If you courageously face what needs to grow, you will overcome your present blockage.

Desires

The Page of Wands Reversed can represent an impulsive desire for a person who has proven they are not ready for a serious relationship. Often this page can signify an addiction to drama. This card may advise you to tame your passion and reactions and exercise self-control and patience. Take a deep breath and think before making your next move.

What the Page of Wands May Be Teaching You

The Page of Wands may be teaching you how to look upon what is currently growing in your life with optimism, rather than as evidence for how life still hasn't measured up. Wands in the tarot appear as tree branches. They are still sprouting leaves and are unpredictably twining toward the light of the sun. The Page of Wands's growth process is free from shame, negativity, and baggage. His good-humored nature takes his personal development in stride, assuring that his goals will be realized before he knows it. He gives himself time and space to grow. When the Page of Wands appears, you may be feeling like you don't have it all yet. You are likely striving toward a happier version of your life that doesn't quite resemble what you are experiencing now. The Page of Wands encourages you to take heart. Don't allow fleeting challenges to destroy your optimism. Eventually, your present growing process will be complete, and an exciting new beginning will leave you wondering why you felt so troubled before.

KNIGHT OF WANDS

The Knight of Wands seizes each day with a spirit of adventure and vitality. He might leave you breathless after your first passionate encounter. The Knight of Wands loves physical activity, movement, and change. He will likely be athletic, enjoying sports or working out. It goes without saying that he also loves sex. His self-confident presence oozes energetic virility. The challenge the Knight

330 The Minor Arcana in Love

of Wands presents is also what makes him so desirably attractive—his roaming spirit of adventure. The Knight of Wands will maintain his freedom for as long as he humanly can. This is not to say that the Knight of Wands can't fall in love or make a commitment *one day*. However, he must be at a life stage when his wild oats have been satisfactorily sown. Waiting for this knight can take a very long time. At his best, the Knight of Wands is thrilling, sexy, confident, honest, free-spirited, travel-loving, and open-minded. At his worst, he is rebellious, noncommittal, evasive, impulsive, and unfaithful.

In a Love Reading
New Relationship
The Knight of Wands represents a thrilling new romance that's hard to stop thinking about. There is an insatiable quality to this attraction, and this person will always leave you wanting more. Try not to get too clingy with the Knight of Wands, or your heart could break. He may spend years traveling, dating, or moving from place to place before settling down.

Long-Term Partnership
The Knight of Wands symbolizes a relationship that has been a wild ride. The very fact you got this person to commit to you is a wonder. Your partnership thrives through travel, freedom, and a change of scenery. This card can also signify a long-distance relationship or a partnership in which both partners spend a lot of time apart.

Intimacy
Intimately, the Knight of Wands can represent an active sex life. Your partner is likely uninhibited and likes to take control. Sex will continue to magnetically pull the two of you together. It's at the very center of your inexplicable attraction to one another.

Seeking Romance
If you are single, the Knight of Wands tells you to enjoy it! Don't be in too much of a hurry to settle down. There will be years to enjoy that future partner who'll be unromantically eating pizza in their underwear on your couch. For now, be free. Flirt, explore, feel sexy, and enjoy your freedom!

Desires
The Knight of Wands desires a partner who doesn't come off as needy, clingy, or desperate. He prefers to do the chasing and speeds away from being chased. Much like the Charioteer, the Knight of Wands must always feel there is something left to conquer. Love interests who radiate nonchalant, fun-loving sassiness ensnare his ardor.

Reversed
New Relationship
The Knight of Wands Reversed can represent a person who has difficulty moderating his fiery passions. They may lack self-control or might be impulsive to a destructive degree. If you are looking for safety, consistency, and security, you may want to seek someone who can truly provide that.

Long-Term Partnership
When the Knight of Wands is reversed, he can represent a noncommittal long-term partner who feels no remorse in stringing you along. Because the initial attraction was so chemical, you may feel desperate to experience the thrill of your initial passion together. You must resist the temptation to rationalize and disregard blatant red flags.

Intimacy
The Knight of Wands Reversed can indicate infidelity or a lack of commitment from someone who is sending mixed signals. One week you experience hopefulness, while the next week you find yourself questioning whether you imagined everything. This card encourages you to leave drama behind to realign with your center.

Seeking Romance
The Knight of Wands Reversed may appear when someone else is stifling your energy and freedom. If you've been feeling stifled, suffocated, or turned off by the actions of another person, it's time to be upfront and honest and free yourself. If it isn't a love match, be honest.

Desires
The Knight of Wands Reversed can represent a time when you feel frustrated that you can't change the erratic behavior of another person. The only thing

you can control is your response. You may need to lay down boundaries that you follow up *with action*. Don't allow desire to trounce reason. It's time to get off the roller coaster even if it once thrilled you.

What the Knight of Wands May Be Teaching You

The Knight of Wands may be teaching you to cherish your freedom instead of being in such a hurry to relinquish it. Your autonomy gives you options, power, and unlimited potential to live the life *you* want. You don't have to ask permission to explore the options of your best life. If you are feeling lonesome or lost, perhaps it's time to plan an adventure and bask in your independence. The Knight of Wands calls you to the exciting, faraway places that restore your spirit and help you escape the limitations of your small pond. The world is wide open and waiting. Make the choice that helps you feel unencumbered, passionate, and free. Exploring new places and making new connections will grant you a fresh perspective about what makes your spirit soar. If you've been feeling stuck in a rut, it may be because you've outgrown your current reality. Follow the adventurous Knight of Wands toward exciting vistas of newness and truly let yourself *live*.

QUEEN OF WANDS

The Queen of Wands possesses a rare charisma that brightens any room. She leaves onlookers starstruck with her noble bearing and radiant light. The Queen of Wands is a lion among sheep. People who follow a herd mentality tend to be uneasy around her. She often finds herself the target of both the admiration and the jealousy of others. The Queen of Wands seeks a partner who is equally strong and confident. In love, she is fiercely protective, showering her partner with attention, warmth, and affection. She expects honor and respect in return. In matters of the heart, the Queen of Wands is devoted and faithful … *but only for as long as her partner is*. If she is dishonored, she has no problem packing up her glittering show and taking it elsewhere. *This* queen plays second fiddle to no one! At her best, the Queen of Wands is warm, magnetic, entertaining, attractive, and confident, and she exemplifies the It Factor. At her worst, she is vain, fixed, needy, and resistant to receiving any form of criticism.

In a Love Reading
New Relationship
The Queen of Wands represents a love interest who responds well to admiration. However, the compliments mustn't be hollow … they need *magic*. As a master of performance, she can spot a fake a mile away. The Queen of Wands appreciates authenticity over image. Be real and let her shine. This card also signifies an optimistic new beginning.

Long-Term Partnership
The Queen of Wands holds a sunflower, which always turns its face toward the light. She will represent someone who is positive about love and her ability to address any challenges. The Queen of Wands can also represent a partner who must feel heard. As long as you give this person loyalty and a sympathetic ear, the future remains bright.

Intimacy
Like her black cat, the Queen of Wands is sultry and seductive. She waits to unleash her full passion until after she's captured pride of place in her lover's affections. This card can also represent a person who projects an air of nonchalance when flirting. Don't let this fool you. This queen deeply desires to hear that *she* is the fairest of them all.

Seeking Romance
The Queen of Wands encourages you to brighten up with confidence. Go on dates, socialize with friends, and just have fun. *Make the extra effort* when it comes to your appearance. Enhance how you display yourself to the world. Allow your external charms to amplify the beauty within. This card always encourages one to stand out and attract attention.

Desires

The Queen of Wands can signify a desire to shine brightly once again. It's time to stop carrying yourself in a manner that appears overly apologetic to others. Don't dim your light for out-of-power people. When you radiate what makes you unique, you attract the people who are on your level. Bask in your brilliance and don't be afraid to stand out.

Reversed
New Relationship

The Queen of Wands Reversed can represent someone who cares too much about what other people think. She may be more interested in maintaining an image than connecting with the source of her authentic power. She may also need constant reassurance of her value. This card can also signify a person who has a hard time sharing the spotlight.

Long-Term Partnership

When the Queen of Wands appears reversed, she can represent a partner whose ego is easily triggered. She has a hard time listening to others and may talk over them. If her pride is wounded, she can lash out thoughtlessly. She may also have a hard time accepting criticism, even when it's valid.

Intimacy

The Queen of Wands Reversed can represent someone who feels overly insecure about her physical appearance. She is a perfectionist who has unrealistic expectations of beauty. This card can also represent a person who uses sex to feel validated or admired.

Seeking Romance

Like her black cat, the Queen of Wands Reversed reminds you that you won't be liked by everyone. No matter how talented, charming, or confident you feel, you may not make a connection with every potential love interest. Believe in yourself. Upright or reversed, the Queen of Wands encourages you to walk away with dignity from anyone who undervalues you.

Desires

The Queen of Wands is known as the actress of the tarot. When reversed, she can symbolize a person who desires maintaining an image over letting others see who she is beyond her performance. Upright or reversed, the Queen of Wands encourages authenticity. There is no need to pretend when love is true.

What the Queen of Wands May Be Teaching You

The Queen of Wands may be teaching you to embrace what makes you stand out. Her black cat sits before her throne, a relative emblem to the proud lions that adorn her banners. The lions symbolize the regal solar warmth she externally shines. The black cat represents her hidden lunar aspect, where her alluring magic truly emanates from. The Queen of Wands not only proudly shines her light, but also allows others to witness her shadow. This is why most people adore the Queen of Wands. She isn't perfect, and displaying her shadow unapologetically makes her relatable, human, and unpretentious. The Queen of Wands teaches you to be yourself and humbly embrace both the light and the shadows that grant your personality dimension. When you can find the beauty in your quirks, imperfections, and contradictions, you will know that you authentically accept yourself. This liberates you from needing someone else to validate you. Clothe yourself in the queen's radiance and take the lion's throne.

KING OF WANDS

The King of Wands likely came up the hard way and survived many trials by fire. In a love reading, the King of Wands appears as a world-wise individual who embodies the qualities of competency, resilience, and perseverance. In relationships, the King of Wands does not play games. He is direct and honest, and you will know exactly where you stand with him. If he is interested in you, he will say so plainly. He is attracted to people who are themselves authentic, honest, and resilient. In life and relationships, the King of Wands is most comfortable when taking the lead. People with the King of Wands's attributes make wonderful managers, teachers, entrepreneurs, or counselors. However, they must always feel they maintain absolute control over their own destiny. At his best, this king is honest, passionate, ambitious, progressive, protective, and wise counsel. He will maintain his honor and integrity. At his worst, the King of Wands can be a control freak who displays a quick temper when agitated.

In a Love Reading
New Relationship
The King of Wands is thoughtful, understanding, and warm. However, he cannot abide dishonesty. You will not have to guess how he truly feels, for this king is honest to a fault. This card can also represent a developing passion where both partners feel understood and can communicate authentically with one another.

Long-Term Partnership
This card represents a mature partnership based on mutual respect. The King of Wands will encourage you to apply the wisdom gained from past to present. No matter what trials by fire are currently before you both, the King of Wands governs relationship bonds that can withstand the test of time.

Intimacy
The King of Wands can be an exciting and passionate lover. Yet this card can also represent heavy responsibilities that draw attention away from shared intimacy and toward problem-solving. Create space and time to play and let loose, where external pressures can be left at the door.

Seeking Romance
If the King of Wands represents you, he symbolizes the survival of many trials by fire. You become your best when times are toughest. Whatever you are currently enduring will only make you better. Maintain your integrity and don't lower your standards for a quick fix.

Desires

The King of Wands desires a partner who is comfortable in their own skin. Superficiality won't cut it. For a younger partner, this king desires a person who displays wisdom and maturity far beyond their years. For an older partner, he gravitates toward an unjaded individual who retains their youthful spirit.

Reversed
New Relationship

The King of Wands Reversed can represent a partner with a sensitive sense of pride. He must feel recognized and appreciated before opening up. This person dislikes feeling contradicted in front of others. Reputation matters to him. He does not respond well if his methods are questioned. He desires respect above all else.

Long-Term Partnership

This card can represent a relationship that has survived many trials by fire. Both partners have a shared experience of suffering that has actually strengthened their mutual respect for one another. Express your talents, warmth, optimism, and playfulness.

Intimacy

The King of Wands Reversed suffers most when he allows his emotions to boil too hot or freeze too cold. He is also an ambitious workaholic and must be encouraged to rest to prevent burnout. He can be very passionate so long as there isn't some other pressing issue depleting his energy.

Seeking Romance

This card can represent a time when you are beginning to doubt what you know to be true or are second-guessing your own perception. You may need to take a break from what is triggering you to see the situation more clearly. When your emotions have simmered, you will know just what to do.

Desires

Upright or reversed, the King of Wands not only desires to share his talents but to *prove them*. The King of Wands Reversed can represent a person who feels insecure about where he falls in social hierarchies and in the affections of his partner. If this person is not getting recognition, he can become apathetic and disillusioned.

What the King of Wands May Be Teaching You

The King of Wands may be teaching you to honor whatever trial by fire you are currently experiencing. In truth, this ordeal is your initiation. Like the King of Wands, you will experience setbacks, disappointments, and trying times before eventually attaining the success and happiness you desire most. The King of Wands reassures you that challenging times are just as meant to be as your happiest moments. The King of Wands also urges you to trust the common sense and instincts you've developed when it comes to other people. You will only perpetuate inner turmoil if you forego your inner wisdom in favor of excuses, rationalizations, or conspiracy theories that don't resemble reality. The King of Wands has a special kind of courage. This card is rooted in honesty. When he appears, he urges you to be honest with yourself about what you are perceiving. The branch of truth will pull you out whenever you feel you are sinking in quicksand.

PART 3

SPREADS FOR RELATIONSHIP READINGS

The pictorial images of the tarot are the *soul* of any reading; however, tarot spreads are the *skeleton*. Tarot spreads help you systematically organize the intuitive information you receive in a reading. They supply structure, sequence, and, most importantly, *context* for card interpretation. A tarot spread can consist of any number of cards, from only one card to all seventy-eight! Each position a card falls in can help you narrow down *how* to interpret a specific card, clarifying its meaning through the spread position's subject. Spreads can help you deduce if the appearance of the King of Wands in your reading refers to you, to the person in question, or to a situation. I have included various spreads that can be tailored to your unique situation.

You can also design your own tarot spreads. Begin by formulating some questions you want answers to. Have fun and use your imagination. Be mindful when choosing how to frame your questions while consulting the tarot. Try to avoid questions that verbalize disempowering beliefs or that set up an expectation of having no control over your own life. For example, don't ask, "Will I ever be happy?" This question implies that the future is set in stone, and that your happiness or future unhappiness is already predestined. Questions like this trick your mind into believing that you have no power to change your life. The future is not some looming, fixed narrative that you'll be passively victimized by. Ask questions that reveal the best choices you can make *in the present,* which can positively change the future *you are creating.* Better questions to ask would be, "What do I need to understand about this situation so that

I can experience a breakthrough?" or, "What empowering traits should I embody when dealing with this person?" Design spreads that encourage the best version of yourself to lead the way.

Tarot is also a wonderful tool for helping you make a decision. It masterfully presents your current options. We can't control every event we experience in love and in life. However, we can choose whether to respond with strength or passivity. Tarot can lead to confusion and disillusionment if you walk into a reading believing that it can promise you a fixed future that will never deviate. Try avoiding words like *ever*, *never*, or *always* in your tarot questions. Instead, reframe your questions to reaffirm your power, such as, "What can I focus on to create more happiness in my life?" "What can I work on in myself to attract the best possible partner?" "How do I respond to this person's behavior to ensure the best possible outcome?"

The following spreads are a launching point that you can experiment with. Feel free to alter the spreads provided in this book to suit your needs. The tarot works best when *your own* wisdom and common sense interact with it. Choose the spread that seems to resonate with your heart's present desire. Experiment with different spreads from other tarot readers from time to time. There are dozens of wonderful books that supply thoughtful tarot spreads that can illuminate your choices. You can also find brilliant spread concepts browsing the social media pages of other tarot readers in the tarot community. Have fun exploring the limitless uses for the cards by exposing yourself to a diversity of perspectives on how to use the tarot.

DO I NEED TO CHOOSE A SIGNIFICATOR?

Many tarot readers begin their readings by selecting a significator. A significator is a card chosen from the tarot deck to represent the querent (the person getting the reading). I usually pick one of the court cards (page, knight, queen, or king) or a Major Arcana card to be the significator. You may want to read through the personality traits of the Major Arcana archetypes or court cards in this book to choose the significator that shares common traits with the person you are reading. You can also designate a significator based on gender, age, or astrological correspondence. The important thing is that the significator card reflects at least one unique symbolic characteristic of the person getting the reading.

Before beginning a tarot reading, I ask my client what their astrological sun sign is. The sun sign in astrology is what you look at in the paper when you read your horoscope. In astrology, the twelve zodiac signs are separated by four elements: earth, air, fire, and water. Each element has three astrological signs associated with it. The earth signs are Taurus, Virgo, and Capricorn. The air signs are Gemini, Libra, and Aquarius. The fire signs are Aries, Leo, and Sagittarius. The water signs are Cancer, Scorpio, and Pisces.

The Minor Acana of the tarot is separated into four suits that each reflect an element. Earth is represented by pentacles, air is represented by swords, fire is represented by wands, and water is represented by cups.

Some people insist on picking kings and knights to represent men and boys and queens and pages to represent women and girls. However, gender identity is not so black and white. Always select a significator based on the gender you or your querent identifies most with. If you are unsure, just ask them: "As a Libra, which card do you think better represents you—the King of Swords, the Queen of Swords, or Justice?" Some men prefer to be represented as queens, and some women view themselves as kings.

For example, If I were going to read for an adult who identifies as female, I would select a queen to reflect that individual. If she were a water sign, I would choose the Queen of Cups. If she were a fire sign, I would choose the Queen of Wands. For a young man, I usually pick a knight. For a mature man, I would pick a king. Pages are gender neutral. Pages can be younger people or people who don't identify as a specific gender.

Astrological identity is flexible, too. You may meet a client who tells you, "My sun sign is technically Aries, but I really don't feel like one. I have a Libra rising and resonate more with Libra." In this case, I would select a card that represents Libra from the swords suit.

I personally like to use significator cards. It helps my deck know that it is reading for a person who exhibits some of the qualities of the chosen card.

There are many fine readers who do not choose a significator. It is totally a matter of preference. Do what works for you!

"IN A NUTSHELL" ONE-CARD SPREAD

This simple spread consists of only one card and does not require a significator. This spread can help you regain clarity amid confusing emotions by summarizing what you are currently learning into one card. This card can also be adapted to answer questions about what a relationship partner might be experiencing as well.

Readings are more effective when you are calm and willing to examine your situation at its deepest level. Take a moment to center yourself before selecting your card. Take three slow, deep breaths and surrender the stress of the day. Unclench your jaw and release all the tension from your shoulders. Begin shuffling your cards. Bring your awareness to your instincts and intuition, which will tell you when it is time to stop shuffling. If fear, tension, or anxiety begins to creep back into your chest, take another deep breath and relax away your worries. Ask,

"What do I need to understand about this issue on my heart?"

Nutshell Spread

Select a random card from your deck. It can be from the top, bottom, middle... trust your instincts. Some people ritually cut their deck and choose the card that ends up on top. When you turn your card over, it may not be what you expected. Try not to prejudge the card you select. Don't automatically dismiss it because you don't like how it looks or assume it means something bad. If you are automatically resistant to the card you selected, that is a big red flag that your ego is running the reading and is trying to stay fixed in denial about something important.

This card you chose was meant for this moment. If you look at the image deep enough, it just might lead you to an epiphany and allow you to view your situation in an empowering context. If the card triggers a fear, sit with that fear for a moment and allow yourself to feel it. Grab a notebook and journal whatever anxieties you are currently experiencing. *Feel your feelings and don't dismiss them.* Examine the card carefully, and study what is happening in the image. What do the actions portrayed on the card remind you about when applying them to the context of your current experience. Once you are ready, look the meaning of the card up in the book. You might want to read the What This Card May Be Teaching You section. Whatever words or personal insights resonate most within your heart have delivered the message.

THREE-CARD COMPATIBILITY SPREAD

This classic spread can help you gain insight into who you are, who your love interest is, and how your combined energies are likely to intermingle in a relationship. This card does not require a significator as the spread itself will grant insight into you and your companion.

Take three slow, deep breaths and surrender the stress of the day. Unclench your jaw and release all the tension from your shoulders. Begin shuffling your cards. Bring your awareness to your instincts and intuition, which will tell you when it is time to stop shuffling. If fear, tension, or anxiety begins to creep back into your chest, take another deep breath and relax away your worries.

Stop shuffling and cut the deck into three piles, from left to right. Select the top card from the left pile, facedown, and place it in position one. Take the top card from the middle pile and place it in position two. Take the top card from the third pile for position three. Gather the remaining cards and set them aside.

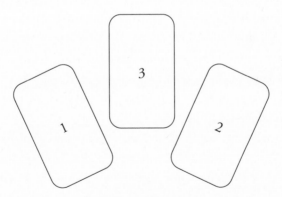

Three-Card Spread

Card 1. Me: *What energy or expectations am I bringing to this relationship?* This card shows what you are carrying in your heart at this time. It will also reveal hidden challenges that this relationship is allowing you to confront.

Card 2. The other person: *What energy or expectations is my current love interest bringing to this relationship?*
This card will reveal what may be going on beneath the surface with the person you are inquiring about. It may also reveal hidden issues this person might be struggling with.

Card 3. The relationship: *What challenges and/or opportunities will arise in the relationship if we decide to be together?*
This card will reveal the health of the relationship and any potential issues that might need to be resolved within your partner or yourself.

SEEKING LOVE SPREAD

This spread can help you reclaim an empowered perspective while you are searching for the right relationship. When we are single, we are often bombarded with messages from society, media, and even family that we must hurry up and settle down with somebody. This can lead to feeling we must find our special person quick, or we will miss all hope of happiness and fulfillment. This fear can quickly turn into desperation and can actually repel potential suitors rather than attract them. This spread will help you be more mindful of what your energy is telegraphing to others and what requires resolution within.

This spread will help you see the gifts of your current independence. It will also highlight areas in your life that need investment, which can bring you fulfillment *now*. Being single grants you the opportunity to do the deep work on yourself and make personal breakthroughs without worrying about how this affects a relationship partner. Being single is freedom, power, autonomy, choices, options, and adventure.

Begin this spread by selecting your significator card and placing it on the table before you. Take three slow, deep breaths and surrender the stress of the day. Unclench your jaw and release all the tension from your shoulders. Begin shuffling your cards. Think about the current issue that's been weighing so heavily on your heart. Bring your awareness to your instincts and intuition, which will tell you when it is time to stop shuffling. If fear, tension, or anxiety begins to creep back into your chest, take another deep breath and relax away your worries. When your intuition feels ready, stop shuffling and cut the deck if you so choose. Lay out the cards.

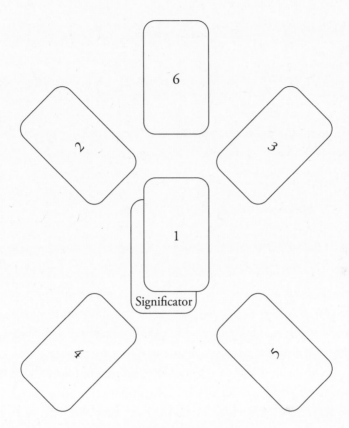

Seeking Love Spread

Card 1. *What am I currently gaining by being single?*
This card will illuminate the wisdom you are acquiring from your present situation. This needed experience must be undertaken by you alone and will help pave the way toward your future bliss.

Card 2. *What is my energy unconsciously announcing to others?*
This card will help you become more self-aware of how you come across to other people. It will also show you if the energy you are currently embodying is attracting or repelling others.

Card 3. *Where is it best to invest my energy to tangibly manifest my heart's desire?*
This card will reveal what actions you can take in the real world to create the life you most desire. It will also highlight strengths that you should embrace or issues that seek resolution to pave the way toward love.

Card 4. *What wisdom have I gained from my past relationships?*
This card can reveal the personal breakthroughs that resulted from letting go of past relationships. This card can also reveal negative expectations, beliefs, or feelings that could be blocking you.

Card 5. *What connections will benefit me this next year?*
This card will represent the kinds of relationships you should be on the lookout for in the coming year. This card could also reveal your potential for romance and where you might discover it.

Card 6. *What will lead me toward true love?*
This card will show you what people, situations, connections, or opportunities will guide you toward the love you seek. If this card discusses positive personality traits, work on exemplifying them in the coming year. If this card is challenging, know that this is where your soul work is taking place. By clearing out the shadows within, you will create a better environment for love to flourish.

CUPID'S ARROW SPREAD

When struck by Cupid's dart, all the world begins to feel intensely exhilarating. However, that pesky arrow can also toss you into a tempestuous sea of uncertainty. This spread can help you keep your wits when intoxicated by fascination with that striking person you just can't stop thinking about.

Romantic love is the best high nature can deliver. However, like any drug, it is extremely addictive and can make you lose your common sense and control. Remember that people will usually show you their best attributes in the beginning. Time is needed to gather more data about *who* this person really is, and whether or not they are good enough for *you*. Use this spread to remain clearheaded while exploring the potential for a relationship with the major crush who has left you infatuated.

Begin this spread by selecting your significator card and placing it on the table before you. Take three slow, deep breaths and surrender the stress of the day. Unclench your jaw and release all the tension from your shoulders. Begin shuffling your cards. Think about this current issue that's been weighing so heavily on your heart. Bring your awareness to your instincts and intuition, which will tell you when it is time to stop shuffling. If fear, tension, or anxiety begins to creep back into your chest, take another deep breath and relax away your worries. When your intuition feels ready, stop shuffling and cut the deck if you so choose. Lay out the cards.

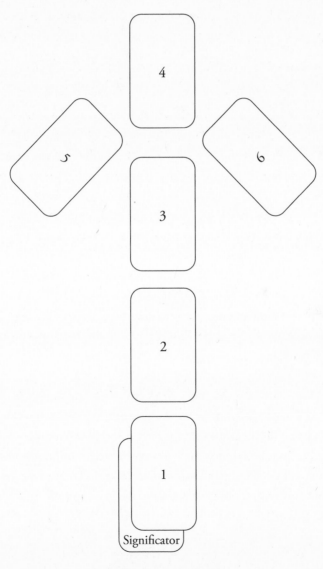

Cupid's Arrow Spread

Card 1. *What is this passion bringing to the surface?*
This card will reveal hidden attitudes, motivations, or issues that this attraction is bringing to the surface. This card will also reveal if you are approaching this relationship with a healthy mindset.

Card 2. *How is this person perceiving my energy?*
This card will reveal how your romantic interest is interpreting your energy. This card may also reveal if your initial attraction is reciprocated.

Card 3. *What is the best way to proceed?*
This card will reveal the best actions you can take when interacting with this person. This card can also offer advice for how to handle your emotions.

Card 4. *What might I not be seeing clearly about this person or this situation?*
This card will reveal your blind spot. In the case of a numbered Pip card, it might reveal a situation you need to be aware of. In the case of a court or Major Arcana card, it may reveal your romantic interest's hidden positive and negative traits.

Card 5. *What is this person attracted to?*
This card will grant insight into what attracts and motivates this person. It may also reveal what qualities you possess that this person finds attractive.

Card 6. *What will help or hinder this relationship's progress?*
This card will reveal the opportunities to grow closer or the obstacles in the way of forming a deeper relationship. This card might also reveal the potential for a long-term relationship.

SHOULD I STAY OR SHOULD I GO? SPREAD

Sometimes we find ourselves at a pivotal crossroads where we must make a difficult decision about whether to continue or end a relationship. Every relationship experiences challenges that must be overcome. If relationship problems are not addressed or resolved, anger and heartache can take the place of the love that was once shared. This spread will help you organize your options. It will also grant insight into the best decision to make for yourself and your relationship.

Begin this spread by selecting your significator card and placing it on the table before you. Take three slow, deep breaths and surrender the stress of the day. Unclench your jaw and release all the tension from your shoulders. Begin shuffling your cards. Think about this current issue that's been weighing so heavily on your heart. Bring your awareness to your instincts and intuition, which will tell you when it is time to stop shuffling. If fear, tension, or anxiety begins to creep back into your chest, take another deep breath and relax away your worries. When your intuition feels ready, stop shuffling and cut the deck if you so choose. Lay out the cards.

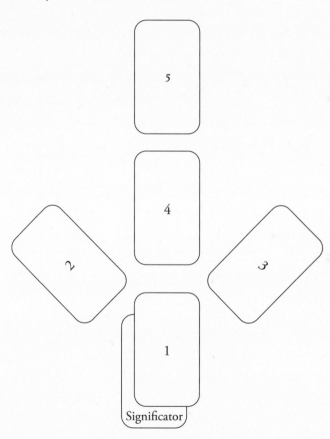

Should I Stay? Spread

Card 1. *What is at the core of my current relationship?*
This card will reveal the foundation of your current relationship. It can illuminate whether that foundation is strong or damaged.

Card 2. *If my partner and I both decide to stay together, what can we do to strengthen the relationship?*
This card will reveal what you both can do to improve your partnership together. It may also show the benefits or difficulties that result from staying together.

Card 3. *If we part ways, how would I fare on my own?*
This card will reveal the pros or cons of leaving. It may also reveal your emotional state and what may need to be supported within.

Card 4. *What is the best possible advice to help with my final decision?*
This card will reveal an important insight that needs to be weighed when making your decision. It may also help you identify what you might not be seeing clearly about your partner or yourself.

Card 5. *What is this choice revealing about me?*
This card will show you what your impending decision is revealing about yourself and your needs. It may also unearth a non-negotiable that you will want to communicate moving forward.

*As a special note: Relationship challenges are very different from relationship abuse. If you are experiencing abuse in your relationship, seek compassionate support from a caring professional. Call an abuse hotline or speak with a licensed therapist. Love is not proven by staying with an abuser. No tarot card in a reading can justify violence, psychological trauma, or emotional abuse. Don't leave issues of your mental and emotional health to the flip of a card. The light you carry is sacred, special, and so incredibly precious. It's the only light of its kind in the whole universe. It deserves to shine, not be diminished. You are never alone, even if you might currently feel that way. Love will never seek to destroy you or make you feel trapped, terrified, abandoned, worthless, or small. You are worthy of the best. Don't settle for crumbs when a sumptuous feast may be awaiting you elsewhere.

THE CELTIC LOVER'S KNOT SPREAD

If you are already in a relationship, this variation of the Celtic Cross spread can illuminate what lies ahead for you and your partner in the coming year. This spread can also reveal areas of disagreement that may need resolution. This spread covers the past, the present, and the next three to six months. The Celtic Lover's Knot can also show what each partner will be focused on independent of one another. Use this spread to gain insight into your own unconscious feelings and to make you more sensitive to your partner's perspective.

This spread can be performed alone or with your beloved. If your partner is with you, allow them to shuffle one half of the tarot deck while you shuffle the other. Begin the reading by selecting a significator card to represent your relationship. You could use the Lovers card, the Two of Cups, the Ten of Cups, or any other card that reminds you of your relationship vibe. Once you have selected your significator card, place it on the table before you. Take three slow, deep breaths and surrender the stress of the day. Unclench your jaw and release all the tension from your shoulders. Begin shuffling your cards. Think about this current issue that's been weighing so heavily on your heart. Bring your awareness to your instincts and intuition, which will tell you when it is time to stop shuffling. If fear, tension, or anxiety begins to creep back into your chest, take another deep breath and relax away your worries. When your intuition feels ready, stop shuffling and cut the deck if you so choose. If your partner is with you, you'll have to decide whose half of the deck gets to be on top! If you can't decide, flip a coin. Lay out the cards as follows:

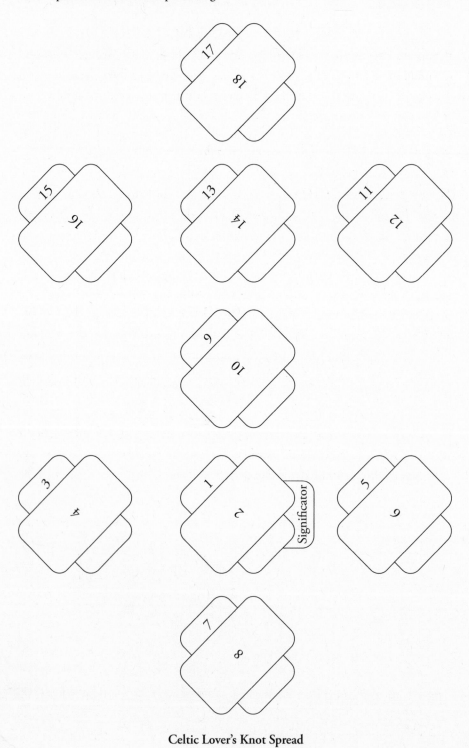

Celtic Lover's Knot Spread

Card 1. *You in the present.*

Card 2. *Your partner in the present.*

These cards will reveal what you and your partner are experiencing presently. These cards can also show you what your individual priorities are and how they currently affect one another.

Card 3. *What's currently on your mind.*

Card 4. *What's currently on your partner's mind.*

These cards will reveal what you and your partner are fixated on at the moment. These cards will also reveal if there is a meeting of the minds or a disagreement.

Card 5. *Your present foundation.*

Card 6. *Your partner's current foundation.*

These cards will reveal the foundational values both people hold dear. They can represent your standards or where those standards are beginning to slip.

Card 7. *Your past.*

Card 8. *Your partner's past.*

These cards will reveal how your individual pasts may be affecting your current situation. These cards can also reveal issues from childhood or a former relationship.

Card 9. *Your near future.*

Card 10. *Your partner's near future.*

These cards can help you understand both the challenges and the opportunities that the next several weeks are likely to have in store. These cards will also reveal if your individual priorities in the immediate future are in alignment or not.

Card 11. *You in the next several months.*

Card 12. *Your partner in the next several months.*

These cards will reveal the challenges or opportunities that will likely occur in the next three to six months. These cards will also reveal how the situations described by card 9 and card 10 are likely to evolve in the coming months.

Card 13. *The people who affect you outside of the relationship.*

Card 14. *The people who affect your partner outside of the relationship.*

These cards will reveal how family, colleagues, friends, or social obligations will impact your relationship in the next year. These cards will also reveal if these people are disrupting or supporting your relationship.

Card 15. *Your feelings in the future.*

Card 16. *Your partner's feelings in the future.*

These cards will reveal the emotional needs of you and your partner in the next three to six months. This position can also illuminate the emotional issues that may need to be resolved or supported.

Card 17. *Your outcome.*

Card 18. *Your partner's outcome.*

These cards will reveal how your individual concerns are likely to resolve. They will also show you how your present issues and opportunities are likely to evolve.

Remember, when forecasting the future, you are looking at a *likely* future. The cards can only reveal what is likely to happen if the two of you don't dramatically change course. If you (or your partner) don't like the direction you are heading in, you can change your future by making better choices *in the present*. Also remember, the only person you have control over is *you*, and the same goes for your partner. Both people need to do their part to keep the relationship healthy. This spread can show you what issues may need to be communicated and what you may need to be more empathetic about with your partner.

HEALING A BROKEN HEART WITH THE EMPRESS

Few things in life can feel as devastating as having your heart broken. This chapter incorporates a visualization exercise and tarot spread to provide compassion and healing with the tarot's most loving and nurturing archetype, the

Empress. The following guided tarot visualization can begin a dialogue between ancient symbolism and the healing energy found within your inner self. This exercise will also create a safe, compassionate space for your heart to release the shock and disappointment it is currently holding. The ancient archetypes of the tarot speak the language of your inner self. This language is not literal but one of symbols. Imagery can guide you back home to your center, where the wisest essence of your authentic self resides.

Before performing this spread, secure a time and space where you and your tarot deck will not be interrupted. Have a journal and pen handy to record your impressions. Choose a safe, quiet room where you can reflect. Try not to speed through the following exercise. A healing heart cannot be hurried. Silence the phone and leave all distractions of the modern world outside. You can help create a sacred space by dimming the lights, lighting some candles or incense, surrounding yourself with comfy pillows or a blanket, and getting comfortable. Take three slow, deep breaths and exhale all the stress and tension in your body. Unclench your jaw and release all the tension from your shoulders. Visualize a soft, golden light slowly filling the room. As this light enfolds you, know that you are surrounded in protection, acceptance, and love. As you let go of all tightness in your mind and body, breathe deeply. Take a slow, deep, nourishing breath and say, "I am present ... I am protected ... and I am ready to mend these wounds."

Now, turn your attention to your tarot deck. Select the Empress card and look upon this image as if seeing her for the first time. What do you notice about her that you didn't see before? Gaze upon the love that radiates from her image. Place her on the table before you. Gaze into her eyes. When you feel safe and ready, begin the journey inward to the broken place.

Imagine you are walking through a wooded forest on a beaten path. The sky is overcast and gray. Each step you take feels heavy and mirrors the sadness you've been carrying with you. The path you are on appears to have been walked many times before. Although it seems familiar, you can't quite recall if you've been here before. As you follow the winding path that bends out of the woods, you come upon a shining meadow. A gate lies ahead, and golden light begins to break apart the gray clouds. A fresh breeze rustles the leaves behind you like a sigh of relief. As you enter the meadow, you feel as if a heavy burden has been left behind. As you walk toward the gate, you notice that there is a garden on the other side, bathed in a golden light. *Write down the first three words that come to your mind as you look around. What do you see on the gate? Is there writing, an ornament, or a symbol? What plants do you notice first in the garden ahead? Write down anything you might feel or see. Don't judge your choices, just write.*

You feel drawn to the garden beyond the gate. It looks safe, inviting, and peaceful. Something within you knows that entering this garden will change how you see things. The gate unlatches and effortlessly swings open as you touch it. The gate makes a low creak as it slowly opens, and your heart wells up with relief. As you step through the gate, you find yourself in a lush, verdant garden, surrounded by flowers of every color and rich sheaves of golden wheat. You look up, noticing there isn't a cloud in the sky, and a gentle breeze with the sweet scent of lilacs fills your nostrils. The light in this garden seems to permeate everything, causing it to shimmer and glow. This radiance brings light to even your deepest sorrows. As you walk forward through the abundance of life before you, you come to a clearing. This is where you finally encounter *her*.

The Empress is seated upon an ancient stone dais inscribed with archaic symbols. Her throne is covered with velvety, silken pillows. She looks like the stately queens from ages long past. She is both young and old. Her beauty is ageless. Her kindly eyes twinkle like a fairy, while her majestic presence fills the entirety of her garden. Her delicate gown is richly embroidered with the fruits of summer, all intricately stitched. The breeze delicately tugs at the fabric of her gown. The Empress wears a glittering crown of twelve stars that dapples your face with dancing light. And yet, the most striking feature of the Empress is the heartfelt expression that emanates from her knowing eyes as she takes in the full measure of your presence, for the Empress can see straight into the secrets of your heart. One look from her validates and soothes the stinging pain she finds within you. She looks to you with both compassion and concern.

She speaks to you in soothing tones:

I know the heaviness you carry in your heart today.
I see and feel the hurt you hold.
I have many names, and like you, many stories to tell.
I am Gaia and my soil has been showered by the tears of every ancestor who ever came before you.
I am Demeter and know the agony of loss and death, despair, and grief.
I know what it feels like to lose what is not coming back.
I am Hera and know the ruthless sting of unjustifiable betrayal. I know the ineffectiveness of words to soothe the seething rage that screams to right the insult done to my honor.
I am Hekate, the guide of all who find themselves lost at the misty crossroads.
I am Persephone, Maiden of Spring, and Aphrodite, Goddess of Love.
I know that journeys to the Underworld are never forever. Even if only one fragile speck of love remains in your heart, there is still hope to grow stronger beyond this.
My promise to you is this:
You always have a home here.
Your heart holds great value still.
My love will be your shield.
Feeling your feelings allows them to loosen their strangling grip on you.
One day, you won't feel this present pain the same way you do now.
Tell me of all your burdens. For the decay of grief and sadness will fertilize the new life that begins here today.

Express whatever is on your heart to the Empress. She can hear. Tell her everything you are feeling and what you've gone through. If words can't be spoken, write them in your journal. Allow your feelings to flow. If you need to cry, let the tears come. If you feel mad, hit your pillows or scream into them. Don't bottle up your emotions. The Empress does not judge them. *Your feelings deserve to be felt.*

The Empress also has guidance for your ears only. Finish her following sentences. Don't overthink the words. Just let them flow from your heart. Write them in your journal if you choose.

I lend you my crown of twelve stars. It grants you perspective to see that—.

I grant you my golden scepter. With it you will—.

The shield at my feet will protect your heart as it mends. There is a message inscribed on the inside of the shield that says—.

The babbling waterfall behind me echoes with wisdom. When you listen with your heart, it tells you that—.

The Empress has one last thing you must understand.

Take your remaining tarot cards and shuffle them. Lay them out around the Empress card as follows:

Empress Spread

(You may want to read the What This Card May Be Teaching You sections.)

Card 1. *How can I best transmute the poison of this wound?*
This card will reveal what actions you can take to release any toxins you still carry in your heart.

Card 2. *What am I learning from this difficult experience?*
This card can reveal the wisdom you are gaining from this situation.

Card 3. *How can I transform this pain into power?*
This card can reveal what opportunity for empowerment lies before you. Like the Empress archetype, you can endure horrible experiences and still retain your majesty and dignity.

Write any further impressions you had while visiting the garden of the Empress. Though you may leave the garden for now, the Empress will never leave you. She is part of your consciousness and is always close at hand when you need her support. You can revisit her garden with any future emotions you may be struggling with. The words you wrote when you encountered the gate will reveal insight into what may be helping you or blocking you from loving yourself. They serve as a threshold to your breakthrough. Your answers to the Empress may change on future visits. You can also design your own meditations to begin a dialogue with the other archetypes of the tarot to suit whatever situation you are confronting.

CONCLUSION

I want to thank you for opening your heart on this most sensitive journey through the tarot. It takes courage to seek authentic love and to let go of that which is no longer worthy of you. Relationships shine a light on our blind spots, allowing us to identify some of the hardest lessons our souls are here to learn. I truly believe the future is in our hands and that we attract love when we do the work of loving ourselves and making better choices. However, I also believe in destiny, synchronicities, miracles, divine patterns, soul bonds, romance, and dreams. Love, like the tarot, intersects with the realm of magic. Continue to find ways to fearlessly connect with the world, and love will continue to find you.

If you are currently in a fulfilling relationship, I want to wish you all the happiness in the world. Don't let a day go by where you don't let this incredible person know how much they mean to you. Having a companion you love and trust is one of life's greatest joys. I hope that the bond you share continues to strengthen and deepen as you continue to create happy memories together well into the future.

If you are single and searching for your great love, *do not give up hope*! Just because your person hasn't turned up yet, that doesn't mean they will never come. Sometimes your truest love comes later than you expect; but believe me, it will be well worth the wait. Only hindsight will reveal exactly why your future partnership needed to arrive when it did. Keep working on yourself. Loving yourself is the best way to attract the love you seek. You are not wasting your time, no matter how frustrating it seems. I can't begin to tell you all the years I spent pining for the love I thought would never come. Everyone's experience is unique, but as long as love still resides in your heart and has not given way to toxicity or despair, there is still hope. Live your best life every day. Enjoy yourself! You don't need to be in love to start experiencing happiness. When you feel fulfilled, love will seem like the cherry on the sundae, and not your last meal!

If you are single and happy, I wish you continued joy, freedom, passion, excitement, and independence! The adventure of your life is in your hands. I hope the love you find in the family, friends, animals, travel, nature, and experiences around you continue to support your best life. There is power in freedom. Relish the moments you are creating now and be present with the beautiful person you are, inside and out.

If you are having trouble leaving a relationship with someone who isn't good for you, be strong! I wrote this book with a past version of myself in mind. I held on to dysfunctional relationships far longer than was healthy. I naively gravitated toward every seductive embrace that my inner self screamed for me to avoid! *Warning sign? No way! That Three of Swords along with the irrefutable evidence that guy was lying to me must just be me misunderstanding things again!* I was so afraid of being alone, unlovable, or lost that I accepted the unacceptable. However, looking back, I am grateful for these heartbreaks. They delivered the lesson I needed in order to grow through that time. I don't regret the past, for it made me stronger and better.

Past heartache has taught me to be compassionate when reading clients who make excuses for their own unhealthy relationship patterns. Being honest about something that causes pain is extremely hard. If you perform relationship readings for others, I encourage you to show empathy and compassion for the people who come to you seeking answers. Give them the truth, but never be cruel with it. Remember a time in your own life when you longingly waited by the phone for the message that never came. We are all here to do work on becoming improved versions of ourselves, and relationships teach the best and often the hardest lessons.

There is not a one-size-fits-all approach to tarot, or to love. Everyone's relationship looks different, and no two partnerships progress in exactly the same way. I encourage you to take the ideas in this book that pertain to your situation and modify the book's content to suit your unique needs. If something didn't resonate with your unique experience, leave it behind. You know your heart better than anyone else.

Have the courage to embrace truth and be honest with yourself when consulting your cards about love. Your future happiness cannot be found in illusion or delusion. True love is straight up, honest, and to the point. True love will not have you guessing if this person really likes you or not. It will be clearer than a cloudless day.

It is my hope that your special relationship with the tarot continues to thrive in the years to come. May your awareness into yourself and your relationships continue to deepen.

Affectionately yours,
Elliot Adam

APPENDIX:
"HOW DOES THIS PERSON FEEL?"
QUICK GUIDE

THE MAJOR ARCANA

The Fool

This person relishes the excitement you share. Lighten up; don't take yourself or this current relationship phase too seriously. Remember to incorporate laughter into your encounters. Your partner loves freedom and can come off as uninhibited, eccentric, or even a little crazy!

Reversed

This person may act thoughtlessly rather than with common sense. Although their behavior may baffle you by its unpredictability, try not to take it to heart. Upright or reversed, the Fool is not intentionally thoughtless.

The Magician

This person admires your intelligence and competency and the interests you share. You both shine best when you communicate. Many of your priorities and areas of focus align. Use your words to encourage their heart to open.

Reversed

This person feels you are coming off as mentally fixed or obsessive in some way. Dial down the intensity. You may benefit from getting a neutral perspective on what you want to say before you say it.

The High Priestess

This person is attracted to your mysterious aura. Revel in the excitement of the unknown and attract this person with what remains to be discovered. Don't reveal everything right away. Your mystique is your greatest glamour.

Reversed

This person feels you are being secretive or not forthright about your true desires or feelings. This might lead to some uneasiness. Express yourself plainly and without hints, clues, or other passive signals.

The Empress

This person feels safe, protected, and nurtured in your company. Your beauty and kindhearted nature will be what draws this person to you. This is an ideal time to express what is in your heart.

Reversed

This person feels like you are coming off as a bit smothering. They might find it difficult to ask for what they need as they're trying to not hurt your feelings. The Empress Reversed can also represent passive-aggressive behavior or neglect.

The Emperor

This person prioritizes maintaining their strength, autonomy, and leadership over their own life's direction. If his power feels challenged, a boundary will be established. The Emperor only respects communication that is direct, assertive, and confident.

Reversed

This person may feel dominated or pressured. You may be surprised by this since your words have not been aggressive at all. Know that the energy of what you are communicating comes through your body language more than through your words.

The Hierophant

This person feels you exhibit goodness, purity, and a clear moral compass. However, you may come off as emotionally conservative, reserved, or a little too Goody Two-Shoes. Lose your rigidity and allow your hidden passion to be seen.

Reversed

This person feels you are coming off as fixated and single-minded about your own desires in the relationship. Try to consider a different point of view. The Hierophant Reversed can also represent a partner who refuses to change.

The Lovers

This person is in love or has been falling in love with you. You share an intense physical romantic chemistry. If you are just beginning a relationship, let it blossom over time without hurrying through the courtship phase. Enjoy the connection you share.

Reversed

This person is struggling to make a choice and may not know how to communicate about it. They are worried about causing disharmony and are avoiding a situation that makes them feel anxious. Create a reassuring space for authentic feelings to be shared openly.

The Chariot

This person feels inspired and confident about how things are proceeding. However, like the opposing sphinxes, the relationship may have external forces pulling it in two different directions. Compromise will be needed to ensure a happy future.

Reversed

This person is feeling indecisive about which direction to take at this fork in the road. When this person doesn't know how to proceed, they likely retreat into their shell. As frustrating as it may seem, you need to be patient and await their decision.

Strength

This person is attracted to your vitality, strength, and self-control. Your charisma also fuels their ardor. Be confident in what you have to offer. This will ensure that you stay in the center of their attention. Be the lion and not the mouse.

Reversed

This person feels something is getting out of control, and they are worried about how they can maintain their power. This anxiety is spilling into other aspects of their life, including relationships.

The Hermit

This person feels you are introverted, intelligent, and shy. This quiet energy is also what attracts them. Your independence will also draw this person to you. For the relationship to work long-term, both partners will need space.

Reversed

This person feels ready to reengage in the needs of others after retreating for a time. They may also be stepping out of a period of melancholy or depression. If you have been in your own separate worlds, it may soon be time to reconnect.

The Wheel of Fortune

This person feels you are acting unpredictably. You could be taking too many chances, though your luck probably won't run out. You may need to return to your center to regain control of your undulating fortunes.

Reversed

This person feels enmeshed in a cycle that keeps repeating itself. The Wheel of Fortune Reversed can also highlight a relationship issue that repeats itself like clockwork. If you are wondering what will happen in the future, look to the patterns of the past.

Justice

This person admires your fair mind and intelligence. Even so, you must express what you are feeling in your heart. Sometimes Justice will signify a difficult truth that must be vocalized. Although it may be hard to hear, the only way forward is through transparent honesty.

Reversed

This person could be feeling that somehow they have been treated unfairly. They may also struggle with seeing everything in the world through binary, black-and-white terms. Although you may not be the cause for the grievance, it is still affecting the relationship.

The Hanged Man

This person feels that external demands require one or both of you to give too much of yourself. These pressures may be interfering with your ability to connect. You may also appear to be hung up about something right now. You both may just need a break.

Reversed

This person feels an obstacle to your happiness has been unblocked. You are more likely to be pleasant company if you remove tension and stress from the situation. Learn to laugh again.

Death

This person feels the relationship is undergoing an intense transformation. The old ways are now being swept away. There may be some fear surrounding a difficult yet necessary change. Your partner may also feel uneasy about issues of permanence at this time.

Reversed

This person feels you are resisting change or overly attached to the past. If something is meant to transform, you cannot force it to stay the same. You may need to accept that the current endings will lead to better new beginnings.

Temperance

This person thinks you are approachable and easygoing. You are moderate and naturally see what needs to be replenished in yourself and others. Your partner is probably very comfortable around you and sees you as an oasis amid life's storms.

Reversed

This person feels there is an imbalance in the relationship. When Temperance is reversed, one partner's cup may feel full, while the other's is running empty. Individual fulfillment found in independent activities may help.

The Devil

This person feels attracted to darkness, risk, and danger. You may be playing with fire. The thrilling passion in this relationship could be masking an unstable foundation. Being honest with yourself can free you from the Devil's seductive chains.

Reversed

This person feels you are making improvements in your life by facing your shadows honestly. They might also feel that you are being less controlling than before. You may still have to guard against obsessive behavior moving forward.

The Tower

This person feels enmeshed in an intense personal change or crisis. You also may be coming off as too intense or volatile at this time. There may be an instinct to avoid talking about the glaring truth. Uncomfortable conversations may be contributing to alienation.

Reversed

This person is picking up the pieces after a major life storm. You may also be coming across as someone who is holding on to a past trauma or insecurity. This love interest will want to move very slowly at this time.

The Star

This person feels relationships must be built on an authentic friendship and a shared vision for the future. Sometimes the Star can indicate that one partner is periodically remote or is physically distant. Space is regularly needed for this partnership to work.

Reversed

This person perceives you as giving but also feels an unseen pressure to reciprocate. Try to give without strings of expectations attached. This partnership thrives when it is a friendship first. Try not to act too coldly. Destiny still needs to play out.

The Moon

This person feels you are alluring and magnetic, but you don't always make sense. You are hard to figure out rationally. Still, your intense emotions create a magic that is bewitching. Give voice to what lies hidden in your heart.

Reversed

This person may feel you are moody or acting erratically. The Moon Reversed warns of being in denial. Try to get some distance from intense emotions so you can return to the situation with clarity.

The Sun

This person feels you are exuberant, attractive, and charismatic. You brighten up the mood of any room you walk into. The Sun is the best card in the deck and leaves everyone with an optimistic feeling about the future. All is clear, so don't bring in the gray clouds.

Reversed

Same as the upright meaning. The Sun represents positive feelings all around. Keep things light and joyous and don't get too heavy.

Judgment

This person feels you are resilient and interesting. They will respect the transformative moments of your life where you reinvented yourself. Although you experienced great loss in the past, you can look ahead to brighter days.

Reversed

This person feels you are acting impulsively. You may be reacting to something without thinking it through all the way. Be very conscious of how you come across when you are communicating at this time.

The World

This person thinks you complement their energy quite nicely. You have just finished a major stage in the relationship or in your personal life and it is time to take the next step. For the relationship, a major phase has come full circle, and it is time to move on to whatever is next.

Reversed

This person feels that the relationship is following a cyclical, predictable pattern. There may be a major issue that needs to be confronted or completed, but no one is talking about the elephant in the room. It's time to have a conversation about how to move past the past.

THE SUIT OF SWORDS

Ace of Swords

This person feels you should speak plainly and honestly without being wishy-washy. If you want something, you are going to ask for it. Be compassionate but also direct. You will gain more respect by wielding your power rather than by shying away from it.

Reversed

This person feels a new beginning in their life has not fully taken root. Something they feel conflicted about has not been resolved. They may not be ready to be completely vulnerable with you. Go slowly and gently.

Two of Swords

This person feels the need to move slowly. There is something unresolved in their own life that is preventing them from acting decisively. Be patient and don't take it personally. They may also feel this relationship is stuck in limbo.

Reversed

This person feels an old cycle has been repeating for quite some time. There is some hesitancy about moving forward. It is time to clear out any misunderstandings with direct communication. Time to step out of limbo.

Three of Swords

This person likely feels something outside of your relationship is hurting the connection you share. This could be another person, a career, or a creative passion. You may have to accept that this challenge isn't going away on its own. Face painful issues honestly.

Reversed

This person feels the need to get their thoughts and feelings in order. Something uncomfortable is being processed. The Three of Swords Reversed can represent a heart that needs to heal before it can open again.

Four of Swords

This person feels the need to take a time-out or a break. Much stress has been adding up, and now there is a desire for alone time. Don't take this personally. Everyone needs to recharge their batteries from time to time. Give them space.

Reversed

This person feels you are restless and anxious. You may need to tone down your intensity. Try to encourage activities that promote relaxation.

Five of Swords

This person is feeling overwhelmed. These pressures could be coming from you, or from others in their life. There may also be a sense of loss or defeat they are recovering from. Try to avoid saddling the relationship with more issues or stress.

Reversed

This person is feeling there is a mess to clean up in their own life before they can be fully present with you. Be patient with any issues that are being confronted.

Six of Swords

This person feels you are both moving forward. The relationship is now progressing toward the next natural phase. The rough waters are being left behind, and smooth waters lie ahead.

Reversed

This person feels you or the relationship is stuck. There may be an issue that is at an impasse. They may need to feel free to make their own choices. The only thing that might get the boat moving again is compromise.

Seven of Swords

This person has a difficult time being upfront or honest about issues that could hurt your feelings. This card can represent a person who has mastered the art of the half-truth. Insist on honesty even if you don't like what you are hearing.

Reversed

This person is feeling you are letting your past unrelated issues affect your present relationship. Try not to be overly suspicious or accusatory. This will just make this person keep their guard up.

Eight of Swords

This person feels you are looking to be rescued or saved. There may be unspoken pressures and expectations placed on the partnership to fulfill a need that wasn't met in the past. Change your demeanor from passive and reactive to assertive and empowered.

Reversed

This person needs to feel free of any pressure to be what others expect. The blindfold is coming off and they are beginning to see what they want for the future. However, they are deciding to prioritize their self first.

Nine of Swords

This person may be feeling a need to withdraw because of a personal problem, depression, grief, or worry. They may not be thinking clearly now, so don't take it personally. It can be difficult to make a person with a skewed perspective see reasonably.

Reversed

This person is feeling a desire to walk away from something that feels toxic. This could be a job, friendship, family relationship, or relationship that has deteriorated. They want to get out of their head and into the world again.

Ten of Swords

This person is likely avoiding an uncomfortable conversation, change, or ending. A difficult issue must be faced honestly. It is better to confront the challenge courageously, rather than passively hoping it will get better on its own.

Reversed

This person has recently recovered from a major life change. Although the dark clouds are beginning to part, there are still some unresolved emotional issues that must be faced honestly. More time is likely needed before diving into the next chapter.

Page of Swords

This person feels defensive about a personal vulnerability. You may be receiving mixed signals. If you are looking for an acknowledgement of wrongdoing, you are probably unlikely to receive it. The Page of Swords can act unaccountably and immaturely.

Reversed

This person is either communicating in a harsh or negative way or is detaching from truth. You may be hearing excuses or rationalizations for poor behavior. You may have to be the adult in this situation and make the mature decision.

Knight of Swords

This person is rushing ahead without thinking or feeling about how it may affect others. There is a compulsive quality to this card. Although the actions are thoughtless, they are not intentionally cruel.

Reversed

This person is indecisive at this time. They are going back and forth concerning an important decision. This card can represent inconsistency or the breaking of plans.

Queen of Swords

This person is making a calculation and will make the decision that supports the preservation of their personal autonomy and power. Your partner is extremely independent and will welcome going it alone when it serves their needs.

Reversed

This person feels you are not understanding what they are trying to say. There is likely an ongoing internal or external conflict. You may need to withdraw for a time if communication is thoughtless or unkind. Standards need to be clarified.

King of Swords

This person feels resistant to change. He has dug in and will not compromise his position. You will not win a battle of wills with this person. To even have a chance of changing this person's mind, you will have to present irrefutable facts.

Reversed

This person is feeling detached from sensitive emotions. He has likely accumulated a sense of grievance. No matter what the truth is, this individual will cast himself in the role of the person who is being treated unjustly.

THE SUIT OF CUPS

Ace of Cups

This person feels great love and/or affection for you. A positive new beginning is at hand. The Ace of Cups encourages you to make a decision that leads toward renewed joy and love in your heart.

Reversed

This person feels they must take care of their own needs for a time. The requirements of others are becoming too much, and they need to check back within. You may need to stand back to allow them to restore what brings them joy.

Two of Cups

This person feels your relationship was meant to be. However, this card also carries a theme of compromise. You may need to negotiate or come to an agreement on how to proceed with an important matter. Be sensitive to what they desire.

Reversed

This person feels you are not in agreement about how to proceed. There likely are communication challenges that must be addressed respectfully. Allow both partners to leave the negotiating table with their dignity intact. Compromise when possible.

Three of Cups

This person feels attracted to the charisma you exude. There is an aura of excitement or pleasure around this union. Create space for laughter to grace the relationship. This card can also indicate a desire to socialize to refortify their spirits.

Reversed

This person feels the relationship has been getting too serious. Sometimes this card can represent a person who is wonderful when times are good but struggles when a challenge arises.

Four of Cups

This person may be unable to see or accept a good thing being offered at this time. They may be ruminating or feeling pressured and stressed by other obligations. You can lead a horse to water, but you can't make them drink.

Reversed

This person may be feeling depleted. They could be ruminating or distracted by an internal issue that is causing frustration or distress. Whatever it is, it is consuming their focus completely.

Five of Cups

This person may be depressed or disappointed. They are likely disillusioned by a past experience that is affecting their current decision-making. It may be difficult for them to regain perspective of their opportunities at this time. Allow space and time for healing.

Reversed

This person may be tempted to cast themself in the victim role. They may be looking at the challenges they are facing as unfair and may not be accountable for their part in the current difficulties. This card can represent a skewed perspective.

Six of Cups

This person is having trouble turning away from the past. They may be romanticizing something that it's time to leave behind. There may be distractions or people resurfacing from the past as well.

Reversed

This person is feeling regret or remorse. There may be something this person is having trouble letting go of emotionally. If you do decide to begin anew, old attachments must be left behind.

Seven of Cups

This person feels mesmerized by a fantasy. They may be projecting an illusion or fantasy that feels too good to believe. Insist that magic is something that can still sparkle in the face of real life.

Reversed

This person feels they must awaken from sleepwalking through life. This may come in the form of erratic behavior that makes no sense. It's time to clarify feelings honestly and insist on reality.

Eight of Cups

This person feels the need to withdraw to regain perspective and clarity. They may be depressed or out of touch with their authentic sense of purpose. The Eight of Cups can also accompany a period of sadness or depression that eventually leads to a breakthrough.

Reversed

This person is erecting emotional barriers and is not facing an important issue head-on. Neglecting uncomfortable truths can result in feelings of anxiety or obsessiveness. Sometimes people need to accept reality gradually, rather than having it all come at them at once.

Nine of Cups

This person enjoys all the pleasurable times you share. They may have a difficult time committing to resolving a serious issue. The Nine of Cups can also indicate a strong sexual attraction that will consistently bring you together.

Reversed

This person is prone to excess. Emotions and behaviors are all amplified at this time. This card can also warn about too much of a good thing. Try to encourage a more balanced perspective. Strive to avoid extremes.

Ten of Cups

This person feels grateful to have you in their life. The rainbow that appears on this card signifies that the storms that have challenged you both have subsided. Enjoy the closeness you presently feel rather than fretting about the possibility of storms in the future.

Reversed

This person is not feeling clear about what you actually want. Instead of dropping hints or subtly avoiding a difficult conversation, speak up. When reversed, the Ten of Cups still signifies future harmony if you can communicate clearly and compassionately.

Page of Cups

This person feels attracted to fantasy more than reality at times. They may try to avoid the adult issues that come up in relationships. Your partner is a sensitive soul and would prefer to avoid confrontation, even if it means leaving an important issue unresolved.

Reversed

This person may have hit their threshold for how much they are able to express. Emotionally, they may exhibit very immature qualities. Try not to personalize where this person is in their own developmental stage. They may not be ready for mature commitments.

Knight of Cups

This person is feeling immensely attracted to you. Knights in the tarot are on horses and always seem to be coming and going. Although this person's affection may not appear consistent, the attraction is still very strong. You might also expect a message.

Reversed

This person is currently pursuing their own pleasure, rather than considering how you might feel. They may rationalize away hurtful actions. This person has no desire to sacrifice their freedom and will likely resist attempts to be pressured.

Queen of Cups

This person is feeling extremely sensitive and may need time to process emotions. They need to sit with their feelings for a time before making important decisions. However, this card will always signify someone with good intentions, compassion, and love.

Reversed

This person feels muddled and confused about their own feelings. They may need time to sort it all out. Try not to apply pressure or express impatience.

Upright or reversed, the Queen of Cups needs time to consider her authentic feelings before choosing a path.

King of Cups

This person feels at home, familiar, and comfortable when in your company. Although the waves of life crash against the king's throne, he remains upright, calm, and unperturbed. Know that whatever turbulence arises, it will not alter your beloved's loyalty.

Reversed

This person has spent years building walls around their emotional vulnerabilities. If upset, they can be extremely difficult to coax out of their shell. Sometimes this card will also appear when a person is brooding instead of communicating their feelings.

THE SUIT OF PENTACLES

Ace of Pentacles

This person feels an immense physical attraction to you. They are also excited about the new possibilities before you. Career is very important to this person; you may have to share their attention with a vocation they are actively pursuing.

Reversed

This person is prone to procrastination. They will take forever to respond to people or issues that need to be confronted. This person will avoid any feelings or people who trigger their anxiety. If you want them to come to the table, it must appear safe and inviting.

Two of Pentacles

This person is waffling between two decisions. Their choices will shift like the waves. There may be a lot of back-and-forth before a decision is reached. Maintain your sense of humor or this current indecisiveness could drive you crazy!

Reversed

This person feels stubbornly resistant to change. They may be getting bent out of shape over anything that threatens their habits or established routines. However, this person can be persuaded through humor or demonstrating that change will lead to excitement or fun.

Three of Pentacles

This person is still in a learning phase. They are still gathering information on what brings them the most fulfillment in their relationships. This card can also signify that your partner needs time to learn more about you before committing to a course.

Reversed

This person seems stuck in their own repeated life lessons. You may have to accept that it isn't your job to teach this person how to grow. It is better to back off than to attempt to control their developmental process.

Four of Pentacles

This person tends to place their feelings in a vault. They may also cling to their privacy. Although this card signifies the potential for long-term security, you may have to accept that there will be limits on how expressive this person is currently capable of being.

Reversed

This person is ready to release old emotional baggage. They are truly making an effort to let go of the past. You may need to be extra patient and understanding during this vulnerable time.

Five of Pentacles

This person may be struggling with career or financial pressures that are negatively impacting their perspective or self-esteem. This card can also indicate that they are struggling with issues of worth or worthiness.

Reversed

This person may be feeling emotionally depleted or physically exhausted. They might also be struggling with a health issue or some other kind of pain. Sometimes the best thing you can do is not require more energy than they are able to give.

Six of Pentacles

This person feels most confident when they are in the role of the benefactor. Sometimes this card can represent someone who needs to be needed. Even though they give much, you should still exhibit an ability to stand on your own two feet.

Reversed

This person is feeling a current imbalance in the relationship. Something important or desired may appear to be withheld. One partner may also feel they are doing all the giving while the other does the taking. Identify what the imbalance is and speak honestly about it.

Seven of Pentacles

This person feels good about your relationship but is still waiting to make a move on something. This card encourages patience. If the partnership appears to be healthy, you may just need to allow it more time to strengthen and mature before raising the stakes.

Reversed

This person feels inclined to wait longer than usual before making a new commitment. This card can also represent communication that is stalled or at an impasse. You may have to take the initiative to speed things up.

Eight of Pentacles

This person feels driven to devote most of their energy to their work or projects. This card can represent an increased workload or an especially busy time. However, the results that will be enjoyed from these efforts are many.

Reversed

This person feels burnt out from expending too much effort. They may just want to retreat or be alone right now. Sometimes this card can also represent a person who refuses to see issues practically. You may simply have two different ways of perceiving the same thing.

Nine of Pentacles

This person is reevaluating their standards and is striving to achieve success. Financial matters or business may take much of their focus at this time. This card can also signify an opportune time to splurge on luxuries and enjoy yourselves more.

Reversed

This person may be feeling frustrated for settling for something in their current life that does not live up to their standards. Although they are upset about this one issue, it seems to spill over into other areas of their life. Other cards may reveal what the unmet standard is.

Ten of Pentacles

This person feels devoted to family, consistency, legacy, and long-term security. Sometimes this card will represent family (or close friend) obligations that may interfere with your time together. However, this card always signifies good intentions.

Reversed

If you want to understand this person more, look at their family, parents, or family history. They may be carrying on patterns established long before you met. This card can also signify opportunities and challenges presented by your partner's family.

Page of Pentacles

This person is enthusiastically engaged in a learning process. Study or focus on a specific life pursuit will require much of their time. The relationship itself may also be what is causing your partner to learn or grow. They may still be new at this.

Reversed

This person may be coming off as overly picky. They may be a perfectionist with unrealistic expectations. Because these standards can be so impossibly high, they can be difficult to satisfy or please … unless you are equally high maintenance.

Knight of Pentacles

This person feels ready to promise more than they can deliver at times. It is important to be aware of their limitations. Although this card signifies possible success in the future, you may have to come to terms with what they can deliver *now*.

Reversed

This person feels resistant to making a commitment. They may be disappointing you by vacillating on an important decision. This card can also represent an impossibly stubborn individual who won't budge from their position.

Queen of Pentacles

This person feels content and happy with how their current life is unfolding with you. Although there may be some anxieties triggered or expressed, happiness remains. This card can also signify a person who occasionally needs to be reassured.

Reversed

This person is feeling overly anxious about their present or future. They may need time and space to calm down before they are able to communicate with you sensibly. Save the discussion for later if this person seems agitated, worried, or stressed.

King of Pentacles

This person feels confident and successful in the external world but may struggle with the realm of intimacy or emotions. They likely wear protective emotional armor to hide vulnerabilities. As with all pentacle cards, they require time and lots of patience.

Reversed

This person is being distant or remote. They may be retreating to the part of their life that they feel more confident in. Sometimes this card can also represent an attraction to a successful but emotionally unavailable person.

THE SUIT OF WANDS

Ace of Wands

This person is feeling passionate, excited, and ready to act. The magic of newness is in the air. Don't be afraid to express your passions, too. This card can also signify a desire to revitalize your sex life.

Reversed

This person is passionate, but sometimes that passion blazes too brightly and burns out. You may need to invent new ways to prolong the excitement by keeping a small part of yourself just out of reach.

Two of Wands

This person feels overly absorbed by something outside of the relationship. This could include a career, personal desire, or goal. This does not mean your partner doesn't care but does indicate a distraction.

Reversed

This person may be feeling unfulfilled with their current life. They feel disappointed that their present experience is not quite what they envisioned. You cannot make this person happy with their current lot. What they really desire is a new goal to strive for.

Three of Wands

This person feels more optimistic about the future. New opportunities are available to help them chart a new course. However, this card can also feel a bit overwhelming due to the enormity of the threshold being crossed. Change is in the air.

Reversed

This person is feeling restless, flighty, or noncommittal. This person does not like to feel attached to anything that will inhibit their opportunities or choices. Where the wind blows, this person follows. If you choose to be with this person, know they must feel free.

Four of Wands

This person is feeling more sociable and ready to connect through fun activities. The Four of Wands is the party card. This person wants to connect in a celebratory atmosphere without pressure. They desire to let their hair down.

Reversed

This person often desires to abandon self-control. They may be acting on impulse rather than with reason. This person may also keep company that encourages them to abandon their accountability. This card can also represent self-destructive excess.

Five of Wands

This person is feeling conflicted. The conflict could be internal or between the two of you. This card has an immature quality to it. They may respond irrationally when triggered. This card can also represent a disagreement that must be resolved with maturity.

Reversed

This person is feeling insecure. They may express this as being competitive, argumentative, or combative in your relationship. Upright or reversed, the Five of Wands represents immature and irrational behavior.

Six of Wands

This person feels very confident and loves to shine. Shower them with compliments and they will lap them up. This person doesn't need validation from others but does enjoy admiration. This card can also represent a partner you have to share with the public.

Reversed

This person finds it difficult to articulate their needs directly. They may have difficulty saying no in an effort to avoid hurting your feelings. This can lead them to avoid speaking about what they need in the hopes that you will take the hint.

Seven of Wands

This person feels the need to stand up for a boundary they are attempting to establish. You may find that there is some pushback, especially if they are feeling pressured. Speak plainly instead of avoiding issues.

Reversed

This person feels adamant about a position they hold. They have a vision for their life and are resistant to deviate from it. This card can also represent a person who has trouble opening up or getting close to others.

Eight of Wands

This person is fueled by energy, momentum, and passion. They will not hesitate to leave messages, notes, or texts for the person they are interested in. You will not have to wonder about their intentions because this individual makes a move fast on what they desire.

Reversed

This person is feeling scattered or overwhelmed. They often bite off more than they can chew. Although intentions are good, they may not always come through in a timely manner. This card can also represent someone who flakes out of plans.

Nine of Wands

This person feels encumbered by emotional baggage from the past. Although they have overcome many obstacles, there are still raw feelings. This card can also represent someone who hasn't quite healed from an old relationship wound.

Reversed

This person has a chip on their shoulder. Many boundaries have been placed around their vulnerable heart. Often this blockage is not apparent right away, but slowly comes into sharper focus the longer you know this individual.

Ten of Wands

This person is feeling burdened, weighed down by obligations, and exhausted. Often this card will represent someone who is in service to the needs of a relationship, family obligations, or their work. Selflessness is their best and worst trait.

Reversed

This person is exhausted from trying too hard. They may have become burnt out from a difficult past. However, a threshold is now being crossed. This individual may be learning to put their own needs first rather than caving to the demands of others.

Page of Wands

This person is an eternal optimist. They are also a free spirit and will resist any limitations that may threaten to entrap them. This card can represent a positive, fun-loving individual whose only desire is to have a good time.

Reversed

This person feels resistant to responsibilities or heavy expectations placed on them. They may display many talents and successes while still being somewhat emotionally immature. This person likes the excitement of the chase, but hates being chased.

Knight of Wands

This person feels adventurous and is always open to trying new things. They are confident in their appearance, charm, and sex appeal. Often this card will turn up if there is intense sexual chemistry. Keep in mind that *sex* and *love* are two different things.

Reversed

This person may find it difficult to keep their passions in check. They will often act on impulse. Watch out for projecting interest on someone who doesn't reciprocate. This individual can be flighty.

Queen of Wands

This person loves attention and admiration. This card can also represent someone who likes to show off their charismatic nature in public. They prefer going out rather than staying home. Shower them with praise and they will purr.

Reversed

This person can care too much about what other people think at times. This individual often puts on a show to cover up their true insecurity. They might also need constant validation, which never seems to be believed.

King of Wands

This person feels best when in control. They feel most at home with people who are resilient and display a strong and honest spirit. Don't beat around the bush with the King of Wands. He prizes authenticity and truth above all things.

Reversed

This person may be feeling frustrated. They must feel there is a chance for upward mobility, otherwise they are prone to apathy and disillusionment. This card can also represent a person who hates to be questioned and stubbornly insists on being right.

TO WRITE TO THE AUTHOR

If you wish to contact the author or would like more information about this book, please write to the author in care of Llewellyn Worldwide Ltd. and we will forward your request. Both the author and publisher appreciate hearing from you and learning of your enjoyment of this book and how it has helped you. Llewellyn Worldwide Ltd. cannot guarantee that every letter written to the author can be answered, but all will be forwarded. Please write to:

Elliot Adams
℅ Llewellyn Worldwide
2143 Wooddale Drive
Woodbury, MN 55125-2989
Please enclose a self-addressed stamped envelope for reply,
or $1.00 to cover costs. If outside the U.S.A., enclose
an international postal reply coupon.

Many of Llewellyn's authors have websites with additional information and resources. For more information, please visit our website at http://www.llewellyn.com.